ALEXANDRIAN AND CARTHAGINIAN THEOLOGY CONTRASTED.

ALEXANDRIAN

AND

CARTHAGINIAN THEOLOGY CONTRASTED.

THE HULSEAN LECTURES, 1892–93.

BY

REV. J. B. HEARD, A.M.,

AUTHOR OF

"THE TRIPARTITE NATURE OF MAN," "OLD AND NEW THEOLOGY."

Wipf and Stock Publishers
199 W 8th Ave, Suite 3
Eugene, OR 97401

Alexandrian and Cathaginian Theology Contrasted
By Heard, J.B.
ISBN: 1-59752-116-7
Publication date 3/8/2005
Previously published by T&T Clark, 1893

TO

JAMES MOORHOUSE, D.D.

LORD BISHOP OF MANCHESTER

A PIONEER

CLEAR, CALM, CIRCUMSPECT

THROUGH THE JUNGLE WHICH LIES BETWEEN

OLD THEOLOGY AND MODERN THOUGHT

THESE LECTURES

ARE INSCRIBED BY PERMISSION

BY HIS OBLIGED FRIEND

THE AUTHOR

PREFACE.

A FEW words of explanation will be enough to put the reader in line with the leading thoughts of these Lectures. Some years ago I had put forth a volume of constructive criticism, bearing the title of *Old and New Theology*. This contrast of old and new inadequately conveyed my meaning, as it set the reader thinking of some "time" test; and it seemed to raise needless offence by the vague hint that the new was better than the old. As yet I had not struck my finger on the true contrast between old and new; but I had not long to wait. Through the kindness of a friend, I was sent an early copy of the Bohlen Lecture for 1884, on the *Continuity of Christian Thought; a Study of Modern Theology in the Light of its History*, by Professor Allen of the Episcopal Theological School of Cambridge, Mass. This able and thorough-going treatise put in my hands for the first time a better canon than that of old and new. I there learned, to my surprise, that what I had described as new theology was in reality the oldest of all. It was that which was from the beginning in the East, and had there been held to as a consistent tradition of truth in Alexandria by all the early Greek Fathers, from Clement to Athanasius. The contrast between early Greek and Latin theology was the key to Dr. Allen's book, and showed that the "traditional conception" of God which has come down from the Middle Ages through "the Latin Church is undergoing a profound transformation." "The idea that God is transcendent, and not only exalted above the world by His moral perfections, but separated from it by the infinite reaches of space, is yielding to the idea of Deity as immanent in His creation. A change so fundamental involves other changes of momentous importance in every department of human thought, and more especially in Christian theology."

This was the contrast between a God immanent and a God transcendent, which is the master-key to the many contrasts between two theologies which I had crudely described as old and new, whereas in reality they were as far apart as the East is from the West. It was to me a joyful discovery that the so-called new theology of modern thinkers was nothing more than a fresh draft of the oldest of all theologies. It was that Logos doctrine of a Word, a wisdom indwelling in men, which is from the beginning. It is as old as St. John, though later Augustinianism had effaced that early type, and set up a new standard of orthodoxy based on Church authority and the blindness of the natural conscience. To this transcendent Deity the whole West has for fourteen centuries blindly bowed, and accepted under the phrase "sovereignty," the Roman magisterial conception of God. There have been protests here and there, but they were only scattered voices, lurid and broken lights seen up and down the ages; but to question the argument from authority was to write oneself down among the mystics, and to lay oneself open to the reproach of indefiniteness. But thanks to Professor Allen's far-reaching contrast between East and West, we have been given a clue by which again to thread the labyrinth of Church history. We are at one dead lift raised out of that uncritical stage of scholarship in which the "Fathers" were regarded as a whole, and Church teaching was considered a body of truth, one and indivisible. Such a work as these Bohlen Lectures of Dr. Allen were to me "epoch-making." They express what I had been hammering at for years without striking the blow home. To thank a writer to whom, in Plato phrase, the τέχνη μαιευτική has been so largely given, will seem wasteful and ridiculous excess. How helpful it has been to me, let these Hulsean Lectures express. It confirms the old remark, that all discoveries are only recoveries. A thought is in the air, and some one has set it in motion. It is they who are the first to recognise its far-reaching importance, who feel that it clears up contradictions between old and new which were before insoluble.

Another writer to whom I wish to express how deep a debt I owe for unexpected help is Dr. Moorhouse, the Bishop of Manchester. His University Sermons on the *Teaching of Christ; its Conditions, Secret, and Results*, are full of suggestive thought. What can be better than his account of the Book of Origins, and his linking together of the Genesis traditions with those of Chaldæa? The concessions which this broad-minded Bishop makes to the demands of the age, justifies his remark that "nothing is nearer to heresy than a stiff and narrow-minded orthodoxy."

But my chief obligation to Bishop Moorhouse lies in his skilful handling of what he describes as the after-thoughts of dogmatic theology. One of the oldest of these difficulties of belief grows out of the theory of Satanic influence on those cases of obscure disease described in the New Testament as Satanic possession. The Bishop here makes good use of Dr. Martensen's theory, corresponding to Schopenhauer's "Will to Live," which must, from its very nature, come into constant conflict with that Almighty "Will to Love," which is God. The devil "so defined," says Martensen, "hungers after fulness of life, and must come for his substance, for the material on which he works, to the world of man." This, like every other great thought, is pregnant of many others, and the whole difficulty of diabolical possession yields up its meaning, and falls into line with law when touched with this one thought of a God who is "Will to Love." All separate life is mere "Will to Live." It belongs to that lower world which is the "creature, which is not subject to the law of God, neither indeed can be."

I hope in these few pages of explanation I have at least acknowledged some of my debts; discharge them I never expect to do, since a fresh writer sets in motion new trains of thought. It is like the "power" let in to the looms of Manchester, which afterwards seem to go on spinning of themselves, as if endowed with perpetual motion. A remark of St. Beuve is here to the point, that to admire with mediocrity is an unerring mark of mediocrity. I hope I have acknowledged the obligations which I owe to these two writers. There are many more, doubtless, to whom I am indebted, but I am not conscious of it to the same extent. If I have erred, I have at least erred in good company. If I have found the key to this standing contrast between new and old in theology, I at least lay no claim to originality. To have found the true thread to the labyrinth, and the root of the contrast between the one and the many, is what multitudes have toiled after, and still are in search of. Catholic and Protestant have each raised their Eureka cry, only to lose it again in some new form of traditional dogmatism. To these two, my masters in theology, Dr. Moorhouse and Dr. Allen, I gladly inscribe anything that is fresh or new in these Lectures.

CONTENTS.

CHAPTER I.

PAGE

Epimetheus Afterthoughts, ... 1

CHAPTER II.

Theology Proper, ... 31

CHAPTER III.

What are Afterthoughts? 58

CHAPTER IV.

Dissipation of Energy, ... 87

CHAPTER V.

Excuse for Afterthoughts, ... 114

CHAPTER VI.

Not to Premeditate, ... 149

CHAPTER VII.

Augustine and his System, ... 175

CHAPTER VIII.

Augustine, his Merits and Defects, ... 201

CHAPTER IX.

PAGE

DIDACHÉ AND DOGMA, ... 229

CHAPTER X.

AFTERTHOUGHTS ON INSPIRATION, ... 260

CHAPTER XI.

REMEDY, ... 275

CHAPTER XII.

THREE TESTS OF AFTERTHOUGHTS—1. UNPRIMITIVE; 2. IRRECONCILABLE WITH HIGHER LIGHT TO BREAK FROM GOD'S WORD; 3. METAPHYSICAL STAGE OF THOUGHT, ... 314

EPILOGUE, ... 334

ERRATA.

Page 243, line 32, *for* "times" *read* "tomes."
Page 249, line 17, *for* "or alter" *read* "in order."
Page 281, line 15, "protagonist" *for* "protagenist."
Page 347, line 32, *for* "*lumine œstit*" *read* "*vestit.*"

CHAPTER I.

EPIMETHEUS AFTERTHOUGHTS.

THE earliest, perhaps the most precious, fragment of sub-apostolic teaching is the "Teaching of the Twelve." It sets out with the contrast between two ways, "the way of life" and "the way of death." A lifetime has taught me the same sharp contrast between two theologies, the one setting out with the first thoughts of God, the other with man's interpretation of these thoughts, which I describe as second thoughts or afterthoughts. The first thoughts, which are God's thoughts, all address themselves to the conscience—they enter in, and they lodge there. As they are the first thoughts of Him who is the Word of God, so, like that word of God, which is quick and powerful, they pierce sharper than any two-edged sword. The unerring mark of the first thoughts of God is that they come, as all Christ's teaching came, with authority to the conscience. They bind and they loose alone in the region of the inner man, while with superb indifference they sweep by, as beneath notice, those ritualisms and Rabbinisms on which smaller teachers lay such store. The self-limitation of Christ is nowhere more seen than in this, that in discussions which to the critical mind seem so urgent, such as the question of the authorship of the books of Moses, He is severely silent. To questions merely curious, such as whether few shall be saved, He leaves us as before in blank ignorance; as an able modern apologist expresses it:[1]—"Judging, however, from His ordinary method of teaching, I should have expected that just as He said to the man who desired Him to interfere in a question of inheritance, 'Who made me a judge or a divider between you?' He would have said in reply to a question about the age or authorship of a passage in the Old Testament, 'Who commissioned me to resolve difficulties in historical criticism?'"

This is a mark of God's thoughts, the note, as we should say, of "Inspiration" in the true sense of the term, and as contrasted with modern notions of a book religion. Christ is silent, severely so, on all subjects on which the human mind is able to find a path for itself. To paraphrase a celebrated line of Virgil, it leaves others to fuse the melting brass, or make cold marble to breathe. Others may measure the course of the stars or pour out streams of passionate eloquence; but for the arts of moral self-control, and to find out the place of wisdom and the place of understanding, then we may turn to the old Book and appeal to it as to the lively oracles of God. These oracles are dumb where the inquisitive mind of man expects to be saved the search for truth. On this wide reach of thought, embracing the whole of science and the whole of ethics and of politics, on its speculative side at least, these so-called oracles are dumb. So much so, that the Gnostic type of mind turns from them with contempt, and describes itself as Agnostic, or indifferent to truths which are hid from the wise and prudent, and revealed only to babes. God's thoughts, in a word, are not as our

[1] *Sermons on the Teaching of Christ*, by Bishop Moorhouse, p. 42.

thoughts; and the Bible in its way of putting truth ever will be a stumbling-block and offence to the merely curious and inquisitive. A sublime chapter in Job sums it all up as to these silences of Scripture. It is silent on mineralogy, botany, biology, and all the antiquities of man and his dwelling-place, but it breaks out only to teach, as—"Unto man He saith, Behold, the fear of the Lord, that is wisdom; and to depart from evil, that is understanding."

Now, contrast with this theology of God's first thoughts the afterthoughts of man, which make up our dogmatic, deductive systems built up on scattered texts and inferences of the hereafter all grounded in our ignorance. These second or afterthoughts all want this true note of authority, and they make up for it by the mock thunder of dogmatism. They are positive where revelation is silent, and they venture to lift the veil which hangs over the future, where apostles and prophets, who should know most, profess to know least. It is instructive to pursue this contrast between inspired and uninspired men and books. As soon as we get out of the Canon into the Apocrypha the difference is apparent. It needs little learning to see why even an uncritical age like that which drew up the Hebrew Canon had to exclude such a book as Tobit, with its strange demonology and still stranger medical magic. It is too obvious; and this same contrast of fine gold with base metal runs through all the later books. Even the Wisdom of Solomon is too "Solomonic" by far. It is an evident afterthought on the hints thrown out by the way in canonical books on the subject of Solomon's wisdom. Ecclesiastes is eponymic, no doubt, and affects a gnomic style such as an ancient king of Israel of the heroic age would presumably write in. But it is sober in comparison to the more than romantic style of the later

Solomon. His love for wisdom is so piled up with phrases which are the echoes of a truth-seeker, not the voice itself, that it compels us to say that no man really wise would descant in such a style. It sets us thinking of the age of copyists, which always sets in when the age of true wisdom is over.

We have, then, in these apocryphal books a ready test of the contrast we are in search of. The first thoughts of God are simple, self-evidencing, and go home to the conscience straight as a bolt to its mark. But when we descend to afterthoughts, we at once enter a lower level of thought. It is less direct, more discursive; it is more ingenious, but less heart-searching. It may be said to begin at the point where Holy Writ leaves off, and to lift the veil expressly on those subjects on which Scripture lets it fall, cautioning us that "it doth not appear what we shall be." It has been often remarked that the Mosaic creation contains no cosmogony, but the reason for this omission is not seen to be as intentional as it is. But at last we have been able to recover the sources of these primitive legends which lie at the base of the Mosaic narrative. The legend of the Creation, the Fall, and the Deluge are all Accadian, and the Cylinder rolls have given a similar version to our Book of Origins. But the contrast is quite as instructive as the resemblance of the Mosaic to these Chaldee legends. The latter are all polytheistic, and the ethical teaching corresponds to it, while the Mosaic are all set to the note of Monotheism. They are grave, ethical, and not inconsistent with the character of One whose "eyes behold, and whose eyelids try the children of men."

This contrast is not accidental. It runs through the whole Old Testament, and suggests to us the true and only Canon of inspiration, which has been so strangely misunderstood by those who take the Bible for what it is not, and mistake what it is. Every scripture inspired by God, according to the apostle (2 Tim. iii. 16), is profitable for teaching, for reproof, for correction, for instruction which is in righteousness. Here the predication unquestionably is not so much with regard to what theopneustia means in itself (that lies quite in the background), or with regard to the channels through which theopneustia flows. These are its four criteria: it is profitable in these four directions—(1) For *διδασκαλία*, which is not so much the thing taught—this would be *didaché*—as the way of teaching; (2) for reproof, or the elenchus of conscience, convincing, as it were, and binding it with cords of a man; (3) for *ἐπανόρθωσιν*, which means a good deal more than correction, and which rather means that re-setting our nature on a true spiritual and moral basis, that edifying which is in love, which is the true note of Holy Scripture. Lastly, the end and aim of all truly theopneustic writing is *παιδεία*, which is a good deal more than mere instruction or schoolmaster's work. Parental education differs from instruction as a whole from its part, or as genus from species. Fatherly discipline more nearly represents the meaning—that "loving correction which makes us great" when it comes from the God and Father of all.

We have only to put these four tests of a theopneustic book together, and we see what the Bible is not and what it is as a whole, and so are able to measure the contrast between the first thoughts of God and the afterthoughts of man. This, as we hold it, is the true Canon of what is to be the Canon. This is the best reason for accepting on the whole (with some reserve, we admit, which modern criticism calls for) the Hebrew Canon. The Palestinian Canonists extruded certain additaments because "found in the Greek but not in the Hebrew." So far, by this expression, they seem partial, and judges of themselves. Alexandria was a rival centre for Judaism, and the Jerusalem doctors of the law naturally became jealous of their rival. So far we can understand the enlarged Canon of the Greek Old Testament and the somewhat abridged Canon of the same in Hebrew. As a matter of fact, since the Reformation at least, our suffrages have gone with the Palestinian against the Alexandrian Jews. We have accepted St. Jerome's view of the matter, and censure the Latin Church for its Vulgate version, which obliterates the deep distinction between the canonical and the uncanonical books of the Old Testament. It is one of the many errors of Rome which in its place Protestant controversialists do not fail to single out for censure.

But the true Canon of inspiration lies not in any decision of Rabbis, who chiefly for linguistic reasons decided for a Hebrew and against a Greek version. This contention, based on verbal inspiration, is no better than that between Samaria and Jerusalem as rival centres of Palestinian Judaism, and would be decided by the Lord on the same grounds, that "while salvation was of the Jews, the time was coming when neither in this mountain nor yet in Jerusalem men should worship the Father." The old Hebrew draft of Law, Prophets, and Psalms has this advantage over the Greek translation, that these apocryphal additions, which have crept into the Greek, have the unerring mark of all afterthoughts. They do not strike the same note as the first thoughts of God—they are not profitable in the same way for instruction in righteousness. Their *παιδεία* is of a very inferior type. They import an angelology on which canonical books are expressively silent. They are effusive in idealising that foreign notion of Chachmah which is not Hebrew but Greek; but these Wisdom echoes of the so-called Solomonic sage lack the one note of archaic simplicity. The canonical book of Proverbs is quite in the true note. When we come to Koheleth, it seems as if we are on the border line, and the low place which it takes in the Hebrew Canon shows the small estimation in which it was held. The Hebrew Canonists would perhaps have done better if they had used the knife more boldly, and amputated more of the later books of the Hagiographa. When we have named Psalms, Proverbs, and Job, we have included all that come up to the full standard of theopneustic books as profitable for moral and spiritual training. There are, of course, in the Bible, as in any "library," lesser as well as greater lights. Our minor poets have their place in any anthology deserving the name. So for this reason we would not exclude from the Canon such a fragment as that so-called Vision of Obadiah, which critics conjecture was an amplification of the last five verses of Amos, and was therefore placed next after the book of Amos. All we contend against is the superstitious sense of finality in dealing with the books of the Old Testament.

We come, then, to this conclusion with regard to inspiration in general and the Canon of the Old Testament in particular, that Mosaism is Monotheism, and that it is this Monotheism which differentiates the Book of Origins from all other origins or cosmogonies like the Chaldæan, on which they are apparently transcripts. Why, in following the current tradition of Semitic and Accadian races, the Hebrews, that is the men from beyond the river who broke off under Abraham from the common stock, who served other gods, should set up new traditions of their own which were like and yet unlike the old, it is impossible to explain if we leave out of account that election of the father of the faithful. The true beginning of inspiration is that which we may describe as the call of Abraham. That was the true birthday of the chosen race, of which the exodus was the baptism, when they were baptized into Moses in the cloud and in the sea. Then began that course of education which we sometimes describe as inspiration and sometimes as revelation; but these are only different names of the same thing, the education of the race under prophets in sundry times and divers manners. Mosaism is only prophetism, since Moses was the first as Malachi is the last of a long chain of teachers, —a chain of many links and of different patterns. The book element was quite subordinate, if it ever existed, in early times. It is an old fallacy of human nature to judge the past by the present, and so to forget that the best teaching is catechesis—it is ear-wise not eye-wise, by the living voice, not the dead letter, that man acts on man and mind opens mind. It is mere modernism to regard us as dependent on books. These modern oracles are the reverse of lively. We have fallen like the Moslems into the same mistake of describing our holy faith as a book religion. To this day Moslems are described by Kaffirs or pagans of Africa as "men of the book." It is with much the same superstitious veneration as Moslems look on the "Koran"—the "writing" where inspiration is its own witness of itself—that we moderns take the Hebrew *Keri* or written text of what the Jews came to regard as canonical, and make a Protestant fetich of it. Our Bible Societies and suchlike agencies do much to deepen this uncritical tradition which passes current under the Chillingworth phrase, the "Bible the religion of Protestants."

Thus Bible and Church religions are in danger alike of

forgetting how they grew up. We have to bring them back from "afterthoughts" to the "first thoughts" of God. His "first thought" is the education of the human race as a whole; and we regard it as the lasting disgrace of all latter-day theology, from Augustine downward, that it so let go this "thought of God's purpose" that it had to be refound. This was done, as is too often the case, by a mere man of letters like Lessing, driven to Deism for want of anything like a spiritual conception of God in the theologies of his day. But that best truth of *Erziehung*, or education, the unfolding of our spiritual life, which is the key to all revelation and inspiration, is also the key to the Bible as a book. It helps us to deal with the Canon on rational grounds, which are also happily the same as those of conscience and our inner spiritual faculties. They are what Luther meant by his golden rule for testing the Canon, *ob sie Christum treiben.* Mosaism is Monotheism—this is its true point of departure, but Monotheism must go on to the sense of God's covenant-relation to man, else it sterilises into mere Deism, and dies as Islamism dies, for want of some sense of God's immanent relation to man, grounded on the truth that we are His offspring. Hence the next stage onward of the Mosaic dispensation is to get on from Monotheism to Messianism. "Jehovah and His anointed"—this is the key to all Old Testament teaching. It also explains the many apostasies of the covenant people. It is against "Jah and His anointed" that kings furiously rage together and people imagine a vain thing. Here comes in the true significance of prophetism. This precious, this priceless deposit, the one vital germ of all man's after-spiritual education, lay in these true conceptions of Monotheism and of Messianism. "Jah and His Christ" is the true end of Mosaism; and as Moses is the first, so Malachi is the last messenger of the covenant, whose last word is not a little expressive. He has to turn the hearts of the fathers to the children, and of the children to the fathers. The Old and the New, that is, must be linked together. The first thought of God, His unique transcendent glory, that He is El-Shaddai, is to be linked with His later name, Jah, which completes the covenant and rounds off Mosaism into one consistent whole. Thus, when Monotheism meets with Messianism, it has found its complementary truth: like the fragments of a broken *tessera* or plate, these two one-sided truths fit into each other—the one of a transcendent, the other of an immanent Deity. Apart, each is defective. They are like the chemical constituents of our food—the starch matter and the hydrocarbons, on which singly we starve, but which when combined nourish us. It is so with these elements of our spiritual life. In the blaze of absolute Deity true devotion dies down into blind fatalism and submission. Such is the state to which Judaism and Islamism alike decline, because they are sterilised truths. The one has rejected its Messiah, and now, like Islamism, is a form of out-of-date Deism. The two degenerate types of a true religion have both wandered down a blind alley with an inscription at the end, "No passage here." They have petrified in both cases into mere book religions, and it would be a sorry day for popular Protestantism should it ever sink to class itself with the mere "men of the Book," as its rivals for carrying the Koran to the fetich-worshippers of Central Africa are known.

But true Mosaism goes on from Monotheism to Messianism. This is its mark of inspiration. Speaking in general terms, we should say that Monotheism is the key-note of all earlier revelation, Messianism of all its later forms. The testimony of Jesus is the spirit of prophecy, and here Luther's Canon is unerring. A book is inspired in the Old Testament in proportion as it is Messianic. *Ob sie Christum treiben.* This is why the second Isaiah, probably a disciple of the first, or, at least, of the Isaian school, a son of the prophets, was, if possible, even greater than his father, the proto-Isaiah. He stands at the very head of inspired writers. His pre-eminence is as unchallenged as that of Shakespeare, who took the drama and poetry and fused them into one as they have never been fused before or since. So with the evangelical prophet Isaiah. He saw the day of a suffering, who was also the ascended Messiah, as none of his equals ever did. He is pre-eminent among prophets, as St. Paul is among apostles. The last Isaiah, as one born out of due time, saw under the captivity much farther even than Ezekiel, who seems never to the last to have shaken off his Jewish altar-clothes, and who was a Levite to the last. The younger Isaiah soared aloft like his namesake, whose call, in the year that King Uzziah died, is nearly the most sublime vision in the Bible. If we knew all, we should probably know that all Hebrew names are chiefly eponymic, which would disperse nine-tenths of our modern matter-of-fact difficulties as to dates and names of authors. Authorship, and the fame of it, was about the last thing which an inspired man would have dreamed of laying claim to. Hence the mistake of our modern way of discussing the books of the Bible and their authors, and repelling attacks on traditional views of the Canon, which are, after all, only Jewish, as if our faith rested on a Canon or rule of faith. We are not yet out of the stage of Bibliolatry in which Coleridge found us. His half-learned father, a country clergyman, used, it is said, to pour out strings of Biblical Hebrew and Greek from the pulpit of Ottery

St. Mary, which impressed the old folk there as not at all pedantic. "Blessed man," they said, "he gives us God's word as He wrote it." This was the Bibliolatry stage which the younger Coleridge, with that spiritual insight given more often to poets than to theologians, helped to deliver us from. Our popular religion is on the move, but slowly, from the platform of an external creed, bound within the covers of a book, to that higher platform of inspiration in the Church and people of God. Holy men of old were inspired, not magically, but because they were holy men: they became either God's witnesses, by deed as Elijah, or by word as Isaiah. Such inspiration has never ceased in the Church; and were it to cease, we should have to cease to believe in the Holy Ghost, who spake for the prophets. We should then deserve Elijah's taunt, that "he is a god who is on a journey, or, peradventure, he is asleep, and must be awaked." Inspiration, like miracles, is continuous and constant, though we still look back, and not forward, for both.

Such, then, are first thoughts and afterthoughts in their leading contrasts. Afterthoughts are in general fossilised first thoughts. They rest on what God has said or done in the past; they seldom glance at the thought that God has more truth to break out of His word. They are like that roll of the law which was shut up in the ark, and in the priests' custody; but the priests were such sleepy custodians of its letter that they forgot its spirit, till it was accidentally rediscovered in good King Josiah's age,—which is a singular parallel to the Protestant Reformation age, when we awoke for a time and then went to sleep again in a fresh sleep of traditional dogmatism. But the first and most lasting petrifaction of Christian theology began, as we hold, with the great Bishop of Hippo. We are not going too far, then, in asking our age to reform root and branch this term "theology" altogether, and to confine it to its first reading out of the word of the "thoughts of God." "For I know the thoughts that I think toward you, saith the Lord, thoughts of peace, and not of evil, to give you an expected end," Jer. xxix. 11. As soon as we know our God in this sense, we are at once out of the region of provisions, of plans of salvation either by faith alone or by sacraments alone. All that we may describe not disrespectfully as "Church clothes" then fall off, and we are at once lifted up in spirit, and are on the mount with God. It is these first thoughts which alone are lasting, which reveal Christ, which satisfy the conscience, and in the end wean us from our unbelief. The other type of afterthoughts only stir up unbelief, and then seek to smother it by some magisterial thought of God. Pascal in his day, Newman in ours, are types of sceptical minds, acting on the old out-of-date idea in medicine, that *morbus morbum pellit.* The Hindus have a saying that to battle sin with sin, and doubt with doubt, is like letting a hungry tiger in to drive another tiger out. Such will be our fate if we go on in this rut of dogmatic theology. The myth of Epimetheus, perhaps, points at the mistake of these afterthoughts. It is a Greek anticipation of a Christian error.

The first myth of Prometheus was, as we now know, like all myths, a disease of language. Ignorant of the meaning of Pramantha, the fire drill, they invented an explanation of their own by coining a word, and so gave to the name of the first fire filcher from heaven the appropriate title of the fore-thinker, the Prometheus. He looks before and after, he provides for the future by the discovery of fire, the first step of man out of primeval brutishness. But, having started the legend, the inventive Greek went on to improve on it. Prometheus, the fore-thinker, must have a brother, Epimetheus, the after-thinker. In the Hesiod version of the legend, this younger degenerate brother of Prometheus lets himself be deceived by Pandora, that fatal gift of the gods. In spite of the warning of his more far-sighted brother, Epimetheus takes to himself this Eve, the temptress, to wife, and so opens the baleful history of sin and misery, all springing out of self-will. It is evidently the Greek version of that old Chaldæan legend of man's first disobedience through the suggestion of woman, which the Hebrew Book of Origins has also incorporated, as it did after purging it of certain fantastic and non-moral details. Thus Prometheus and Epimetheus stand as the types, to the Greek mind, of that contrast of character between the fore-thinker, the wise man who looks ahead, and the after-thinker, who is only wise after the event, which has been described as the exactest definition of a fool. To learn no lessons from the past, to remember nothing, and to forget nothing, as was said of the Bourbons after the Restoration, this is that type of folly which brings on revolutions, and then goes far to excuse their excesses. On such persons the great lessons of history seem lost, since they are lapped in such self-conceit that they never seem to see that they have been sowing the wind, and must, therefore, reap the whirlwind.

But it is when we turn to Church history that this Epimethean temper is seen in its most striking form. No one is so dangerously near self-delusion as the divine who, presuming on his infallible chart and compass, overlooks the one loophole of error which lies in his own fallibility. It has been often said that, admitted the truth of infallibility either of book or Church, where is our guarantee that we have read the book aright, or that the Church is plenarily inspired when teaching *ex cathedrâ?* If the members are singly and even collectively fallible, how can we be sure all is changed because pope and council, as head and members, lay their heads together to extract new definitions out of old dogmas. Errors in theology are never, then, slight, like the mistakes of politicians, who are mere opportunists or tide-waiters. Such men get tripped up to-day, and pick themselves up to-morrow. But the divine who sets out with the note, "Thus saith the Lord," is in grave danger of going on adding error to error, till we stand aghast at the measureless miscalculation which, like errors in astronomy, do not stop till they break down beneath their own weight of absurdity.

Such is the Epimethean mind in theology. It is so conservative of the mere hull and husk of truth, that it sometimes forgets that the corn of wheat must die to bring forth any fruit at all. It is so concerned with the details of the faith and their defence, that it forgets that a living faith is in reality its own best defence. The two theologies, then, which we contrast as Promethean and Epimethean diverge at once at this point, that the faith of the one centres in a living Person; that of the other, in the doctrines and duties, the *credenda* and *agenda,* which are only the after results of faith in that living Person. The one theology we may compare with the seamless robe of Christ; the other is that raiment of needlework in which, in the expressive phrase of the Vulgate, the bride is brought to the king. The Church is, in more senses than one, *circumamicta varietatibus.* The phrase *varietatibus,* too, well expresses the many hues of that dogmatic deductive theology "received by tradition from the Fathers." It is that *supellex* of superfluous dogmatism, which is as gaudy as the paraphernalia of bridal array of Pharaoh's daughter when brought to King Solomon. It saddens us to think how much the Church loses when she recedes from the simplicity which is in Christ Jesus. How unlike her afterthoughts are to the faith delivered once for all (*ἅπαξ*) to the saints.

If we are asked for a simple test to distinguish between first thoughts and afterthoughts, we should say that first thoughts are few and afterthoughts many. The first thoughts touch life and conduct, and are "according to godliness." Afterthoughts, on the other hand, make up the body of what is known as polemical divinity. The Churchman is seen to be armed at all points when he puts on this Saul's armour of afterthoughts; but how weak he is in reality, the history of polemical divinity, Catholic and Protestant, of Latin and Greek Church controversialists, alike attest. The one unites the most, the other divides most. How many there are, especially among young and ingenuous minds, who, if presented with the truth, as, for instance, Justin Martyr was, and brought to them as a message coming from one who had found it to be true, would, as Justin did, lay aside the philosopher's cloak and put on the baptismal robe of faith. But it is these afterthoughts of theology which stop the way and hinder their coming in. Either it is the claims of book inspiration which bar all honest criticism of either authorship or contents, or it is some narrow theory of atonement or satisfaction for sin which strike the conscience as repellant and unworthy of a God who is justice and love in one, and who acts not on the bare rule of an autocrat—"Whom He wills He kills, and whom He wills He keeps alive." Or, again, it is some predestination theory of the extent of the atonement which spreads like a mist over the face of the whole heaven and darkens the very eye of God, which is good to all. Now, if we can succeed in showing that all these theories are among the mere afterthoughts of theology, which never would have been thought at all, unless some prying, presumptuous Epimetheus had opened this Pandora's box of curious questions and puzzles of half-learned minds, what a relief it will be, what a riddance of so much top-hamper, and how we may thus lighten the ship of our faith, and again make it seaworthy.

The so-called Reformation was a golden opportunity given and lost—though where to assign the blame it is hard to say off-hand. The very zeal of the Reformers probably defeated its own object. They betrayed that it was a revolt against a single form of tyranny only when they inserted that clause into the Litany, soon afterwards expunged, "From the intolerable tyranny of the Bishop of Rome: good Lord deliver us." But mere revolts never go to the root of the evil. They end in exhaustion, nay, they even invite reaction, as soon was the case under Elizabeth. The queen and her astute advisers soon saw that the Crown, on taking over the papal supremacy, had to take over a good deal besides with it, which the early Edwardian Reformers had regarded as the wardrobe of Rome, the livery of the woman in scarlet. The royal supremacy led on to a kind of Byzantinism, as Döllinger calls it, the Cæsaro-Papacy, in which the Crown decided, and that for reasons of mere statecraft only, what ceremonies of the old cult were to be retained and what rejected. It was a compromise, and, like all compromises, pleased neither extreme, and so the Elizabethan settlement contained within it the germs of those acute dissensions which came to a climax in the feuds of the Puritans and Prelatists, and which ended in an appeal to the sword under a weak and sentimental Stuart king.

It is no use regretting the past. But we may, at

least, learn a lesson from it, and see how to do better should an opportunity for a new Reformation offer. Jewell, Hooker, and the best of the Reformers, were on the right track in holding up the principle of continuity, and of the unbroken descent, so far as it could be maintained, of apostolic doctrine and discipline. So far, they stood out for a truth which the Edwardian school of Reformers had nearly let go and forgotten, viz. the continuity of the Catholic Church. But in an uncritical age, when the Renaissance and the revival of Greek letters was itself a novelty, it was ill understood even by the handful of scholars gathered around Erasmus and Colet. The Greek Fathers were little read and less understood. The great name of Augustine overshadowed the whole West. The one heresy was to differ from this one doctor of all the Schoolmen and of all the Reformers alike. Bishop Cox once ventured to take Queen Elizabeth to task for reading Chrysostom's Homilies. Those of Augustine were, as he said, much more wholesome fare — much more distinct against "what the Pelagians vainly talk." Had our Reformers been riper Greek scholars, had they travelled farther to the east than Carthage, and studied in the early schools of Antioch and Alexandria, they would have met with a theology ready to their hand, on which Reformation doctrine might have modelled itself at once and for ever. Instead of that, they uncritically stopped short at the rigid type of narrow theology which Augustine had fixed on in his day, and beyond which the West has not since made any real advance. The result has been a call, in our day, for a new Reformation. What is known as "broad" theology, or "new" theology, is summed up in the two phrases—1st, the Logos doctrine of the inner light; and 2nd, the education of the human race with salvation open to all here or hereafter. But these two truths would not have been stamped out as crypto-heresy, or driven into a corner to take refuge as the hidden gospel of certain mystics and Cambridge Platonists, had the Greek Fathers been better known and more widely read. As it was, the English Reformers, with scarcely an exception, differing widely as they did in the lengths to which they pushed their Augustinianism, agreed, at least, in this, that the great Carthaginian was the true fountainhead of theology, and the one unerring interpreter of the "Teaching of the Twelve."

The result of this initial error was more serious than we might at first suppose it would be. But we know that no lie is of the truth, and, consequently no error, which is a kind of lie in the germ, the scorpion in the egg stage, ever remains a single error. It genders of its kind. Need we wonder, then, that the history of theology is the history of afterthought, or of wrong hypotheses—cycles on epicycles scribbled o'er, as in the old geocentric theory of astronomy. Vinet saw this in his day, when he hinted that there was some tremendous error in the popular theology which the next century would stand aghast at. It is a pity Vinet was not more explicit; but, as a revivalist of the Réveil movement in Switzerland, he had to move on the same lines, and not stand aside and criticise the current Calvinism, with its limitations and shortcomings. A much bolder spirit was that of Beccaria, who, setting out as a law reformer to displace the vindictive theory of punishment by the reformatory, he went on consistently to point out that error was the rule, and truth the exception, in all three faculties alike of law, physic, and divinity. "The story of human progress presents to us," he says, "the picture of an immense sea of error, in which only a few in confusion, and at a vast distance from each other, emerge to the surface of truth." Censures bold and unsparing such as these may pass unchallenged in any secular science, but to charge the Church universal, the "witness as well as keeper of Holy Writ," with deliberately misconstruing the document on which her charter rests, this sounds presumptuous in a Christian advocate. Does he not put himself out of court by this rash assertion that the current interpretation is all wrong, and the precedents which have hitherto ruled in court are based on a grave misconstruction of the terms of the last will and testament of the testator himself?

So serious a charge must have strong supports, which we are now prepared to give it. The testament or will of God to men must have certain interpreters who are authorised, because first hand, as well as others who are mere glossarists or case lawyers, because they have no first hand knowledge of the will or its maker, but only gather the intentions of the devisor from certain phrases of the document which have little or no bearing on the will as a whole. Let us begin in this way by trying to find out the true construction of the "will" from the teaching of a single interpreter, the apostle of the Gentiles, whom all agree to accept as final and authoritative. The Old Testament being the record of God's exclusive dealings with His covenant people, does not presumably travel outside the inner circle of the covenant. It is silent with regard to the hereafter,—silent as to the purposes of God with the mass of mankind in this life,—much more, therefore, with regard to the dim, unknown world to which we all pass at death. The beyond is briefly named as Sheol. What meaning the term Sheol gives up I leave Hebrew critics to say. We may exclude, then, the Old Testament, with no disrespect to its teaching as a "sealed book," with regard to God's general purposes towards the mass of mankind here or hereafter.

I go farther. I make bold to say that of the inspired writers of the New Testament, the apostle of the Gentiles alone seems to have wrung out the meaning of God's ultimate purpose in the call of the Gentiles; nor let this seem strange, as if we disparaged the "Teaching of the Twelve." The apostle of the circumcision distinctly limits his teaching to the circumcision. When he writes a letter, it is to the Diaspora of certain provinces who were the elect remnant out of the mass of his unregenerate countrymen. In his "brother Paul" there were things hard to be understood—probably referring to that universalism, that wide gospel, to all, which, as from sad experience since we know, has never been proclaimed as the gospel, but ignorant and unstable men have wrested it unto their own destruction. God's dealing with the Gentiles, and salvation here or hereafter, lay outside the covenant, and waited till a new commission was given and a new apostolate was raised up.

In this sense the Apostle St. Paul magnifies his office. He is never weary of telling us that his message is a new gospel, an everlasting gospel, a message so wide in its bearings that it was a mystery which had been kept silent for æonian ages, but now at last was made known to the sons of men. That mystery of which he was the steward and minister, and which he was required to be found faithful to, was the revelation that the Gentiles were to be fellow-heirs and one body in Christ. The equality of Jew and Gentile in the general Fatherhood of God was to have no stint. True, that for a time these Gentiles were only the "little dogs," and entitled to nothing more than the crumbs from their master's table. But all this was past from the day when the veil was rent in twain from the top to the bottom, and more significant still, if possible, the middle wall of partition was taken down. This is the Apostle Paul's ministry and commission. It has been so deeply misunderstood, almost from sub-apostolic times, that a legend could grow up uncontradicted to our day, that the two apostles, Peter and Paul, were the joint founders of the metropolitan Church of Rome. The legend itself is beneath criticism; but the ignorance it betrays of the contrast of Jew and Gentile shows how little those ages knew either of the limitations of one apostle or the world-embracing commission of the other.

Returning, then, to the Apostle St. Paul as the one authorised interpreter of the New Testament as the covenant or will of God to the mass of mankind in the gospel of His Son, we soon discern how far his knowledge in that mystery went. It is so comprehensive that he is a debtor both to Jew and Gentile, and seems possessed of a kind of enthusiasm of humanity to carry his message as far as to Rome, and even to set up no altar to Terminus there. Rome itself is only a stage on his journey to Spain; and whether he bathed his feet in the waters of the wide ocean, and stood like another Cortez "silent as on a peak of Darien," we leave legend to conjecture. In any case the spirit was willing, though, as the prisoner of the Lord, the flesh was weak. Now, in his letter to the Romans he distinctly declares that he was not ashamed of the gospel of God, for it was the power of God unto salvation unto all them that believe, both Jew and Greek. Would he not have been ashamed of his gospel had it been the same as that modern version of it, which, like a rift in a stormcloud, only shows a gleam of light on the few who are saved during the short years of man's life of ignorance and error here on earth? That this is the view—with all its Augustinian limitations of grace to those who believe and are baptized—of these honest translators of our English version, is only too apparent from the construction which they and others have put on the following paragraph, in which the apostle goes on to speak of a wrath of God revealed from heaven against all who hold back (not merely hold, as our translators misconstrue it) the truth of unrighteousness. The apostle, like the righteous Psalmist, was "terribly afraid for them that forget Thy law." He looked out on distant Rome as he once looked down on Damascus, the city of sweet waters; but to his spiritual vision Rome was a hell-pool of wickedness, a pest-house whose moral fetor was sickening. Had he been a seer like St. John, he might have had visions of the doom of this spiritual Sodom,—this Babylon of the West,—cast like a millstone into the sea: "Thus with violence shall that great city Babylon be thrown down." But he did not see Rome in this seer-like spirit, or even as Augustine four centuries later, who in his strange philosophy of history drew up a "tale of two cities"—the City of God and the City of Destruction.

To the apostle's larger, saner mind it seemed that the wrath of God was revealed, as it must be, against sin; for sin is its own tormentor. The fires of lust once kindled within burn, as all cases of spontaneous combustion do, till there is nothing left to consume; "self-fed and self-consumed" till "evil on itself shall back recoil, and mix no more with goodness," as Milton grandly describes it. But God's wrath against sin—this spontaneous combustion of evil from within, adding hate to hate and lust to lust—is no part of the gospel as such, as some would describe it of mercy after wrath. It is an incident, a terrible incident, which was sent to quicken his pace as the messenger of mercy; but the revelation of wrath is not part of the message itself, or even its background. Here it is that the afterthoughts of theology, the second unwiser thoughts about God, enter in. Men say that God is an angry God, and His fires on earth are hot; but hotter still those of hell. To preserve some at least from that hottest of all fires, this must be the genuine gospel. The real remedy begins and ends with the rescue—

> " Fly, Christian, to their rescue fly,
> Preach Jesus to them ere they die."

The second line of this sing-song hymn conditions the first. It is now or never. "At last," as the apostle teaches, the appointed time, the day of salvation, has come. But our Augustinian theology of afterthoughts reads the quotation forward not backward. Hereafter there is no appointed time—no day of salvation beyond the grave. This may or may not be so, but it is not the teaching of the passage.

But the apostle is strangely misunderstood, and God's gospel dishonoured, by reading into it these afterthoughts of traditional theology, which all date more or less from Augustine, when they were at last fixed as the reigning theology of the West. Discarding if we can—and it is not so easy as we think—all these prepossessions of current teaching, let us see what was the first thought of the apostle which fired him with such pity for Rome, such a longing to reach there, and to quench this flaming fire of sin and lust which seemed to him like a revelation of the wrath of God from heaven. Was it that unless put out in time it never could be quenched in eternity? He nowhere says so; all he teaches is that the gospel is such a sovereign remedy, the power of God unto salvation, that as soon as we believe, the fires of our hell within die down, we are no longer slaves to sin, but sit clothed and in our right mind at the feet of Jesus. The gospel, in a word, is *the* remedy for sin—the one antidote to the poison of diseased selfhood. God is not angry with His children because, like the lunatic boy of the Gospels or the man with the legion of devils, he cries out, What have we to do with Thee, Thou Son of God? God is not angry, but He is sorry; and all the more grieved when His ignorant disciples, these theologians of afterthoughts and of man's gospel, try to cast out the evil spirit and fail, and that only because of their own unbelief. It is no slight mistake when we make God responsible for our mistakes, and throw on His purposes, as Augustine and Calvin did, the limitations which arise from an ignorant practitioner misusing a remedy which in itself is a specific for all manner of sin and disease.

That the salvability of all men does not require *ex vi terminis* the ultimate salvation of all men, no serious thinker has ever asserted. Hence all anti-Augustinians, such as Origen and the Eastern Fathers, who were generally Pelagian, throw the responsibility on man as the shaper of his own destiny here and hereafter. So the moralist reasons that acts make habits, and habits character, and character once formed is fixed for ever. No one had been able to snap that fatal chain, the links of which Aristotle had firmly riveted, save Christ. It was He who came to destroy the works of the devil, and to whom demoniacs cried out, "Thou art the Son of God." But we have grown afraid of this limitless gospel of love, ashamed of it, as the apostle certainly was not. This power of God unto salvation is mighty to save; and even the will of man cannot weave a chain of acts, habits, and character which the grace of God bringing salvation cannot break. Why, then, men ask, if the gospel can break all chains, why do we not see them snap at the preaching of Christ crucified? The answer is, Why do we not see last year's snow ?—because it is *last* year's snow. But it is still the winter time of our existence in this prison-house of flesh. Many are called, but few chosen here. The reasons for the limitation of the gospel at present lie thick around us, like the thick-ribbed ice of an Arctic winter. The resistance of man's will is only one of many hindrances; the feebleness and unfaith of her ministers, the allurements of sin, all that is meant by the lust of the flesh, of the eye, and the pride of life, make up the rest. All these choke the word, and it becometh unfruitful. But we are no judges of what lies beyond. Even the apostle judged nothing before the time, and did not rush in, as modern universalists do, with an easy "Eureka" cry, since it is no longer regarded as damnable heresy to indulge the larger hope which a poet's phrase has now made a household word. On this subject the silence of God is expressive, and none should lift the veil till the time come and the day shall declare it. But the fault lies the other way with the dogmatic decisions of the Church of the past, which forbade that larger hope, and condemned the one Church Father who was too explicit in teaching that type of Christian Platonism, the key of which is that all punishment is remedial. The vindictive notion of punishment reigned in the Roman law courts, and passed thence unquestioned as an axiom of theology into Roman and Reformed scholastic divinity alike; and here we find it entrenched to this day, and met only by a timid protest here and there. Sometimes the "heart in wrath" stands up to say that there is some lie latent in the logic of that head religion, in those afterthoughts of theology which all deplore, but few have the courage to face on Scripture grounds.

What, then, we return to ask, was the real mind of the apostle, which we can only gather from a few hints up and down his letters? Was it Augustinian, as the majority hold; or would he have turned on Augustine a look of wonder for so perverting his gospel? That he is a universalist in idea none can dispute. "As in Adam all die, so in Christ shall all be made alive,"—a most incautious expression of Augustinianism, is the legitimate outcome of Paulinism. But ingenious minds remind us that there may be truth in *idea* which does not become true in *fact*. God's intention to put all men into a salvable state may fail in fact through an unbelief, and then free will and its abuse is the short and ready explanation of this logical antinomy, this surd or insoluble problem. But the simpler way out of the difficulty is to confess that none of us know what eternity means, and what dispensations lie in the scenes beyond, all folded up like the colour and perfume in a rosebud. Unfortunately for Latin theology, the three Carthaginians, Tertullian, Cyprian, and Augustine, more Carthaginian than Christian, more Pessimist than Platonist, moulded a theology for us, into which, as time went on, the minds of men became fixed, and out of which they are only slowly emerging under two influences, one on the side of the new jurisprudence, the other on the side of the new geology. The law reform of our age is that all punishment is, or ought to be, remedial. This is no longer a piece of pure Platonism, one of the many abstractions of an ideal republic. It has been tried, and to some extent succeeded, and so at least it has set men thinking, that if our criminal code is rising slowly, and after many reactions, to the reformatory stage, may we not so think of the great Judge and Father of men as a Father first and a Judge afterwards, and that His very judgments are mercies disguised? Then, again, Science as well as Law has her analogies of good days to come. All points to a past without form and void, all points to a future when kosmos will overtake chaos; man's ape-like qualities will be dwarfed, the rational and the spiritual be developed, and so the great purpose be reached, man the crown of all things, and the final stage be reached of the evolution of the second Adam out of the first, as the first Adam was an evolution out of many lower forms of animal life. These are some of the lessons which law and science have to teach theology.

But it is needless to go farther into this. We shall never explain why the gospel, in its breadth, length, depth, and height, has not as yet been adjusted to our little systems, for which it is too great. Let us be thankful that we have not lost more of the message in its fulness under the accretions of error. Instead of denouncing these afterthoughts as apostasies, let us admit there is a kind of economy in the dispensation of a gospel whose unclouded splendour would have made it still more incredible than it is. To a pure and sinless angel this message of God's measureless love is intuitively seen to be true, because worthy of God. To men in a mixed state of being, selfish, self-regarding, and who can only get as far as the notion of a "moral governor of the universe"—a gospel of limitations and reserves for men as shut into the Church under the one key of baptism was the only gospel credible. To this day no other is really popular among earnest souls who enter the kingdom of heaven by violence. Universalism is justly stigmatised as "easy going." It may suit philosophers who are half sceptics already, but for an orthodox Churchman or a truly converted Christian to let his thoughts go out in the direction of salvation hereafter, is to put a sleeping potion to the soul. From that day out his yearning to make all men know what is the fellowship of this mystery is tainted by the indulgent excuse that they will some day come to know it, and if so, why press on them to flee from the wrath to come?

But all this arises from men taking sin and the punishment of sin to be two separate things, whereas they are really one and indivisible. All punishments are natural, as all sin is its own self-tormentor. Men invent hell, as the poets did, to make tyrants know that remorse would reach where the dagger of the assassin could not. The reason and the reasoning seem sound, that even if men can slip through God's fingers here, they cannot escape hereafter. It is *because* men so reason (though wrongly, for no sin ever escapes instant chastisement) that Christ's parable of *Dives* was cast in that form. Here was a man who fared sumptuously every day, and of whose torments of conscience there is no Tacitus to write the annals. But that he did not escape these furies of the soul hereafter, if not here, this was that sound element in popular thinking which our Lord wished to strengthen and confirm. We are coming to a time, however, when punishment will be seen to be inherent in evil. Every transgression and disobedience receives its due recompense of reward. With nature, as Huxley teaches, it is a word and a blow. We are struck, though we do not feel it at once, the instant we violate a single law of health. Such is the gospel of modern sanitarians, and theology is learning the same lesson. For this reason there is no longer the same great gulf fixed between retribution here and hereafter. Sin is the same tormentor in this world as in the next. When the vindictive element of punishment is evaporated, there will still remain the sense that the wages of sin is death, and that sin can gender nothing but death and torment here or hereafter. The immoral type of universalism which overlooks this is discredited even in America. It is a calumny on those who preach God's measureless love to say that they leave the door open to men to live as they list. No great truth ever dawned on mankind but owls and bats and birds of night flapped round to hoot at it, and warn us that this comes of too much sunlight. Milton saw this in his noble defence of liberty. It always throws reactionary minds into a fit of alarm that this must end in a century of sects. But truth is great, and must prevail. Afterthoughts, which are later births of time, do not live on in honour for ever, like the elder-born heirs of God, and joint-heirs with Christ of the kingdom of all things. Let us, then, go forward and rejoice in the liberty of our day, when we have freedom to say not only what is truth, but also to say out boldly how much error has mixed with that truth, like sand with gold, as it rolls down the river of time.

CHAPTER II.

THEOLOGY PROPER.

BEFORE we can enter on the subject of these afterthoughts of theology, we must set out with a clear conception of what we mean by theology, since no sound reasoner would attempt to deal with the pathology of the subject until he had first gained a clear conception of its physiology. So it would fare with us, if, as dogmatists too often do, we discuss the theology of any age before first deciding on what we understand, what we mean by theology in itself. Nor need we be at a loss for a definition of theology, since the Master has Himself deigned to define it. At the crowning stage of His ministry, in summing up all He had been given to teach, He thus sums it up: "And this is life eternal: that they might know Thee the only true God, and Jesus Christ whom Thou hast sent."

Theology, it will thus be seen, is not any knowledge of God as the Absolute. As the Absolute this God-conception is a branch of metaphysics, and a barren one, as all who have dipped into later German theosophists can recall to their sorrow. Nor, again, is theology to be confounded with what was once known as natural religion, and which, ever since Kant's *Critique*, has retired into comparative obscurity, together with ontology, cosmogony, and other such proofs of a Supreme Being. Theology, rightly considered, is the knowledge of God in His relation to us, the cardinal point of which lies in the truth which the old Greek poet had glanced at. "For we are also His offspring"—this is the true keynote; and theology, setting out from this kinship between us and God, we at once soar, as on wings of a spiritual intuition, across the abyss between creature and Creator. At any other point of departure theology is confronted with a primal difficulty, that its teachings are unthinkable, and that the only response of the baffled understanding is blank Agnosticism. Theology as taught in the schools is to a great degree responsible for raising many of the difficulties which it is unable afterwards to solve. It is in vain to invent a new meaning for the term faith, and to ask us to believe *because* we cannot understand. Such tricks with thought, such as that arch-sophist, the author of the *Grammar of Assent,* has attempted to popularise, only recoil on those that use them. Not to enter on the psychology of faith and its relation to reason, which is beside our subject, it is enough to remark here that faith is simply consent of the will, grounded on a previous assent of the understanding. It is no mere leap in the dark, as the theological mystery men would have us assume. Reason and faith run together, like the two disciples, to the same tomb, and though faith, the younger and more ardent of the two, outruns reason, yet it enters not in till the elder inquirer follows, to investigate whether these things are so or not, and to make sure that we have not followed "sophisticated myths," as the apostle assures us was not the case.

Faith, then, is not, as some divines teach, a new faculty, which enables us to swallow down mysteries whole and assimilate them after, in some ostrich fashion. Scholastic divines are largely responsible for conjuring up much of the doubt which they afterwards denounce as devil-born. Let us see to ourselves that we take the right departure in theology, and truths will then fall into their proper place, which when arranged in any other order refuse to come together, like the pieces in a child's dissected map. Out of Deism, when taken as our point of departure, nothing comes but confusion, with its demands on us of a transcendental faith to explain the way in which a transcendental Deity could be found in fashion as a man. The transcendental God of the old deistic theology must remain a being apart, like the Jahveh of the Hebrews or the Allah of the Kuran; and it is because Jews and Turks have been asked to conceive what to the human mind is inconceivable, and which, if accepted as a mere dogma, only opens the door to idolatry, that Monotheists outside Christendom have rejected the incarnation altogether; while those inside the pale have explained it away in some Arian or Crypto-Unitarian fashion.

But as soon as we replace the transcendental by the conception of an immanent Deity, our point of view is altered, and the stone is at once rolled away from the grave of a stolid unbelief. God is light: this is His first stage of immanency; and as light He broods over the darkness, though the darkness comprehends Him not. We are here on a stage of lower and lifeless being, and where consciousness has not so much as dawned. Then the next stage of immanency is when the light passes on into life, and earth and water swarm with beings who have all our senses, save one, the sense of selfhood and the yearning for some other self which we call love. Now we are on the threshold of the third and last stage of immanency. Light has passed up into life, and life now dawns into love. *Licht, Leben, Lieben;* this is Herder's Triad.

It is inscribed as his best epitaph and the sum of all his teaching in the Herder-room at Weimar—this is the true point of departure of theology. This, it is needless to say, is the theology of the beloved disciple; and it is mainly because, with the exception of the early Alexandrian Fathers, this has been nearly a sealed book to all but a few mystery and inner-light men among the Churches of the West, that theology has only made a stumbling-block of the incarnation, instead of its being the key to open all mysteries.

Happily, in our day the long eclipse is over, and the true light is beginning to shine. We have done speaking as our Puritan forefathers did of the attributes of God, justice and love and the rest, and of the provision whereby these warring attributes of justice and love are all alike harmonised in the sacrificial death of Christ. This mode of thinking has not been refuted merely by pitting text against text, much less by contrasting Pauline with Johannine theology in the way that Baur of Tübingen taught the *tendenz Kritik*. In a better and a more excellent way we have outgrown all this, by discovering the root of our mistakes, which lay in setting up a transcendental Deism, such as that of Descartes and Leibnitz, as the foundation for our faith in God "manifest in the flesh, justified in the spirit." Out of the data of Deism nothing but Deism can emerge. Each philosophy, in so far as it is a *prima philosophia* at all, genders after its kind. No discussion, as Sir W. Hamilton used to remind his pupils, can emerge in theology which has not first emerged in philosophy. As far as the east is from the west, so far is the intuitional thought of God as "not far from any one of us" from the mechanico-physical conception of God common throughout the whole West, regarded as He is as the Maker and Ruler of the universe, the Judge of all moral agents, and the Redeemer of the race.

The first afterthought of theology, its πρῶτον ψεῦδος, then, was to elide or overlook that Johannine conception of God, that in Him is light and no darkness at all, that light goes on to reveal itself as light rational and moral in all moral and rational agents. Nor is this all: the last word is love. The life was manifested. In man it found its true *nidus* for the incarnation; that incarnation, instead of a conception, repellant to thought, is the only explanation of these "fallings from as vanishings," that yearning of the pure in heart to see God, that hunger and thirst after righteousness which nothing but God in person can fill. The love of God which passeth knowledge can have one meaning and no other. It is integral and internal. To the Calvinist as to the Moslem, God is will—a mighty resistless will; and if He predestines some to eternal life and passes by others, who is he who can resist His will? To such demands the heart can only say in reply, "This is no God to adore; but, like the devils, we believe and tremble." Or, again, to the Deist of the mechanico-physical school, God is the wise artificer who has made all men, and hateth nothing that He hath made.

Let us be thankful that we have emerged at last out of the horrible pit of predestinarian sovereignty. But we still have not entered as yet into the "secrets of the Lord." We dare not say our Father unless we get deeper into God's character than as the mere *causa causarum*, the antecedent cause of all effects. In this sense God may be said to be the Father of the dew, the all-Father of the human family, in the sense that He is our maker. But when we say God is love, we predicate of Him not one attribute out of many, as the old Deistic school supposed. We affirm His inner essence, the fontal origin of all His perfections, to be love. As theologians use the special term "procession" in describing the Trinity, the

Son proceeding from the Father, and the Spirit again from the Father through the Son, let us put these three conceptions in their order of subordination—Love, Wisdom, Power or Will. The Father is Love, the Son is Wisdom, and the Spirit is the operating Will which enters our will, and which makes our wills—which are our own we know not how—at last to become Thine. Love is then supreme. It is this drawing of the Father, under the sense of our orphanage and crying for a Father's love, by which we come to the Son, and the Spirit takes up His dwelling in our spirits. Theology, then, has to get back to this fatherly conception before it can even unlearn its own afterthoughts, and one by one filter them out and separate the truth from the error.

Here let us observe that errors never enter in single-handed. The old saw is true, *Chimæra chimæram parit.* An inadequate conception of God, the obscuring of His fatherly by His magisterial character, began as soon as Roman, or rather Carthaginian, conceptions of God had replaced those Greek and Alexandrian concepts which faded away at last in mysticism. It was towards the end of the second century that Christendom was called on at last to develop itself, and, as we venture to think, it took the wrong turn. Singularly enough, two North African cities held out distinct ideals, the one hierarchical, the other educational, and the Church as a whole took the one and refused the other. Such offers in history are not repeated. With the rise and decline of the catechetical school of Alexandria, and all within the space of less than half a century, there grew up and passed away the one serious attempt to set up Christianity on the basis of the education of the human race. The school, as we admit, has ever held a certain secondary place as a valuable adjunct to the Church; but never before or since has the attempt been made to identify the school with the Church. The "Schoolmen," properly so called, moved on entirely different lines from those of the catechetical school of Alexandria. By the twelfth century the Church had made good her position as the ruling spirit of the age. She had conquered the barbarian conquerors of Rome itself, and was seated on the vacant throne of the Cæsars as the mistress alike of faith and morals, of law and religion. Out of her cloisters there stepped a race of monks who undertook to scatter the seeds of letters among the masses, and, at the same time, to watch over thought in its infancy, and see that it never broke bounds, or dared to depart from the traditional lines of Church teaching. It carefully set out with a *credo ut intelligam*, and only allowed of philosophy at all as the handmaid of faith. As soon as Abelard dared to turn the sentiment round the other way, and put knowledge as the condition of faith, instead of faith as the condition of knowledge, Church authority at once closed on him, and quenched at once a spirit of revolt from authority. Criticism has dared to assert itself openly only six centuries after Abelard was banished from Paris, and the first interdict put on the new learning.

But the catechetical school of Alexandria were scholastics of a different type from either Anselm or Abelard. It grew up as a protest against the Judaising, legalising party in the Church, and was an attempt to set forth Christianity on distinctly opposite lines from theirs. The question thus came up for decision towards the close of the sub-apostolic age, as to what shape the Church was finally to take. Two types were set before her to choose from—one the Hebrew-Latin type, as we may call it, into which, unhappily for her, she finally settled down; the other the Hellenist type of a Demos, or commonweath of free citizens, all equal, all alike kings and priests unto God, and whose moral and spiritual growth was left very much to the initiative of each member of the community. In Alexandria, as the meeting-point of all nationalities, and where Judaism itself had tried to set up a new type of thought, eclectic between Hebraism and Hellenism, and comprehending what was best in both, naturally enough there grew up a Christian type of electicism corresponding to that of Philo. This was represented by the catechetical school of Alexandria, the most remarkable attempt ever made to include the whole Church in a school. The Church had outgrown its congregational or synagogue stage, and the mould was preparing for a rigid hierarchical caste of priests, into which the still molten metal of the primitive faith was to be poured. Just at that critical moment, when the Church was in transition, an attempt was made to set up a totally distinct ideal. The Church was no longer to consider herself a sect cut off from the world, it was rather to become a school or porch to prepare the world for the higher truth. Philosophy, like Mosaism, had long been a training-ground for elect spirits, but philosophy—especially since Stoicism—had narrowed its portals. It had degenerated precisely in the same way as Judaism did. It had narrowed its mind, and to party give up what was meant for mankind. The new Platonism of Alexandria had fallen into the same excesses of spiritual pride and exclusiveness which had withered up Judaism. There was the same Pharisaism of the porch as of the law. The initiated were the elect; and as for the rest of mankind, they were as swine, too brutish to be of any final account.

Into this seething world of rival sects and races the Alexandrian school of catechists threw themselves, and made a noble attempt to rescue the Church, the synagogue, and the Stoics alike from the one bane common to all—the dangerous delusion that the truth was for them, not they for the truth. Setting out on the assumption that God's purpose was the education of the whole human family, they saw in the Logos doctrine of St. John the key to harmonise all truth, whether of Christian sect, Hebrew synagogue, or Stoic philosophy. At various stages of spiritual growth the Logos has been the light of men—to some, as Gentile truth-seekers—to others, as made under the yoke of the law; and lastly, in the fulness of times, as the Word made one flesh with us that we may become one spirit with Him. To educate all men up to this standard seemed to them the true ideal of the Church. True Gnosis was their keynote; and the Gnostic, as Clemens loves to describe himself, was to them the pattern philosopher and Christian in one. They regarded, moreover, a discipline of at least three years as imperative; it was the preliminary condition of entrance into the Christian Church. During the first year the catechumen was trained in the doctrine of the Eternal Father, the fountain of being, the first cause of all. In the second, the doctrine of the Son, under the two central mysteries of His incarnation and redeeming death. Then, in the third year, the final stage was reached in the doctrine of the Holy Ghost, and the mystery of His indwelling in the hearts of the regenerate people of God.

It will be easily seen from this sketch that theology proper, or the doctrine of the Father, Son, and Holy Ghost, made up the entire circle of Christian teaching in Alexandria. This is its real contrast with the theology of the West, into which other considerations of sin and salvation, the Church, its sacraments and ministry, entered in and raised discussions on which the early East had not so much as entered. It is impossible to understand the afterthoughts of theology, unless we so distinguish these first from the later drafts of Christian teaching. Had the school of Alexandria carried the day and fixed its type of religion on the world, it is not improbable that the world's history would have taken a different course. There would have been no such reaction as that of Justinian, who, under clerical prompting, at last shut up the schools of philosophy at Athens; there would have been no Byzantine type of sacerdotalism, no Roman attempt to reproduce a universal Church and State theocracy, no revolt from Rome merely to take up with a debased type of Augustinianism, such as the Reformation settled down to. Church history as we now read it would have been a blank, and then those insignificant sects of Mystics, Quakers, and Cambridge Platonists, who are all who can claim direct descent from the Alexandrian school, would then have expanded out of the sect stage, and become the great Catholic Church of the whole world.

Why it seemed best to the All-wise Father of spirits that this interesting educational experiment should have died still-born, as, we may add, the Cambridge Platonism afterwards did, it is not for us to say. Enough that it was so. It reminds us at least of that wise saying of Aristotle, ἐρᾶν βελτίστων νόσος τῆς ψυχῆς, The desire for perfection is a disease of the soul. Our ideals may be too lofty to be practicable, and in that case God takes the education of the human race out of our hands and passes it on to ruder, less spiritual instruments, who shape it less perfectly than we could do, but in the end, perhaps, more fittingly for future use than any mere idealist could do. At the same time, there are failures which are more instructive than any successes. The catechetical school of

Alexandria, by holding up the flag of an intuitional idealist religion, reminds us in this day what the goal is we should advance to. That goal is something which Rome and the Reformation have alike missed, with their Church and State controversies. It points to an age, millennial perhaps, when the Church itself shall become a school of prophets and teachers, and society at large, merging its old contrasts of sacred and secular, shall again rise into a theocracy such as Israel was designed to be, and when they shall no more teach each man his brother, "Know the Lord," but when all shall know Him, from the least to the greatest.

Why the Alexandrian type of theology proper failed to fix itself on the Church as the true type, while the Carthaginian or Roman dogmatic type succeeded, would lead us too far afield to inquire into here. On the whole, the Baur theory commends itself, not only as the most ingenious, but on the whole as the most historical. He sees in Church history a repetition of the old Roman instinct of government—

> "Tu regere imperio populos Romane memento."

The Church, plagued with Gnostic types of heresy, and failing to see, as her better instincts should have taught her, that truth can only fight error with weapons of its own forging, fell back on authority. It listened to the insidious excuse of Tertullian for pleading prescription. Much must be said for this short-sighted plea. Greek philosophy had joined hands with Jewish theosophy, and the Church knew not where to look for help. So serious did the danger seem, when it was assailed at once and from opposite sides by Jewish and Greek types of Gnosticism, the one from the monotheistic point of view impugning the Godhead, the other for the Docetic side explaining away the manhood of Christ, that the Church, in despair of beating error by mere apology, fell back on the method of authority. The Church was the only safe keeper of the deposit of sacred tradition; whoever impugned that tradition, let him be put out of the communion of saints. The next step, then, was to lodge that central authority, the power of the keys, in one man, who was the bishop or president of the Church. It was probably at first the bishop in council, as he sat *in cathedrâ* or seat of office, the arch-presbyter, from his apsidal throne, surrounded by his fellow-presbyters. From this there was but one step more to full-blown magisterial rule in the Church. To borrow Baur's metaphor, the Church drew into a kind of fortified camp, as the legions did when on their march. Unlike other armies, who lay down with their arms and trusted to chance against a night surprise, the Roman legionaries marched in a kind of moving camp. Every night there was a fresh stockade thrown up, a fresh *vallum et agger*, which, however rude, served the purposes of defence. This instinct of a nation of born soldiers passed from the prætorium to the basilica. Nor is it without significance that the courts of law in Rome became the earliest churches. To say nothing of the temples being utterly unsuited for congregational worship, the early Church saw in the tribune the pattern of her true holy place, and in the curule chair of the magistrate, her pattern of the holy table. It was the place where Jesus Christ her Head had witnessed a good confession before Pontius Pilate, and probably before any thought of Jewish altars had entered the mind of the early Church—which was a much later afterthought of a still more corrupt age—this correspondence of a basilica and a church had fastened itself on the thoughts of the second and third century Christians as a pattern to be copied when they should have rest from persecution.

Be this as it may, we do not care to lay too great stress on a correspondence which, after all, may turn out partial. There is little doubt that Roman ideas of jurisprudence and strategy largely entered into and modified the simpler draft of Christianity found among the Churches of the East. It is enough for our present contention if we lay stress on the thought that theology proper had its home in the East, while the Latin Fathers, almost without exception, took up much lower ground, on questions, such as of sin and redemption, of grace and church order, which do not touch the centre in the same deep way. That uncritical phrase the "Fathers" is the root of all our mistakes. Till we sift our Fathers in a critical sieve, passing Greek theology into one class and Latin anthropology into another, our study of the Fathers will be sterile, because wanting the light of true criticism. This contrast of East and West is by no means original; but it has been generally assumed as linguistic only, and then passed over as of no particular importance. It is the key, as we hold, to all our thinking on the subject. We are not insensible to the spiritual greatness of the Carthaginian school, and most of all to the great merits of the doctor of the Latin Church. His spiritual insight was penetrating and profound, and his deliverances on the Trinity, the Incarnation, and all other subjects bearing a theology proper, were of permanent value. But this was not the sphere of his true activity. As a theologian, he spent his strength on controversies, the importance of which he unduly estimated. We shall return to this subject elsewhere. All we contend for here is, that if theology be understood in its strictness as the knowledge of God in His triune relation to us as Father, Son, and Spirit, it is to the East we must look for light and leading. The West was "orthodox" on all these truths, but wanted the Logos doctrine, which is the clue to the mystery. It is sometimes *sermo* and sometimes *verbum* with which it tries to express the Greek *Logos*, and we have only to try to use either of these poor equivalents to see why, and in what sense, the West were not theologians in the sense that theology was understood by St. John and his disciples of the East.

It is the first thought of God which colours all afterthoughts. Such as we set out with, such is our conception of the great Supreme to the very end. Awe must enter in from the first and abide to the last; but there is the awe of filial fear, and the awe of the slave who would make some composition with his dread taskmaster. The theology of the West has been largely coloured with this debased conception which belongs to the primitive savage, and which soon ripens into superstition and priestcraft, unless it is purged out by a purer revelation of God such as the name of the Lord as revealed to Moses. This magisterial view of God on which His majesty overshadows His goodness, will descend and darken the whole field of theology; God's true character will be eclipsed; one half of the truth that "power belongeth unto God" will be taken at the expense of the other half, "also unto Thee appertaineth mercy," and the result will be disastrous to the whole. It is a libel on the Old Testament to describe God as a God of terror and wrath, who is only softened down in later times under the milder whisperings of a more humane age. We fail to see how much the superior civilisation of the age of Hezekiah over that of the Judges succeeded in humanising the half-savage conception of a local Jahveh, the patron Deity of the Hebrew tribes, who, bursting out of Egypt, made a clean sweep of the Canaanites. Taking the sacred text by itself, and not reading into it the inferences of later criticism, it seems that Moses stood at quite the same spiritual elevation as

Malachi. The prophets, in a word, were the purifiers of spiritual conceptions which had become debased by time, and the dead discharge of mere ritual functions by a caste of hereditary priests. But they were not the discoverers of a new and nobler conception of God than that which Israel had reached on the very dawn of its career,—at the height where Abraham stood when he looked down on the cities of the plain, and priest-like interceded with God for them,—at the height where Moses stood when he communed with God face to face on Sinai's peak, or when on Pisgah's height he looked out on the goodly land he was not to enter, and died there under the kiss of God. It seems to us that the phrase "progress" is a little unmeaning when applied to our spiritual intuitions. The covenant with the chosen people was entered on when Abraham was called out of Haran to serve the living God,—this was the true education of the race. True, there were advances,—the law and the prophets were each a stage on towards Messiah's times, but the advance was only given to meet and overcome serious relapses. The law was added because of transgressions, and the prophets in their turn came to replace the priesthood when it had sunk into formalism, that ritual of the letter out of which the typical meaning had departed.

All this teaches us that the first thoughts of the covenant people were their best thoughts. As for the after-growths, they were at best expedients to meet and overcome the deepening of corruption of the times. Nothing was really added to the covenant by these afterthoughts. The river as it broadened and deepened swept down certain impurities and also oxidised others, the volume remaining on the whole much the same, a mixed tide of good and evil. So we should say it has been with that later revelation of God as contained in the gospel. Those who set out with the Fatherhood of God have had little to learn. Their theology, like that of Abraham, the father of the faithful and the friend of God, stands at a height of spiritual elevation which we in later times may come up to, but certainly never can surpass. To know the true God, and Jesus Christ whom He has sent, this is the whole meaning of the message;—what can we add to it or take from it? The only way in which we can possibly attenuate its meaning, and so dim the glory of the gospel, is when we descend from these heights, and put up with that servile conception of our relation to God which the elder son is ever too prone to, while he is in the fields doing mere task-work of dry, dull, religionism, and grudging the Father's goodness towards returning prodigals. It is this root mistake of measuring the heart of God by our poor standards of love and duty, thinking "wickedly that He is altogether such as we are," which lies at the root of all these miserable afterthoughts which make up nine-tenths of our popular evangelical theology. They have been often refuted and exposed. By no one was this done so acutely and unflinchingly as by the late Thomas Erskine, who laid bare the Lutheran dogma of solifidian salvation, and also the Calvinist dogma of a mere arbitrary election.

We have nothing here to add at this stage of our argument, unless it be to press home the thought that afterthoughts can be swept off our spiritual sky only in one way. The north wind driveth away rain; so an angry countenance a backbiting tongue. A just jealousy, in a word, for the character of God—this must be our best, our only safeguard against that evangelical legalism which creeps in, as all afterthoughts do in later times, to steal away the hearts of men from the simplicity which is in Christ Jesus. We have maintained that the home of this misconception of God was in Latin rather than in Greek theology, arising chiefly from the magisterial view of God which the West was more inclined to than the East. Still, it would not have wrought all the mischief that it did in the West, but for those hard thoughts of God which sprang up in the wake of Augustine's predestinarianism. It was the singular quality of that perfervid African, that, having begun to brood on a particular line of thought, he never could rest till he had rounded it off by rejecting all those concessions and compromises which men run to in practical life. The best use of a theory when constructed was, according to Turgot, to demolish it and set up another in its stead. Not so thought Augustine. But, having passed over from his earlier and better stage of Christian Platonism, he moved altogether, and so went on to elaborate that coat of mail with predestination as its first link, and the final salvation of an elect remnant as its last link, with all the stages of grace worked up between. Canon Mozley, whom no one can accuse of any bias against Augustinianism, has struck at the root of the mistakes of this prince of dogmatists. He observes, "If revelation as a whole does not speak explicitly, revelation did not intend to do so; and to impose a definite truth upon it when it designedly stops short of one, is as real an error of interpretation as to deny a truth which it expresses."[1] Augustine, whose method was the vicious one of all dogmatists, which is first to lay down certain propositions, which are little else than our own philosophical conceptions, and then to turn to the Bible for verbal proof of these rash overreachings beyond that which is written, is thus an example and a warning. In his *Enchiridion* he piles up one assumption on another till we stand amazed at what a flimsy support

[1] Mozley, *Augustinian Doctrine of Predestination*, chap. v. p. 156.

the whole structure of this theology rests on. The angels who fell were to be replaced by an elect remnant out of another race created on purpose so to fill up the gap. We should like to have some better authority for this than Augustine's *ipse dixit.* It is a bold leap in the dark as to the reasons which moved God to create man. Then, as the sin of our first parent was all foreseen and provided for, he goes on to assert that "the restored part of humanity shall, in accordance with the promises of God, succeed to the place which the rebellious angels lost." So persuaded is he that actual *sin* as well as *guilt* becomes an inherited taint, that he discusses the question whether "children are involved in the guilt, not only of the first pair, but of their own immediate parents." He seems to feel that it is difficult to decide whether the sins of a man's other progenitors are imputed to him. There is much more of this gold-beating in the *Enchiridion* which we need not discuss here; but it is curiously illustrative of that temper of mind which is unable to stop short of conclusions till rounded off and admitting no question. He discusses, for instance, the text whether God will have all men to be saved, as 1 Tim. ii., and the conclusion he comes to is most sophistical: "who will have all men to be saved" means only "that no man is saved unless God wills his salvation; not that there is no man whose salvation He does not will, but that no man is saved apart from His will." Such evasions of the plain meaning of Scripture are so common in Augustine, that when we meet them in later writers we should know where they come from. It is only as we know the usual way of those who, having made a system of their own out of the *obiter dicta* of Holy Writ, seem surprised when reminded that truly inspired men are strangely negligent of their logical cobwebs. They state apparently contradictory truths about man's free will and God's purposes, faith and good works, and other such antitheta, in the sense that Dr. Mozley wisely remarks: "The two ideas of Divine Power and Free Will are, in short, two great tendencies of thought inherent in our minds which contradict each other, and can never be united or brought to a common end, and which, therefore, inasmuch as the essential condition of absolute truth is consistency with other truth, can never, in the present state of our faculties, become absolute truths, but must for ever remain contradictory tendencies of thought going on side by side till they are lost sight of and disappear in the haze of our conceptions, like two parallel straight lines which go on to infinity without meeting."

These wise reflections of Mozley seem an echo of the Hamiltonian teaching of the limitation of our faculties to construct a philosophy of the Absolute. But they had not occurred to Augustine, who, setting out on the single track of the eternal purpose of God, had to push aside, one by one, every other theory of life which conflicted with it, till he had reached the last stage of determinism. Not all at once did Augustine make this final breach with the purer traditions of the early Church; and nothing, we may add, would have drawn him down such an abyss of fatalism but the unhappy dogmatism of Pelagius in the contrary direction.

But this is the old story of all dogmatism, and is the warning against afterthinking theology which we are in search of. The test is whether it conflicts or not with our intuitive sense that "God is good and doeth good." Any misconception, such as that God, as Lord of all, must be master, and must lay down His own rules of right and wrong, is at once a deadly wound to truth. In this sentiment lies more Atheism than old-school theologians suspect. It is the "damned error," though pious brows may bless it, and approve it with a text. All afterthoughts, then, must come up to the bar of our "intuitions" or first thoughts; and if the complexion which they then show seems revolting to conscience, and hard to accept, we are bound at once to reject them as among the presumptuous conjectures of those who would say, Lord, are there few that shall be saved?

"Can tyrants but by tyrants conquered be?" we are tempted to ask; is there no escape from dogmatism but by dogmatism? Is the age to reel for ever and stagger like a drunken man, between the affirmations resting on bare authority and negations quite as unwarranted, and only leading down to gulfs of despair? Some restoration of belief is the cry of the age, but it must be on other, better grounds than the old dogmatism. It must rest on the threefold support of conscience, the average agreement of the Christian world, and the testimony of the historic record.

To this cry of pain we think we can offer a satisfactory reply. There is such a type of thought; there is such a body of truth, which is both catholic, *i.e.* expressive of the Christian consciousness, and also of the needs of the awakened conscience, and which is living water drawn direct from the fountainhead of Holy Writ. But to get it we must make a clean breach with dogmatism in all its phases. Theologies are such tyrants, that unless discarded they return by back doors and again assert their mastery over us. We are only safe when we discard dogma altogether, and fall back on the simpler Biblical phrase *didaché*, or the teaching. One is our Master, and all we are brethren. If doctors of the Church give us doctrine, let us thankfully take it for what it is worth. We shall venerate it in proportion as it comes from a venerable source. Antiquity is an immense presumption in favour of any teaching, but it is a presumption which may disappoint us if it approaches apostolic times, and yet seems to fail and come short. We want the signs of an apostle when we speak of apostolic teaching.

Dogma, on the other hand, strikes a totally different note. It comes with authority; it bears us down with the peremptory requirement, "Accept this or reject Church teaching;" and, after all, what is it but δόξα fossilised. Such and such a Father expressed an opinion; the majority came round to that way of thinking, and the consent, or rather the indolent assent, of the many is assumed to have given to an *obiter dictum* a finality which it never otherwise could lay claim to. This attitude of mind, common enough in theology, but utterly foreign to all other branches of thought, must have a root somewhere, either in some great virtue or in some striking defect of human nature. This limpet-like clinging to the rock of tradition and antiquity must be either a sterling quality, or the note of some strange halting of the mind in reaching after the things of God. It is to the latter side of our nature that we assign it.

Whenever men lay hold of a sense of God as the living God, then they wrestle with Him as Jacob of old did. They will not let Him go. "Righteous art Thou, O Lord; yet let me talk with Thee of Thy judgments." They sometimes rise, as the prophets do, into passionate pleadings with God, "Doubtless Thou art our Father, though Abraham acknowledge us not." They are like that Syro-Phœnician woman, ready to retort upon God, "Truth, Lord, yet the dogs eat of the crumbs." Such is faith at first hand. It is a persuasion and assurance that whatever else God is, He is not the mere omnipotence of a distant Deity. Sovereignty, unless it be of loving-kindness, is the very last, not the first and only thought of God. Such a misfaith as that of Ahaz, "I will not tempt the Lord by seeking a sign," is that atheism of the heart, the very sin of sins, which the record condemns from first to last.

But dogmatism at once brings us to a lower level of thought, in which systematic theology lives, moves, and has its being. It has its arrangements, covenants, creeds, and systems. The machine is so very perfect in itself that it is never to be taken to pieces, much less supposed that it is a mere provisional arrangement. The men of the first covenant were shocked at the prophet who hinted at another covenant founded upon better promises. We of this latter day have come to think his words "inspired," and admire the predictive power of Jeremiah; but the men of his own day saw no inspiration in such "blasphemous words against Moses and the law:" and because he was a prophet he earned a prophet's reward. The religious world was not worthy of him, or he of the religious world. Such is dogma in all ages. It lacks the one element of living faith, that grand discontent with things as they are, and the sublime determination to turn the world upside down rather than let them remain as they are. Faith, unlike dogma, must "know" God; it will put up with no mere eidolon or second-hand representation. Presentative truth is, in the Hamiltonian phrase of the Scotch common-sense school, to know things as they are: as long as we only know appearances, and have to put up with notions, our knowledge is representative only. It is a presentative truth only when perception and sensation exactly tally, and the real thing and our real idea of it are one and in harmony. Are we never to "know" God in this sense? If not, then Scripture misleads when it promises the pure in heart that they shall see God, and know Him in the only way that He can be known, by reflecting His moral perfections. To love God is to know Him, as conversely to know Him must be to love Him. On this relation of love to knowledge all true theology turns. It is the *pou sto* of the lever which moves the universe.

Not cognition, then, as an intellectual act, but knowledge in the intuitive sense that we know God to be light, and in Him no darkness at all,—this is the point where *didaché* and dogma part company. It is here that the Church ceases to be primitive, as she wrangles over words after their true meaning is exhausted. Every fossil was once the shell of some molluscous thing which had life in itself; so we admit it was with the old phrases of our old creeds. There was a time when the timeless generation of the Logos was worth contending for, as Athanasius did against the world. But when the Logos doctrine lost its true meaning, as it soon did in the West, it became mere logomachy, whether we hold with Tertullian, that God made the Word in time to be the first-born of every creature, which is plain Arianism; or whether we hold the opposite, which is the orthodox view. So essential is it to see that we not only hold the right faith, but also hold it in the right way, and as a living stock springing out of a living root. To know God as He is, —this, in a word, is theology proper; all outside this belongs to those afterthoughts of theology on which dogma lives, as on its native element.

To trace, then, the course of theology proper as compared with its afterthoughts, we must adhere to the strict etymology of the term. It is the doctrine of God and of His relations with us. Abstract theology or ontology, properly so called, lies too far in the background. It is abstruse and metaphysical, and beside the purpose of a revelation, properly so called. In the other extreme, theology, when it enters into anthopology, and takes up ground such as that of St. Anselm in his *Cur Deus Homo*, declines in the other direction from the true bent and bearing of theology. It is singular that the same St. Anselm, who in his Monologium and Prologium attempted to rest the existence of Deity on strict ontological grounds, should also have passed in the other extreme into a class of conceptions in his *Cur Deus Homo* in which theology is merged into anthropology. He loses the sense of Divine justice by assimilating it too much to the forensic conceptions of a Roman magistrate. The law became an abstraction to be set beside the throne of God Himself, and to which His other attributes must bow, or at least conform. His theory of a *satisfactio activa vicaria*, on which all modern teachings of the doctrine of the atonement rest, draws the idea of God too far down to a lower level than that of the scriptural standard to which the earliest ages conformed. In these opposite extremes of Anselm's teaching, we have an instance how ill able the West was to move in that inner circle of truth, the knowledge of God in Himself, which was the native element of theology in the East. The proper knowledge of mankind is man, is a smart epigram in Pope which sounds original. It is in reality a reflection of the whole mode of Western thinking on all subjects, theology not excepted, from Augustine's day and downward. With the exception of the Mystics, who were always regarded as only semi-orthodox, and bordering on Pantheism, Western divines made no disguise of confounding theology proper with anthropology. The incarnation and the Trinity itself were treated as "regulative" truths, or as incapable of speculative handling, but which assist us to approach the true kernel of the question which lay in the plan of salvation and the mode of God's reconciliation with sinners. The interest of the West in all questions of theology proper was quite subsidiary to the question of how God could be just and yet the justifier of them that believe. We are far from implying that the West was indifferent to the Arian controversy or to those discussions at Nice over which a Western theologian, Hosius of Cordova, presided as the representative of the voice of united Christendom. But its interest in these later discussions, on which Eutychians and Nestorians rent the East with their rival cries, was always comparatively languid. On the other hand, that Pelagian controversy to which the East was utterly indifferent, siding on the whole with Pelagius rather than Augustine, these disputes, which have their roots in anthropology, not in theology, were those which stirred the West to its depths.

This contrast is not accidental, but goes to the root of the whole question. For theology proper, we have to turn to the East: we there find ourselves in a region of thought where we can breathe freely, if we delight to dwell on a class of conceptions such as those which breathe throughout the whole of St. John's writings. What sounds "mystical" to our more practical Western needs, seemed to be the very vital air which they breathed. Take the orations of St. Athanasius, which to the superficial reader seem only echoes of a strife which we have laid to rest in condemning Arius and his opinions—to the careful student they come out as the breathings of a devout nature, to whom the Eternal Logos was much more than a mere abstraction, unmeaning apart from the incarnation. In our ignorance we smile at the zeal with which he contended for the eternal generation of the Son of God. To Athanasius and the orthodox East this was much more than a contention of words—as if it were a dispute of a diphthong, as Gibbon sarcastically describes it, justly enough from the mere deistical point of view. To Athanasius and the East this contention for the Homoousian carried the whole question of the Logos, to which the West was strangely insensible from the first. In Latin, such is the poverty of the language, there is no term at all equivalent to the Logos. Probably the reason of this—for speech is but the reflection of thought—was because this inherent plurality of persons in the Deity was only a dogma to Latin theology—infinitely important, no doubt, but still a dogma, which found no support in their fundamental conceptions of God in Himself. As long as we are content with a mere contrast of creature to Creator, there seems no need to go beyond the grounds of "regulative" theology, as we are now taught to phrase it, since Dean Mansel stole it from Kant's ethics and applied it to theology. We may be Monotheists with Jews and Moslems, or Tritheists with the orthodox East and West, but our Tritheism rests on the mere letter of certain texts, and has no warrant beyond the page of revelation. But to Athanasius and his school, the Logos, as the only possible mode of self-manifestation of the Absolute to the Relative, of the Infinite Father of all to the finite universe, this was a conception so vital, that the whole of revelation stood or fell with this truth of the eternal generation of the Son, or rather of the Logos, since sonship and fatherhood are relative terms, the one implying the other.

We never do justice to Athanasius unless we thus place him on his throne as the greatest of all theologians, because he contended to the death for this foundation truth of all theology. Disregarding the Logos doctrine and all it implies of mediation between the finite and the infinite, the Homoousian and Homoousian of Athanasius and Arius must seem a mere wrangle of words. Orthodox Western divines never say so, but they certainly imply as much; and the wide spread of Arianism, as well as its long duration, among the Gothic and other races converted to Christianity in the West, is easily accounted for by that tendency of Western theology to set out from a Deistic set of conceptions, on which Trinitarian teaching comes in as a kind of afterthought or awkward accommodation. The frequent lapses of the West into Arian and Unitarian view of God in later times are accounted for in the same way. Assuming Deism as our base line on which we rest our belief in God, Trinitarianism invariably rises like a building from an insecure foundation. So it has always struck the best and devoutest thinkers; hence the desire of our day to recast theology by revising its foundation conceptions of God. Deism or *l'être suprême* is no foundation on which to rear such a superstructure as that of Father, Son, and Holy Ghost. But when we set out with the Eternal Father, who through the Logos instrumentally, and by the Eternal Spirit effectively, has moved out into creation, we are then on ground out of which the Christian doctrine of the Trinity springs, as a building out of a rock into which its foundations are dug deep.

All that we mean by theology proper is contained in that text, "This is eternal life to know Thee, the true God, and Jesus Christ whom Thou hast sent." In proportion as we get back to that position, and rest in it as the Alpha and the Omega of our thinking, our theology becomes sound and stable. Without that, our theology will be only a house on the sand, as too much of our afterthoughts of derivative later theology is found to be. He is a theologian in the true sense of the term, who keeps close to that central truth, and then the knowledge of the living God never can be barren and unfruitful. It never can lie like a dead dogma in the dormitory of the soul; it must ever quicken us to fresh strivings after fellowship with Him whom to know is life everlasting.

CHAPTER III.

WHAT ARE AFTERTHOUGHTS?

HAVING seen what are the first thoughts of theology, and that they all centre round the doctrine of God in Christ, we are in a position to go on to consider what are afterthoughts, and how they take their rise. Theology is at its best and purest stage when it is intuitive; it is based on our spiritual instincts; its only logic is that best of all logic, when there is one single step, as it has been well said, from the premiss to the conclusion. "We know that the Son of God is come, and hath given us an understanding, that we may know Him that is true; and we are in Him that is true, even in His Son Jesus Christ. This is the true God, and eternal life." It is all contained here. The philosophy of the faith—if we do not wrong it by so describing it at all—is here all summed up in a phrase or two. What, then, we may ask, are our spiritual intuitions? Here we see that with a defective draft of human nature we have reached wrong conclusions with regard to the Divine nature. It could not be otherwise, since "in the image of God made He man;" and the result is that our bald and meagre psychology has resulted in a dogmatic defective theology of afterthoughts. By an intuitional theology we mean one grounded on the fundamental conception that man is the child of God, and something more than His creature. Into the scriptural proofs of this we need not enter; the genealogy of the second Adam, traced up through ancestors to the first Adam, who is said to be the son of God, may suffice. We come from God and go to God. The first and the last links of the long chain are fastened to the throne of God. Any other theory, such as that held by the whole West, which excludes this conception of the original and indissoluble relationship of the race to God under the one headship of Christ, must be an "afterthought," and must be rejected as such. It may not be impossible to harmonise the two theologies, but surely we must admit that it must be by interpreting afterthoughts in the light of first thoughts, and not the other way about. "Let God be true, and every man a liar,"—so we must conclude that if our eschatological inferences impugn the Divine perfections and dim our vision of God, we need scarcely ask which of the two must go overboard. So much the worse for afterthoughts.

It is only when we are familiar with these deep and lasting contrasts between Latin and Greek theology that we get hold of the master-key by which to determine what are, and what are not, afterthoughts in theology. In a word, we learn in this way to distinguish between a genuine and a spurious evolution in theology. The Greeks, at least until they had sunk into the slough of Byzantinism, after the removal of the seat of empire from old to new Rome, always understood the term theology in one definite sense only. It was the doctrine of God in His relation to man; but not conversely of man in his relation to God. Greeks invariably set out at the other end of the chain from Latins,—the one left off where the other began. But it will be said this comes to the same thing,—whether we box the compass east to west or the other way about, west to east,—we come to the same point at last. Not so. The difference is more than verbal, whether we make man or God the starting-point of our inquiries on this subject. Setting out with man, we have to take him as we find him, blind and insensible to spiritual things. We have to find an explanation of this strange fact—we have to begin with a theory of original sin, a tradition of the fall, and the problem of evil in general. We get out of our depth all at once in a kind of theodicee, which lands us at last in a dilemma which no thinker has yet overcome, and which J. S. Mill admitted to be logically insoluble. Either God is all-goodness, but not all-mighty, or He is all-mighty, but not all-goodness. Pelagians and Augustinians, Arminians and Calvinists, have beaten their wings against the bars of this cage ever since Latin theology replaced Greek, as it did soon after Augustine's day, and we are no nearer a solution than ever.

On the other hand, setting out, as the Greeks did, at the other end of the problem, all unfolds itself in a simple and natural order, and there is no room for these gloomy afterthoughts which have made earth a prison-house, and evil a kind of Manichæan partner with good in the government of the universe. Let us notice the order in which the early Fathers of the Alexandrian school approached the problem. Their point of departure was the general Fatherhood of God,—of a God, let us add, who was not so much transcendent as immanent in the world. The opening verses of the Gospel of St. John is the key to all that is distinctively Hellenist in contrast with the Latin or magisterial conception of God. The Logos is *σπερματικός*, or germ-like, in the world; that Logos in man becomes reason or thought in its twofold manifestation of speech and action. At a loss for a Latin equivalent for the Greek *Logos*, the Latin mind lost hold of the primitive and deep significance of the thought that there was a Wisdom which was one with God, and yet which had its habitation with the children of men. The *verbum* of the Latins was bald, and carried with it no such connotation of terms; it awaked no such far-reaching associations, such latent adumbrations and anticipations of the incarnation. It has been well said by Bishop Lightfoot, that what the word was to the world, that Christ the incarnate Word is to the Church. Redemption is thus the pleroma of creation, the completing work of Him who filleth all in all. In any other sense than this, the description of the Church as His body, the fulness of Him who filleth all in all, is unmeaning. The most fruitful and original of Justin Martyr's opinions is that concerning the λόγος σπερματικός, the germinal word, the word that is sown as conscience in the hearts of all men. It is on the ground of this λόγος σπερματικός, this light which lighteth every man, this anticipation of Immanuel God with us, as the God in us of the light of conscience, that the Greeks maintained the true ground of the λόγος προφορικός as the Word manifested in the flesh, and by which the Holy Ghost was given without measure to Him who as Son of God was also Son of man.

The Latins, lacking the Logos doctrine, never could see the true grounds of the incarnation which were laid deep in the original and unchangeable relations of God to men. What Liebnitz describes as the sufficient cause is the only cause which adequately explains the effect. It leaves it no longer a bare phenomenon suspended in the air, open to sense perception, but accepted then as a final fact. The sufficient cause is that which, as soon as it is reached, transforms what was before arbitrary into a necessity; it renders it reasonable and consistent with all other views of things, thus impressing us with a settled sense of its truth. In this point of view Latin theology never has been "rational" in the sense that the early and best type of Greek theology harmonised reason and revelation. To the Hellenist mind there was no strained reconciliation between reason and faith. Such a rhetorical phrase as that of the Carthaginian Tertullian, *credo quia impossibile*, would have seemed a senseless swagger, if not a sin against true selfhood. The contrast between two theologies, for which we have to thank Aquinas, the one known as natural and the other as revealed, never so much as occurred to Greek thought when at its best and earliest stage. All revelation was an orderly process upward and inward. In this it anticipated what we now describe as evolution, and which old-school dogmatists, having hastily denied and derided, are now only too anxious to make their peace with. To the Greek the Eternal was from eternity immanent in the universe, and has manifested Himself in time under three stages, as Light, as Life, and as Love. It is at the last and highest stage, as Love, that He breaks into consciousness, as the intelligent and spiritual agent, revealing Himself to man by that which, in the early Hebrew record, is said to be the voice of the Lord. "Where art thou, Adam?" is the first utterance of God in which we see the first link of the long chain of recovery of God-consciousness let down to the erring child from his offended Father in heaven. All after-revelation is nothing more than the unfolding of that far-reaching cry, "Where art thou?" History may be said to contain two chapters, and only two—one in which man seeks after God and loses himself in the search; and a second, in which God seeks after man, and seeks, as the shepherd after the lost sheep, until He finds it.

Speaking, then, generally, we may say that early Greek theology held fast by this clue which Latin never seems to have known. The best apologists, who are without exception of the Greek school, all keep to this leading principle, which the Latins lost sight of, that secular and sacred history are only different sides of the same truth, corresponding to the Word in the world and the Word in the Church. Philosophy was to the Greeks the same propædeutic that Mosaism was to the Hebrews. In both cases men were placed under tutors and governors. Hence the keynote of the Greek is the education of the human race, certainly not its probation, much less that last afterthought of a too logical theology, its reprobation. All those gloomy inferences from the known to the unknown, which make up the body of what is known as Augustinian theology, were unheard of in the Church until the close of the fourth century. They were echoes of the despairing cry of a dying world which had laid to heart only too seriously the *extra ecclesiam nulla salus* dogma. Is it accidental—we think not—that three Carthaginian doctors, Tertullian, Cyprian, Augustine, are responsible for that arbitrary magisterial view of religion which is more Roman than Roman law itself? This is too often the colonial type of mind, to exaggerate the qualities of the mother country. American Puritanism ran to seed the home type of Calvinism, as we know, before the middle of the last century. Predestinarianism in New England reached its last term of Determinism, in which that pure and spiritual conception of election, as the progressive purpose of God to redeem the many through the few, which runs like a river through Holy Writ, is lost in the sands of a dark and hopeless fatalism. This was the point reached by Jonathan Edwards, when the outraged public conscience took the matter in hand,

and restored the balance by asserting the suppressed truth. It reasserted all the moral attributes of Deity. It set up a form of Deism which for the time concealed, if it did not deny, these trinitarian truths, to which a dominant Calvinism had given a twist. In any case, the protest against the God of Jonathan Edwards ran its course, and in the way that we might expect; and at last the Christian consciousness of America has set itself to build up a new theology to replace the old. It has set out from the low ground of Deism, passing on then through transcendentalism, intuitionalism, and other vague phases of thought of the Emerson school, it has reached at last the same point from which theology began to decline in the wrong direction, when by the third century Alexandrianism began to give way to Carthaginianism.

It is to three Carthaginian doctors, then, that we trace this development of the Latin Church in the line of extreme dogmatism. All three were rhetoricians, and of a debased provincial type. Tertullian, the father of this deviation in the wrong direction, brought into the service of dogmatics a fierce temper, which would have disgraced an advocate of the worst type of hired sophistry. The prescription of heretics, which was the poisoned weapon first brought into use by Tertullian, may be said to have led the way to rack and dungeon, to *Dominic* and his *domini canes*, Alva and the blood-bath of the Netherlands, Spain and its Inquisition. All lay, *as the eagle in its egg*, in this one misconception of truth by this fiery Carthaginian. His noble confession and martyrdom must not blind us to the sad fact that Cyprian was on the same line which Tertullian had laid down, on which he only too faithfully followed. *Da magistrum*, Give me my Master, was, according to Jerome, the phrase with which Cyprian, the father of the hierarchical, as Tertullian was of dogmatic, theology, took down these treatises which he never passed a day without perusing. It has been said by Harnack, that Cyprian polished the language that Tertullian had made; he sifted his thoughts, rounded them off, and turned them into current coin. *Nisi Lyra lyrasset, Luther non saltasset*, may be more or less true, for the filiation of ideas is often more mixed than we suppose. But it is as certain as that Socrates taught Xenophon and Plato, so Tertullian set in motion the hierarchical principle, the Roman regimental view of religion, which Cyprian took up with such determination. This theory, when passed on to a still abler Carthaginian, became in Augustine's hands that appalling conception of the Ecclesia Clavigera, with its two keys of baptism and extreme unction, with which, like a janitor, it stands at the two doors of life, passing the new-born babe by one sacrament into the visible communion of the faithful on earth, and by the other passing the dying into the dread world, with its vast spirals, upward and downward, on which the gloomy genius of Dante threw a lurid light of imagination in one direction, as Milton did in another.

To discuss all these afterthoughts of theology, sin and salvation, heaven, hell, and purgatory, grace and its two channels, faith and the sacraments, would be to write the history of Augustinianism in its many phases. Criticism of Augustine is like plying a pick on a rock of basalt. There has been too much waste of good hand labour of this kind by divines of the type of Jeremy Taylor and the liberal school of Anglicans, who, in a day before criticism was born, seemed to feel that mixed feeling for the great doctor of the West which the poet felt to his mistress—

"Nec tecum vivere possum nec sine."

Unable to trace the error to its true source in a departure

from the Greek conception of theology as beginning and ending with the knowledge of God in Christ, they stopped short at one of these half-way houses, which, whether we call it semi-Pelagianism, or in more modern phrase Arminianism, it disheartens us even to look into. To say that Augustine was right in his contention against Pelagius is quite to understate the truth. The Pelagian theory was little else than an afterthought of an afterthought. The ascetic theory of salvation by self-righteousness ran to seed in Pelagius, and to stamp it out was the smallest of Augustine's services to truth. Unfortunately it became a case of stamping on Plato's pride with greater. The anti-Pelagian Augustine not only came out of the fight victorious, as he deserved to be, but also burdened with a doctrine of grace so ultra-Pauline, that we feel it impossible to describe it unless by Joubert's phrase, "Les Jansenistes font la grâce une espece de quatrième personne de la sainte Trinité." The key to this mistake, which has been the bane of theology, Joubert strikes his finger on in one memorable phrase, "*Personnifier les mots est un mal funeste en théologie.*" This explains why the Church, from the first, favoured realism and consistently discouraged nominalism. Nominalism, which is free-thought in the germ, is death to dogmatic traditional theology of the Latin type. It was a true instinct which drew the Schoolmen to the side of realism; for as soon as mental concepts are taken out of the subjective sphere of concepts, and treated as ultimate, undeniable truths to be accepted as data of thought, behind which we dare not go, or ask the why or the wherefore of, at once slavery begins. Conscience is dethroned, and in its place is set up a director, he may be a father confessor or a popular preacher with a gilt-edged Bible,—but at once the new note of authority is struck. Dogmatism, in one of its two forms of an infallible Church or book,—it comes to the same thing whether in Church or book we have our one infallible interpreter,—becomes the doctrine of theology, and truth has to get back into its well, or muffle up its meaning in mysticism, if it is even allowed to whisper its thoughts at all.

To the last and greatest of the three Carthaginians we trace this strange aberration, by which he sought to compensate for that other aberration of his early life, the Manichæanism to which in a sense he returned in his very recoil from it. It is the irony of history that, as Tertullian set out orthodox and ended as a heretic, so Augustine began in heresy and worked back into straight orthodoxy. But the error and the truth in both cases were congenital, and congenial to the nature of both. There was that same fiery temper in both characters, mixed with a certain Punic faith, which is unable to understand that truth wants no champion, no challenging of error, no riding up and down the world and running a tilt against the smaller sectarianisms which grow out of men's earnestness, dashed as it is with ignorance. Far wiser is Coleridge's golden saying, "Presume yourself ignorant of a man's understanding until you understand his ignorance." This is the key to the highest type of toleration, which is that of being tolerant of intolerant people. But the saint-worship which throws an aureole round the head of the second and third of these Carthaginians, while the saintly prefix is refused to the first of the three, who was the undeniable master of both, is consistent with the monkish ignorance which denies to Origen a distinction allowed to men like Demetrius and Epiphanius,—men so contemptible that nothing but their rancour against Origen has helped to keep them in remembrance.

But enough of these contrasts between the first, second, and third redactors of the theology of the West. For all its later exorbitancies its first three teachers are not fairly responsible. The immoral fiction of sin imputed to the unconscious posterity of the first Adam, and the strange logic of the Westminster Confession on the subject of elect infants, this is an afterthought of an afterthought. In the case of Augustine, there were two mitigations to his cruel Carthaginian theology: he had reserved a *limbus infantum,* with its inarticulate wail of *infanti perdudi,* and he had emphasised the pious desire for an intermediate place lying not quite beyond the reach of our prayers on earth. It is fair to Augustine to add that he was the first doctor to do so, as consistently enough he had closed the gates of mercy on mankind. With a horrible inconsistency which alone explains the counter-Reformation, the Reformers went on to teach one-half of Augustinianism without the other, Zwingli always excepted,—the one Reformer to whom justice has never been done in orthodox or Anglican circles,—the Reformers turned the afterthoughts of Augustine into a strange mass of thorny contradictions, which it would tax a logician to cut his way through. The race, all endowed with separate immortal souls lodged in mortal bodies, enter the world one by one a foredoomed race, "hell-deserving sinners," as the old phrase was. Still, having lost the day by one probation, which turned out a defeat in Eden, they are sent into the world in a second state of probation, to form characters which are foredoomed to failure on account of some antenatal defect for which the race is not responsible, but which clings to it like the Nemesis in some Greek tragedy. Thus the probation of man is meant only to exhibit—justify it never can—this reprobation at the last day. Out of this fatal circle the semi-Pelagian and Arminian school, such as Jeremy Taylor and the Anglicans, and also Wesley and his followers, try to escape only to impale themselves on still greater difficulties. If we are the makers of our own character, and responsible for the whole issue on which eternity hangs, why is it that beings are flung ashore in life like that coming of Arthur born in a storm, and ending like that passing of Arthur in the din of battle? All this is more than perplexing on any of the two theories which, since Augustine's day, hold the field of the old orthodoxy.

But as soon as we get behind Augustine into a stratum of thought more primitive than that of the later Latin theology, we discover, as the German proverb has it, that "behind the hills there are people." There were brave men before Agamemnon, and so there were theologians before the austere doctor of Carthage, to whom the whole West has agreed to bow with unquestioning submission. In the apse of St. Peter's the four doctors of the Church, who are supposed to support the chair of Peter, are Ambrose, the administrator and statesman-bishop; Jerome, who gave the West its Latin version of the Scriptures; Gregory, the great model of the Papacy in its best estate; and Augustine, who, if not *summus episcopus,* is regarded as the one *doctor incomparabilis.* He surpasses them all in this unique quality, that he has formulated the whole theology of the West, and fixed it in a type which it has never since diverged from.

The dogma of original sin, out of which the whole of Augustinianism grows as a building out of its foundation, never held the same place in Greek theology as in Latin. It had been referred to indistinctly by Tertullian and Cyprian, and certain intimations of the two headships of the two Adams looking in that direction are to be found in the writings of Ambrose. According to this dogma, when taken in its harshest form, humanity is absolutely separated from God in consequence of Adam's sin. In the guilt of that sin the whole human race is implicated, and has therefore fallen under the wrath and condemnation of God—a condemnation which dooms the race as a whole as also each individual to a future of unending woe. So deeply is Augustine interested in establishing this position, that the redemption of the world by Christ inevitably assumes a subordinate place, and is practically denied. Adam, and not Christ, becomes the normal man, the type and representative, the federal head of the race. There is a solidarity of mankind in sin and guilt, but not in redemption—a solidarity in Adam, not in Christ. There stands, as it were, at the opening of the drama of human history a quasi-supernatural being, whose rebellion involves the whole human family in one common sentence of doom. How Augustine could have so misunderstood the apostle as to assume that the headship of the two Adams was not coextensive, is not apparent at a first glance. But unless we get back to Augustine's point of view, we shall fail to trace this afterthought of theology to its true tap root. It lay in the exaggerated conception of the "two cities," and that salvation depends on an act of grace on God's part, and of faith on man's part, to remove us out of the one city into the other. All the well-worn Old Testament illustrations of Noah and the ark, of Lot escaping out of Sodom, of the exodus out of Egypt, were pressed into the service of this one aspect of personal salvation. It was a case of spiritual subjective experience on Augustine's part, the sense of conversion and consequent salvation, which he extended into an obligation of all to pass under a similar experience. Conversion based on the text, "Ye must be born again," grew up in Augustine's mind into a kind of new decalogue. The rescue of a doomed, imperilled soul became the whole duty of man. "Hell-deserving sinner"—the phrase excusable, perhaps, as coming in the heat of the moment from a street preacher with a message to deliver, and calling for a response of "now or never"—passed into dogmatic theology, and underwent there, as words do, a silent transformation. Men forget the law of connotation of terms, and that a teaching might be experimentally true but dogmatically false. So it was that Augustine and his followers reached the startling conclusion that guilt passed from Adam to his unborn posterity, through forgetting that the moral consequences of evil are quite distinct from that physical sequence which we now call the law of heredity.

As a taint or defect, evil may pass on *per traducem;* but traducian guilt, or the forensic fiction of sin imputed, even though set off by a counter fiction of merit imputed, lands us in conclusions which the moral sense of mankind revolts at. The imputation of Adam's sin to his as yet sinless posterity is a strange exaggeration of the Pauline expression, that death passed over all, for that all have sinned; or, as the other rendering is, "all sinned in Adam as their federal head." But Augustine and his school forgot that the apostle, as if startled at his own conclusion, throws in considerations which go far to neutralise its apparent harshness, "not as the offence, and not as it was by one that sinned." He meets the obvious injustice of thus making the innocent suffer with the guilty. He remembers Abraham's plea, "That be far from Thee to do after this manner, to slay the righteous with the wicked;" so he throws out two considerations, first, that if it is dreadful to think that the mass of mankind suffer for the transgression of the one, on the other hand, to the mass of mankind (οἱ πολλοί) the grace and the gift of grace which is by one man "abounds." In the next verse he restates this truth, that "where sin abounds grace much more abounds;" for he adds, if the judgment was by one offence to condemnation, the free gift is of many offences unto justification. It comes, then, to this, that if one sinner made many sinners, and one sin brought many offences in its train, the remedy is co-extensive with the disease. It reaches to all, yea, it abounds. Apostolic language is exhausted in order to bar the strange perverse conclusion which Augustine, and after him Calvin, drew from his statement of the universal spread of evil from the sin of our first parent. It was a conclusion quite foreign to the Pauline type of thought, which was to set the second Adam's headship as, at least, coextensive to the headship of the first, and even something more, in so far as He was greater. We are thus able to say that we have gained, not lost, by the fall—

> "What Adam lost and forfeited for all,
> Christ keepeth now, who cannot fail or fall."

It puzzles us at first to see how the Augustinian school could have gone wrong. It seems that their afterthought of particular redemption grew out of the dogma of the salvation of the elect only. They reasoned, as men sometimes do, backwards: from their estimate of what the end must be to their opinion as to the provision for meeting that end. They reasoned on this disjunctive syllogism, either Christ died for all the sins of all men, and then all will be saved; or for some of the sins of all men, and then none will be saved; or, lastly, for all the sins of some men, and then some will be saved. Our only comment on it is the wise words of a greater than Augustine, his spiritual father in Christ, Ambrose of Milan,

"Non in dialecticâ complacuit Deo salvum facere populum suum" (*De Fide*, i. 5, s. 42). It is this logic in theology which has undone both logic and theology. Rules of reasoning are all very well, but when the distribution of middle terms is of our own making, the whole conclusion is arbitrary and worthless—we are weaving spiders' webs which even flies can push through. What kind of distribution of terms is that which speaks of sins and sinners as separable conceptions. It is mere logic-chopping to divide between all the sins of all men and some of the sins of all men, as if in God's sight there was any quantitative measure of evil at all, or as if salvation were a mere ransom for the penal consequences of sin. It was in the West, more than the East, this magisterial mode of thinking of evil grew up, and with it theories of the atonement which, though riddled through and through with criticism, have lingered on to this day. Even yet they are not argued out of the field; but we are outgrowing them, and may leave to the twentieth century to report that the doctrine of equivalence or compensation has passed out of the statute book of theology, like other pale ghosts of a jurisprudence now seen to be barbarous. Like all "afterthoughts," this notion of *quid pro quo* retribution went on till it reached the breaking point of self-contradiction. Equivalence, to Calvin's mind, suggested that as the elect were "hell-deserving" sinners, it was necessary that the Substitute should taste death in the sense of a *descensus ad inferos* never dreamed of before, and which would have revolted Augustine himself. Calvin held that eternal torments were undergone by Christ during that time when, as St. Peter teaches, He was preaching to the spirits in prison, whatever that means. Such a distortion as that of Calvin's has only to be named to be rejected, as it has been, even by his followers.

But it is as well to fasten on this *magister* of French logic some of the heretical conclusions which he does not spare others. If the representative of the redeemed endured eternal torments, only in a temporal sense, what is this but turning hell into purgatory, and so upsetting his own narrow creed of an eternal-punishment theory. The quibble that the intensity of Christ's sufferings made up for their non-eternity is worthy of its author; but it may be left to others to say that if this be "logic in theology," the less of such logic and the less of such theology the better for the true interests of morality and religion.

But the question remains, How are the sundered relationships to be restored? What is redemption, and how is it applied? The place of Christ in Augustine's scheme is not a prominent one, since humanity, as a whole, has not been redeemed. Augustine continues, it is true, to speak of Christ in the conventional way; but he no longer finds in His work any bond which unites God with humanity. The incarnation has become a mystery. God chose to accomplish human salvation, but as far as we can see He might have adopted some other method. Unquestionably in this criticism of Augustine there is the key to the deep contrast between East and West. The East is Johannine, the West exclusively Pauline in its Christology. Are we, then, to set these two apostles in opposition, and describe them offhand, as the Baur theory would do, as the respective heads of two rival theologies, in the same way as Paulinism and Petrinism are opposed in the Tübingen version of Acts. There is no need whatever to go so far as this. The East never effaced or ignored the sense of sin and the need of redemption. The teaching of St. John in his Epistles is quite as distinct as that of St. Paul on that subject; and the Alexandrian Fathers are quite explicit on the redemptive meaning of

Christ's death, as well as of its peculiar value. But they sought to hold the analogy or proportion of faith; and this same law of subordination, which they saw and taught in the doctrine of the Trinity, they also held in setting forth the work of Christ. As the Father sent the Son to be the propitiation for the world, so also the incarnation not only precedes the atonement in the order of time, but there is the same subordination to be traced between the two dogmas. The birth of Christ, in a sense, necessitates His death, as the seed of corn must die to bring forth much fruit. Fellowship with man carries with it as its complementary truth a fellowship with His sufferings and obedience to death, even the death of the cross. All this the East saw as clearly as the West. But to the devout but uncritical mind of Augustine, a few phrases in a single chapter of one of the Apostle Paul's Epistles seemed enough on which to build up a whole theology of two covenants, one of works and one of grace, of two federal heads of humanity, a first and second Adam, and then by a strange twist of the apostle's argument to draw an inference the very opposite to the apostle's true teaching, viz. that the redemption was not coextensive with the ruin. Universal damnation in Adam, and particular salvation in Christ. This seems a strange inference to draw from the twice-repeated expression, "Not as the offence, so also is the free gift," and again (see text in Rom. v. 15, 16), "And not as it was by one that sinned, so is the gift." Twice over the apostle is careful to explain (which the English translators, steeped in Augustinianism, have quite overlooked) that the many or the mass, if included in the ruin of the first Adam, are also included in the redemption of the second Adam. So wide, in a word, does the apostle throw open the gates of a universal salvation in Christ in the fifth chapter of the

Romans, that he has to explain the meaning of his own expressions in the sixth chapter, and to point out that his teaching does not lead up to an immoral universalism (too common to-day in America as a reaction against Calvinism), but the very contrary. He emphasises the true meaning of salvation, which is delivery from that form of sin which is selfhood; a redemption which has not even begun in us till the death of Christ produces in us a corresponding death to self, and we reckon ourselves to be dead indeed unto sin and alive unto righteousness.

It would lead us too far into exegesis, if we were to turn aside here to discuss how far Augustinianism is a narrow, misleading draft of the true Pauline teaching as to the race and its destinies. Enough here to remark that at the point where the turn was to be taken, the Bishop of Hippo turned the wrong handle, and so, like a careless pointsman, switched the theology of the West on to a wrong track. The Augustinian theology, as Dean Milman observes (*Latin Christianity*, i. p. 172), coincided with the tendencies of the age towards the growth of a strong sacerdotal system; and the sacerdotal system reconciled Christendom with the Augustinian theology. This explains the paradox, that two widely contrasted systems the Pelagian theory of creature merit by ascetic exercises, and the doctrine of grace without works, nestled together in the same Church, and only broke asunder when the true Augustinianism of grace without works was dug out of the mud of mediævalism by Luther and Calvin, and set up as the keynote to their teaching. Neither set of rival doctors, the Reformers nor the anti-Reformers, dared to traverse a single text of Augustine. Both were equally interested in upholding his reputation as almost, if not quite, on the level of Holy Writ, and the result is an unquestioning acceptance of Augustinianism through the whole West, with some exceptions which we have already glanced at.

It is no longer, then, a vague charge which we bring against the dogmatic theology of the entire West, that it is one long afterthought traceable to three Carthaginian teachers. Criticism has already begun to trace a contrast between North African and Alexandrian teaching; but, generally speaking, the verdict has gone in favour of North Africa. The overwhelming weight of prescription was so much in favour of Augustine, Cyprian, and Tertullian, that to set Tertullian and Origen in opposite scales, or Clement and Cyprian, or even Athanasius against Augustine, would seem to the uncritical mind to exchange brass for gold. Ruling ideas are not all at once overturned—these idols of the tribe and theatre are not turned out of doors like the idols of the den, and treated as our mere private delusions may be. Still, the tide has already turned, and is beginning to carry all with it, except a few old hulks moored on mud-banks high and dry beyond the reach of tidal waters. Even in Scotland and the States, where the high-water mark of dominant Augustinianism was reached a century ago, the reaction is too marked to be passed over. The Westminster Confession goes down every ten years into a deeper lumber-room than before, among the muniments of a now fossilised type of thought. The general Fatherhood of God, once so strange an expression, that when employed by Irving in a small Scotch church in London, it drew Brougham and Canning to hear a preacher of so singular and so unique a type of thought, has now passed out and become the common property of all. Scotch professors like the late Doctors Candlish and Crawford have disputed over the sense of Fatherhood—Is it adoptive only for the elect, or is it natural, and extended to the whole race in its relationship to God?—but even that phase of the controversy is now out of date, and with a great price the Church has gained her freedom to say "Our Father" over the race in general.

But never let us fail to admit the debt which we owe to the late Thomas Erskine for helping us to break the chains of Augustinianism, which even Butler contentedly wore a century ago. The "state of probation" theory of life remained an unchallenged dogma, although Lessing, a few years after Butler, had questioned it in a short treatise, only known in this country when Dr. Temple popularised it in an essay, the first of the *Essays and Reviews*, once so notorious. It is Erskine's distinguishing merit that he seized on this stronghold of the old theology, the probation theory of life, and turned the "position." For the term "probation" he substituted "education," and this changes our whole view of existence. That we come from God and go to God is the whole account of man. Passing through life we enter the foul and turbid stream of humanity, and so are befouled by our surroundings. The environments condition all life, whether of plant or animal; they modify, but do not wholly control it. They modify by elevating or depressing, and at certain extreme points may actually make life impossible. Within these limits there is room for the education of man to go on here below; but does this bar or forbid that education being carried on under more favourable conditions when transplanted to some fairer clime? Such is life at present, as in the lively allegory of Milton life is compared to the plant Hœmony, which "presents a small unsightly root, but of divine effect. The leaf is darkish, and had prickles on it; but in another clime bore a bright golden flower, but not in this." Such is life at present. The error of the

Augustinian school has been to shut us in to a short probation here, with "finality" written broad across the portal of the exit of life. But as soon as we replace the term probation by education, all these eschatological difficulties, which make the gospel according to Augustine a hard saying to many who are neither scoffers nor infidels in heart, will pass off of themselves. It was all the better that this alternative term "education" came, not from a trained theologian, but from a layman, whose training had been forensic, and who early in life had begun to suspect what lengths of error this Latin forensic theology had run to, when it turned the death of Christ into a transaction between three parties—the Judge, the prisoner, and his Advocate, who was also his Substitute, and paid the penalty in His person.

It has been truly said that no Eastern divine would have ever asked the question, *Cur Deus Homo?* which makes up Anselm's celebrated argument for the atonement. In the first place, a Greek would never have set out with a *cur* at all, a why and a wherefore, for the incarnation. Clearly to the mind of Anselm, as of all Latins after Augustine, the incarnation was a kind of afterthought of God. Sin and salvation were the facts of a morbid experience which he set out with. It is not man so much as the child of God, but man as a fallen, guilty rebel, that he sets out with. To forgive him freely might be the fatherly instinct of God, but these Latin theologians, steeped in Roman conceptions of forensic jurisprudence, saw that there was a bar to mercy in the demands of justice. There must be satisfaction and equivalence of punishment to guilt before the claims of justice could be discharged. Out of this grew all those theories of the atonement which we do not enumerate here, much less discuss. One immoral theory Anselm has the merit of laying to rest, for which later Greek theologians were more responsible than the Latins, viz. that man was the lawful prize and slave of Satan, and that the slaveholder's claims must be discharged before the ransom could be complete. Anselm took the dogma out of one difficulty only to land it in another. The debt or guilt of sin was due to one attribute of God. The schism was thus set up in the Divine nature, which has been closed only when Christ, Curtius like, leaped into the gulf, and so reconciled, not only man and God, but more than that, reconciled God's mercy and His justice. The incarnation, then, in Anselm's point of view, is not an end in itself, but simply a means to an end; and this exactly indicates the deep divergence between the older Greek and the later Latin theology. His coming as man is a mere preparation or condition, to give value to His death in the Latin view. To the Greek His coming alone lifts man up to the stage of becoming a partaker of a Divine nature, to which his whole training and antecedents were preparing the way.

It is needless to follow further these contrasts between East and West. To all liberal divines they have this consoling aspect, that we are not so heterodox as we were at first considered to be. When appealing against the school of Erskine as teaching another gospel different from the good old gospel of an angry God reconciled by a dying Son and Saviour, we can now lay our appeal for orthodoxy before any educated tribunal. To the question, "Whose are the Fathers?" we reply by asking, Which Fathers? If it be said the Fathers of the Latin Church, from Augustine downward, then we admit judgment goes against us. But if we lay our appeal to the Fathers of the oldest theology of all, that of Alexandria and Antioch, then we claim to be orthodox "old Catholics," and our opponents are the neologians. Nor is this all. Singular as it may seem, it is the oldest and the newest theologies which harmonise best. During the long interval of sixteen centuries, error has had the field almost to itself. Nor need we be surprised at this. When jurisprudence awoke from its long sleep under the humanitarian tone of last century, jurists like Beccaria were startled to find how strong was error, how weak was truth. Punishment in those days was almost exclusively vindictive, and, as Bentham puts it, it took out in severity what it lacked in certainty. "If I catch you, I'll skin you alive," seems to have been the merciless cry of the carnifex; and he was so often baulked of his prey, that, like a hungry beast, he did torture when he could catch a victim. "Luke's iron crown and Damien's bed of steel," such were the conceptions of the century which brought on the French Revolution.

It was in the dawn of that age that Beccaria lived and struck the note which has revolutionised our jurisprudence. He saw that severity had to give place to certainty. He did not go so far as Plato and the Platonist divines did, who held that all punishment is, or ought to be, remedial. But then Beccaria was only a jurist. He had to deal with crimes and punishments from a magistrate's point of view. His horizon was bounded by time. But if his view was limited, he saw clearly within these limits. He saw that error was the rule, and right opinion the exception all through life. "La storia," as he expresses it, "del progresso umano cì da l'idea di un immenso pelago d'errori in quale, pochi, e confusi, e a gran distanza, verità soprauuotano."—The story of human progress gives us the idea of a vast sea of error, in which only a few in confusion, and here and there, emerge to the surface of truth. If jurisprudence has thus seen and corrected its mistakes, it is time for theology to drop its old dogmatic note, and admit, with Vinet, there is some tremendous error in our popular theology which it is our duty to find out and expose.

This is the only class of criticism which is wholesome, and by which alone we can put down dogmatism. If we can get divines once to admit that they may be wrong in the dogmatic theology as much as jurists have been in jurisprudence or physicians in medicine, the point is carried. Our contention on the evil of afterthoughts is at an end, and the remedy in sight.

We have nothing more to add than the demand—surely a moderate one—that as one set of "ruling ideas," the Roman forensic, largely drawn on in the Augustinian theology, had set us on a wrong track, so we should leave each age to mould its own theology according to the "ruling ideas" then dominant. Far be it from us to seek to bind our grandchildren, or to pledge them to our conceptions, as if God had no more truth to break out of His word. This is the very temper we revolt from, and it is sad to remark that there are divines of the school of the larger hope who seem dogmatists turned inside out. They have given up some old fortress only to entrench themselves in a new. It comes with very bad grace when the heretics of one age turn round and play the persecutors of another. Shocking as the murder of Servetus by Calvin was, it deepens our horror when we know that Calvin almost played into the hands of the bishop of Vienne, taking care that he should be torn by the young leopard of Geneva lest he should fall into the fangs of the old lion of Rome. This crime of crimes darkened the bright promise of the Reformation, and prepared the way for that reaction in which the Spanish Jesuits were near making an end of it. After that day the dogmatic temper again drew breath, its deadly wound was healed, and all men again marvelled at the beast whose wound was so healed, and in such a singular way.

To us the lesson should not be lost. Let there be no more fossilising of truth by these afterthoughts of any kind, coming in from any quarter. *Antiquam exquirite matrem* should be our note, especially to those who lay such store on antiquity and the note of Catholic consent. It has been often said of Vincent of Lerins, who laid down the oft-quoted test of true catholicity against false, that this is nearly begging the question; but it has been little supposed that it was formulated by Vincent, not in blind submission to the reigning Augustinianism, but as a flag of revolt to its teaching. It was a recognition that these anthropological disputes as to sin and its heredity, and as to salvation and its extent, were in reality novelties, and failed of the true note of catholicity. They were not part of the teaching as laid down by the Church from the beginning, but derivations from doctrines which had been accepted as beyond dispute, that man was a sinner, but that Christ's salvation extended to the sin of the whole world. "Augustine's doctrine," as Mr. Allen truly remarks, "concerning original sin and its remission by baptism, as well as his views upon predestination, were regarded at the time as innovations, as well as a dangerous disturbance of the faith of the Church." Theodore of Mopsuestia, the greatest among Eastern theologians in the fifth century, ascribed Augustine's lack of insight into the Christian faith to his ignorance of the Scriptures. He called his doctrine of original sin a novelty recently set forth; he reflected on his lack of reverence and true fear, in asserting things about God which human justice would condemn, and with which no wise man could agree. But the most remarkable opposition to the Augustinian theology came from the remoter West, and was formulated by Vincent of Lerins in his famous motto, by which he sought at once a principle of Christian certitude as well as a convenient test for detecting error, "That should be held for Catholic truth which has been believed everywhere, always, and by all." Judged by this standpoint, the teaching of Augustine lacked every one of the three essential marks of truth.

It is probable enough that this widespread ascendancy of Augustinianism would not have maintained itself so long but for the utter decay of the Greek Church, under that debasing servility of the Church to palace intrigue, which is known as Byzantinism. It has been truly said that, just as the rise of scholasticism in the West was an attempt of the Latins to Hellenise, and so let a breath of philosophic thought pass over the stagnant morass of dead dogmatism; so, on the other hand, Greek theology in the age of its decline showed a tendency to Latinise, and to fall away from the high intuitional view of spiritual realities, by mixing its gold with the clay of legal conceptions. The result of this falling away of Greek theology into Byzantinism, by the adoption of a magical external type of ceremonial religion, has been that Reformers have ceased to look any longer for new light from the East, and have steadily set their faces to the far West. We have ceased to think of the Church of the future as a revised orthodox Church. That dream seems to us to-day to be out of date, and as hopeless as the Old Catholic movement, which, since Dr. Döllinger's death, seems to be given up by its most hopeful friends. So, in the same way, the well-meant attempts of our Patriarch of Canterbury to renew communion with the Patriarch of Constantinople has led to nothing; it is forgotten, and is as a sentimental dream, doomed only to pass out of the gate of ivory. This is only what we may expect as long as the East continues sunk, as at present, in a sleep of traditionalism. Naturally enough, in the absence of any other type of national life, Greeks clung to their priests in the same way as the Irish did. But just as the breath of independence coming from America has stirred the Irish Nationalists into an attitude opposed to priestly dictation, so it may, and probably will, come about in the East as soon as the last traces of Turkish ascendancy have passed away.

Then it may be possible for a Greek Church to arise, such as the Church of Athanasius and Chrysostom, and then, perhaps, we shall reach a higher unity in a complete setting aside of Augustinian afterthoughts by a new theology, which we shall discover to be older than the old. "So runs my dream; but what am I?" and so we may indulge hopes which may be realised, though not in our own time or in our way. In any case, *Magna est veritas.* It is not from one point, but from many, that the light breaks in at morning: it is not in one creek, but all along the shore, that the ocean swells the channel with the incoming tide; and so, when the time comes for larger thoughts and sweeter views of what God has prepared for them that love Him, our evangelical legalism, under names as great as Augustine, will pass away like an evil dream. This is the time appointed by the Father. He knows best why an evangelical legality should have overshadowed the whole West for fourteen centuries, and why tutors and governors should so long have held the yoke over the children. But the end must come at last, and this is the true reunion point of Christendom. This is not to be some new type of ecclesiasticism, born out of base compromise; it is a return to the point where dogma melts into doctrine, and theology recognises its true mission, which is to be an educational process. In this sense theology at its best is philosophy and ethics in one, vitalised and energised by the sense of a living, loving God and Father. Then shall our ancient discords between nature and grace, between law and gospel, between reason and faith, cease — we shall enter at once into that grand sense of unity summed up in the "one God, one law, one element." Instead of afterthoughts, theology shall at last yield back its first precious juice of the grape, and in that sense the mystical words of Christ may be said to attain their meaning, "I will henceforth drink no more of the fruit of the vine till I drink it new in my Father's kingdom."

If "charity be the blood of Christ as faith is His body," in the striking saying of Ignatius, then we can see in what sense He will drink this fruit of the vine new in His Father's kingdom. The kingdom or rule of the true Father of men has not yet come; but it is coming. The old wine of legality and doctrinalism is nearly spent, and the new wine of charity is ready to be poured out. The wine of charity poured out in the cup of comprehension, or a return to Catholicism in its true sense, awaits us in a future at hand but not yet come; and the signal of its coming will be the breaking up of sects and parties, and the return of the Church to such a simple and primitive standard known as the apostles' doctrine and fellowship, so that even those who stand outside will do so in the attitude of seekers, only to find it here or hereafter in the bosom of Him who is the Way, the Truth, and the Life.

CHAPTER IV.

DISSIPATION OF ENERGY.

THE "dissipation of energy" is the scientist's phrase for expressing the theory that some forces of the universe, such as much of the light and heat of the sun, go off into space infinite, and represent so much pure waste. On this subject we dare not venture an opinion; we know too little of the forces of the universe to hazard an opinion whether there is any waste at all, and whether forces which seem lost may not return like comets whose paths we are unable to calculate. But at least in the thoughts of men we may speak of a dissipation of energy. We may say of some thoughts that they wander through eternity

> "Swallowed up and lost
> In the wide womb of uncreated night,
> Devoid of sense and motion."

Such are these useless discussions [1] as to what might have been had events happened otherwise, had there been no

[1] The ingenious author of *The Unseen Universe* has discussed this question, Whether in the wheel of life all that comes on may not go off and leave not a rack behind? "Are we not inevitably led to conclude that our present state cannot last even for a lengthened period, but will be brought to an end long before the inevitable dissipation of energy shall have rendered our earth unfit for habitation?"—*The Unseen Universe*, p. 196, London 1884.

evil, no pain, no ruin, and no redemption. This type of thinking has happily gone out with the age of the Schoolmen. These disputes of Scotists and Thomists as to contingencies of other worlds outside our own, represent only the common-room talk of monks in their refectory,on which it was as idle to make books as it is waste of time for us to read them. The Church has gained this at least from the Kants and Lockes of philosophy, that she knows the limits of the human mind; she does not let down the plummet of reason too deep into the ocean of the hidden purpose of God. She has learned to be silent at least concerning the hidden things of God; and this is no small advantage gained on the side of truth. It is a deliverance from the tyranny of old outworn dogmatism.

At the same time, we have to see and determine at the outset what are and what are not the afterthoughts of theology. Some deductions we should describe as legitimate—they are no Epimethean afterthoughts, inquisitive reaching forth unto the unknown, or impertinent inferences that certain consequences must flow from certain admitted verities most surely believed among us. There are Promethean as well as Epimethean truths in theology, and we have now to seek for some canon or criterion by which we may distinguish between the two.

A text in St. John's Epistle seems to offer a simple and easy test. The apostle, having spoken in the previous verses of two truths of experience,—first, our knowing that whosoever is born of God sinneth not; and, secondly, our knowing that we are of God, and that the whole world, or rather the world as a whole, *i.e.* all that is of the world and its lusts, lieth in the evil one, and is placed in the sphere of his influence,—goes on to sum up that which is the whole of the knowledge of God, and that truth which "makes one thing of all theology." It is all contained in this, "We know that the Son of God is come, and hath given us an understanding" (*διάνοια*, a solecism in St. John's writings, and so all the more noticeable) "that we may know Him that is true" (*i.e.* the original norm and pattern of all things, any false representation of which is a mere idol, whether of the tribe, the theatre, or the den), "and we are in Him that is true, even in His Son Jesus Christ. This is the true God, and eternal life." To which St. John adds in a postscript full of significance, "Little children, keep yourselves from idols. Amen."

In this passage, as we venture to think, we have the criterion of what is the true and what is the false gnosis in theology. The true Gnostic is the theologian who does not read into theology what he afterwards reads out of it, anxious questions, chiefly anthropological, as to man and his dwelling-place here, or his destiny hereafter. Much that we call Augustinianism, for want of a better term, is of that theanthropological character. It may be true, it may be false; but it is of that mixture of philosophy with theology which, like all mixture of drinks, spoils both. Let mental philosophy, like physical science, go its own way. But this infecting of theology with metaphysics, and too often with muddy metaphysics, accounts for that degenerate type of dogmatism best described as the afterthoughts of theology. The strict sense of the term theology, which we must always insist on, is that knowledge of God as *ὁ ἀληθινός*, the true and genuine God, any refraction of whose rays, as through a prism or by diffraction, from these rays passing round the edges of some opaque object, must lead us to see only an *εἴδωλον*, some false image of God, which to adore or worship, under any pretext, however pious, is of the essence of idolatry.

What are known as Atheists should in charity rather be described as antitheists. They are, to borrow their favourite phrase, only iconoclasts of some image of God which to them seems devil-born. We need not discuss this further, but here will remark that true theology not only begins but ends in the knowledge of the true God. In a sense the centre is also the circumference. Of Him and to Him and through Him are all things. Any inquiry beyond this of knowing the true God as the Father in the Son, can be no Gnosis at all; it is that Gnosticism falsely so called which in the reaction fosters the growth of Agnosticism. Not a few Christian apologists in our day waste their time in replying to Agnosticism. They would do better in distinguishing, with Clement of Alexandria, what is the true from what is the false Gnostic. Gnosticism and Agnosticism being relative terms, the best argument against the Agnostic is, by his own admission, to drop that dogmatic, arrogant temper too common among certain divines, who, professing to hold the key of an inspired book in their hands, claim to have opened by it all doors and unlocked most if not all mysteries. As soon as the orthodox Gnostic begins to take up more modest ground, and to say with the wisest teacher of his day, "that the whole scheme of Scripture is not yet understood, and that if it ever comes to be understood before the restitution of all things, and without miraculous interpretations, it must be in the same way as natural knowledge is come at. Nor is it incredible," as he goes on to add, "that a book which has been so long in the possession of mankind should contain many truths not yet discovered." This cautious temper of Bishop Butler, which is the only antidote to Agnosticism, acts, as we may easily see, as a febrifuge would do by lowering the pulse of the old orthodox Gnostics who add inference to inference, and so build up a whole scheme of dogmatic theology on the deductive method only.

As soon, then, as theology begins to give up these outworks, as we have described them, of the defensive dogmatic method, men fear she will have nothing to fall back on. She will become, it is said, a bare skeleton, or rather the mere *simulacrum* and shadow of what she once was. But is this so? What remains of it after theology has surrendered one by one her afterthoughts? To this our answer is simple, What remains is theology properly so called. Theology etymologically means a discovery of the true God and of His dealings with us; but all knowledge being relative, we do not push on to transcendental theology, or the philosophy of the Absolute, which ends in mere word play. Dismissing all this as the new German scholasticism, as arbitrary as the old, we take our stand at that point where St. John is content to rest. To know God as He is in the person of His Son—this is theology; this is that eternal life which was with the Father, and is now revealed to us by the Son through the Holy Ghost.

There are, then, these first flowings of Scripture which we describe as theology proper; nor do we deny that there are certain legitimate inferences from them which all serious divines must go on to draw for themselves. They circle, in a word, around the Incarnation and that triune relationship of the Absolute which we call the doctrine of the Trinity. Here, as we have remarked, our centre becomes also our circumference. God has been defined as a circle whose centre is everywhere, but whose circumference is nowhere; which is only an antithetical way of saying that God is the Infinite Being; He is the ocean on whose shores we play as children with pebbles, unable even to conceive what we mean when we speak of that infinite which contains and surrounds all finite things. It is He who sitteth on the circle of the earth; but the centre is that which is present everywhere, and of which alone we are conscious. It is the awful presence of one whom we can never flee from or evade. This is the lesson which Jonah had to learn in one way, as perhaps we have to learn it in another; since, some by land and some by sea, some in the day and some in the dark, try to hide from the presence of the Lord God. A theology, then, which is not full of God, charged with the sense, not of His perfections only as mere abstractions, but of His presence as the one reality of life—such a theology is a mere second-rate draft of a grand original. Such has been too much of the theology of so-called systematic divinity. *Gott-ertrunkenes* has been the reproach against these pantheistic types from Spinoza to Schleiermacher, whose sole justification was that they were reactions against that Dutch flat of Deism into which the orthodoxy of last century had subsided. The mystics may have pushed too far this desire to make one thing of all theology. But at least it was a healthy reaction against that way of regarding God as if He were only another name for distributive justice, and doing what He wills with His own. Such shadows as these lie thick around us, while we are in the lower walks of life, and as mere field hands doing drudgery as hired servants, when we might have an elder brother portion. "Son, thou art ever with me, and all that I have is thine."

Far be it from us to rob any one of the least and lowest sense of the Great Supreme, to whom we must give account. But it is too true that those who describe God as their great taskmaster generally do so as slaves. Their service is only eye-service, and any worship only lip-honour, breath which the poor slave would fain deny but dares not. It is because men are too generally unspiritual, and, what is sadder still, content that it is so, that theology keeps as a rule to this region of "afterthoughts," with its provisions of pardon and its plans of salvation. We drive Jacob-like bargains with God, that in return for so much faith and works (and how much the schools and sects are not quite agreed on), we covenant that He shall be our God, and we will erect our little Bethels in token of such a covenant. But as soon as Jacob has wrestled with God and prevailed, and is known by his new name of Israel, men of the better sort get beyond this theology of afterthoughts, with its Lutheran, Calvinistic, and other glosses, and get up to the first thoughts as they flow from the inspired pen of a Paul or Peter or John. Theology then reasserts its true sense, described in the first clause of the Westminster Confession, that man's chief and highest end is to glorify God, and to enjoy Him for ever. But to glorify God, unless we know Him to be altogether glorious, is like the clashing of cymbals by slaves in a procession in which they have no part but as slaves. Too much of man's worship has been of that kind; and if the conception of God of these Westminster divines was all that was left us to hold on by, doubtless some of us might fall out of the ranks and describe ourselves as Agnostics.

Against this falling away from the "faith once delivered to the saints" there seems to be one and only one remedy. This is to decline to pay lip-homage to these "afterthoughts," and to point out how debased a copy they are of a glorious original. On this subject the tone of cultured men is deplorably weak. They see the falling away caused by confident negations; they know and admit that vamping up the old apologetics is of next to no use; that the usual apologies for the supernatural, for book inspiration, for the authority of the Church and its claim to be a witness and keeper of God's word, are all as useless as sending wooden ships into action with iron-clads. They persist in this to their own discomfiture. It may fortify the faith of those who believe already, to receive assurance that miracles are not incredible on the assumption of a personal God, that revelation with its corollary of plenary inspiration is also equally reasonable on the same data of a personal God, and that, lastly, the Church and her functions are also the necessary accompaniment of such a revelation; for the word without the witness of the Church is as incomplete as the Church without the warrant of the word. But the orthodox forget that this chain of deductive *à priori* reasoning from a personal God to His last incarnation or inhabiting of the Church by His Spirit, must, like all chains, depend on the strength of each separate link. If faith loses only a single link, then all is lost. This is the real objection which scientists feel to deductive reasoning in theology. To assume and then build up a whole theology on the personal will of God seems to them a mere anthropomorphism. It is the setting out with an assumption to which science presents a blank negation of Agnosticism. It may be so, the naturalist replies to our assumption, but nature knows nothing of it. Behind the *natura naturata* there is no doubt a *natura naturans,* but its relation to the universe is the same as that of art to nature, it aids and improves it; but it is always the case that nature is made better by no mean, but nature makes that mean. The scientist as such declines to take a single step outside the charmed circle of phenomena and their antecedents. The first cause which the Deist demands as a postulate, is to him a postulate of pure reason, which he neither affirms nor denies. Even Kant could only cut himself out of this charmed circle into which Hume had lured him, by a new dogmatism as audacious as the old. He laid down the categorical imperative of duty, and here with his back to the wall he faces all-comers. Eternal honour to Kant for this invention of the dogmatism of duty, which rears the temple of worship again out of its ruins, God and duty being the Jachin and Boaz on which this new temple of natural religion rests!

But if there be no categorical imperative, no demand of duty to which the youth may not reply with a side glance at consequences, where are we but back again to the great dismal swamp of scepticism under the mask of scientism. A new school of American transcendentalists have put Kant's Ezra-like reconstruction of the old temple in a couplet—

"So very nigh is God to man,
Such honour in his dust,
When duty whispers low, You can,
The youth replies, I must."

But the assumption of the first line carries the whole question of spiritualism against scepticism. "So very nigh is God to man,"—if this is a mere *petitio principii*, where are we? Alas, we have to say it is so in some cases though not in others! To one it is self-evident, and he turns to God and duty—in a word, he cometh to the light. To another this is a mere *que sais-je*, and he describes himself in a new phrase which Montaigne would have repeated with delight, as an Agnostic to intuitional truth.

The intuitive spiritual school who set out with the vision of God,—not an open vision, we admit, but the vision of God given in this tabernacle to the pure in heart,—to them theology can mean only one thing, the display of the Divine perfections, and the sense that the more perfectly they are displayed before the eyes of men the more disposed they will be to say with the Psalmist, "Oh, come let us worship, and fall down and kneel before the Lord our Maker!" But this must be the free service of sons, not the mere marching in procession of slaves, clashing cymbals of traditional and unverified belief.

The criterion, then, of what are forethoughts and what are afterthoughts is simpler than many suppose. Cutting ourselves loose from the traditions of men, and going up to the true fountainhead of God-consciousness, which is laid up in our own spiritual consciousness, let us work out a theology on lines, let us say, such as those of Barclay of Ury, the first apologist since the early Alexandrian school who rested the argument from revelation, not on the fall and darkness of nature, so much as on the light born with every one coming into the world. Revelation is thus supplementary to, not in place of, any knowledge of God gained from other sources. Simple as it may seem, this is the key to the standing controversy between the claims of natural and revealed religion. If it be that we come into the world with some seminal germs of spiritual light (the old innate ideas, as they were once inaccurately phrased, and as such quietly disposed of), then revelation becomes antecedently probable, and the foundations are laid for a spiritual theology deep in the rock of man's constitution as a child of God, though a lost and orphan child. The presumption that our heavenly Father will not leave us orphans, but by His Son and through His indwelling Spirit that He will come to us and in some way reveal Himself, is at once so strengthened that the antecedent difficulty begins to change sides. It is now no longer antecedently improbable that God should come and dwell among us and Shekinah among the children of men. On the contrary, we may throw on our opponents the way of showing that it is not so. The fool may say in his heart, "There is no God," *i.e.* he may put the thought of God from him with a peevish Tush! But the revelation of God has begun beforehand, when that candle of the Lord was lighted in our conscience, and which from our birth has given off some glimmers, though it be only that of the "smoking flax." As soon as we take our stand at that point, nine-tenths of the difficulties of harmonising nature and grace, the natural order and the supernatural, are seen to be of our own making, and arise from two exaggerations, to neither of which we need approach. If, on the one hand, man is a mere intellectual animal, and wholly dark and destitute of any spiritual instincts or cravings, how can he be illuminated *ab extra*? This is the puzzle which no orthodox theologian of that type can explain. "War nicht das auge sonnenhaft," as Goethe puts it in his inimitable lines—

> "Wie konnt'es in das Licht erblicken
> Lebt nicht in uns das Gottes eig'ne Kraft
> Wie konnt'uns Gottliches entzücken."

Were the eye not apprehensive of light, no amount of sunshine could ever produce in us the sense of seeing. This correspondence between organ and function runs through the whole of man's nature, and the fact that he craves some one to worship and adore, some one above his soulish self to keep him from sinking into a brutish self,—this must be our first evidence that God exists, and exists to us. To argue, as some short-sighted people have done, that we exalt revealed religion when we take the ground from under natural, deserves the contempt into which it has fallen. An obscure sect of "Bereans," as they were called in Scotland, held that opinion; but the worthy Dr. Archibald Campbell, who a century ago maintained, Hutchisonian-fashion, that the knowledge of the existence of God was derived from revelation alone and not from nature, has not left his mark outside his little sect, the very name of which is probably now forgotten in Scotland. The error in the opposite extreme is much more diffused, that all that can be known of God is known already through the open page of nature, so that no special revelation can ever be needed. If our sense of God is so confined that we are content with a *Deus Artifex*, who is also *vindex et Judex*, then these two leaves out of the open book of nature may suffice. Men with a superficial ethical code, content to dwell in decencies for ever, with no sense of sin, no ideals of holiness unsatisfied, no longings for the betterment of mankind at large—men of the world of this type may accept things as they are in this the best possible of all worlds. But easy optimism of this kind sits with an ill grace on those who profess to leave well alone, but who in reality only leave ill alone.

Setting aside these exaggerations, right and left, of those who deny that there is any natural religion, and of those who say that it suffices, we set out at the point of our being sons of God, but sons who are orphans or infants crying for the light, and with no language but a cry. Unless we strangely misread God's character, it follows from this that He will undertake man's education, and meet him exactly at the point where our gropings after our Father in heaven have gone wrong. What is idolatry but the attempt to get from nature more than she can give. She is our foster-mother, and with all the foolish fondness of fosterage does us no little harm.

"Yearnings she hath in her own natural kind,
And e'en with something of a mother's mind,
And no unworthy aim;
The homely nurse does all she can
To make her foster-child, her inmate man,
Forget the glories he hath known,
And that imperial palace whence he came."

These idolatries or nature worship, springing as they do out of sense, must lead downwards. This is why all cults outside the covenant only deepened the degeneration of man—they arrested progress at the beginning—they paralysed philosophy under the withering charge to which Socrates fell a victim, that it was a setter forth of strange gods. Never was morality able to disengage itself from the cobra-like embrace of immoral superstitions. The fountain of humanity was tainted at its source, and unless the Son of God had come forth Himself and dried up the fountain of pollution by making nature cults impossible after His coming, we should have lain in the same helpless state in the West that they are to this day in the East. In India there are debased and ugly symbolisms of nature to which a race in its childhood still pays pujah. As soon as the schoolmaster gets abroad in India, this pujah ends; but the educated Babu has nothing to put in its place. A new syncretism has sprung up, which seems a weak imitation of the English Deism of last century. It may be left to the fate of all imitations; it has no roots in itself. Hindus will not be slow to see that, like Babu English, it is our discarded clothes, and that only an inferior race wears cast-offs, or wears them long.

The true basis of man's spiritual nature lies in the thought that he is a son of God, and made in His image, though the sense of sonship has been forgotten through our long orphanage, while that image has been defiled by sin. For this reason a revelation is more than possible, it is probable. The presumptions are all in its favour; and to unfallen angelic natures the surprise must lie the other way, that man has lain so long grovelling in error and ignorance, and that God has looked on so long and with such apparent indifference to the cries of this Ishmael, our outcast race. Redemption and ultimate restoration of the race, root and branch, seems the conclusion which we are shut in to, and the only outstanding difficulty is this, why God moves so slowly and in such wide circles of sundry times and divers manners. Analogy is at best cold comfort. It is very true that the Saurian age, when "dragons of the prime fought and battled in their slime," may be an ugly foreshadow of the world as it now is. Well, then, does the prophet exclaim, "Oh that Thou wouldest rend the heavens and come down!" to which a psalmist's cry, "Why pluckest not thou thy hand out of thy bosom?" seems only too true an echo.

To argue that because revelation is only partially understood, that its partial extension is also designed, may have suited Butler's over-cautious temper. But this half-scepticism in one direction, mated with a half-scepticism in the other, only helps us a little way on out of the horrible pit of unbelief. As soon as we leave behind the stagnant marshes of Deism, and get up into the clearer air of a spiritual order of things, all our prospect brightens. In God's light we see light. Then our theology draws up a train of deductions which are not mere afterthoughts, because they do not spring from a mere governmental view of God. The first is that, as the Father sent the Son to be the Saviour of the world, so it is His will that the world should be saved; but every man in his own order—first the head, then the members—first the elect, then the remnant, that *massa perditionis* whom we have described as not of the election of grace. That a design of universal salvation should emerge in a universal home-bringing of younger sons, seems to be a deduction so obvious, that the wonder is it has been ever disputed. Nor would it have been, but that Catholic antiquity, in its recoil from Origenism, some of whose theories were too fantastic to deserve reply, had fastened on this, the least objectionable, on which to show that kind of Jehu zeal for Jehovah which is too often the note of a dead orthodoxy which mistakes formulas for faith. Augustine, as the late Dean Plumptre[1] truly remarks, shrank from the term Origenista, as the framers of Article XLII. of 1552 shrank from being classed with the Anabaptists or others who revived Origen's wider hope in the sixteenth century, and was led to disclaim more emphatically any approach to the special view of Origen. On the other hand, he continued also to assert, even more definitely, his own view of a purgatorial punishment for the baptized. Even in him, however, there is at times a strange absence of the horror and alarm with which the assertion of the hope of universal restoration has not unfrequently been met in later times. He admits that that view was held by *nonnulli immo quam plurimi*, who were led from feelings of human pity. He does not accept it, but he allows men to believe, if they like, that there will be a *mitigatio* and *levamen* of the punishment of the lost.

But some will say our afterthoughts in the direction of the larger hope are just as much *ultra vires* as those deductions of orthodoxy, that salvation is limited to the present place of being, and to men who, in the days of their flesh, had been enabled to walk, not after the flesh, but after the Spirit. We admit that all such reachings forth to the hereafter, whether in the direction of particularism or universalism, are mere feats of levitation, such as that of sleepers who, in their dreams, yield to delusions, and leap the life to come, and who suffer for their presumption. The true attitude on eschatology is that, since Scripture is silent, it is for us to keep silence,

[1] *Spirits in Prison*, p. 144, by Dean Plumptre.

and wait for the day. On this subject of the hereafter we stand precisely on the same footing as the children of the old covenant. Warburton's paradox, which, like all paradoxes, had its grain of truth, maintained that Moses sought to wean the people from the eschatology of Egypt, with its elaborate scheme of rewards and punishments held *in terrorem* over the heads of the ignorant masses by a caste of priests who were members of the governing body. Against this official type of a terrorising religion Moses entered the expressive protest of silence. He knew nothing, taught nothing of a God who winked hard at wickedness during the years of man's lifetime on earth, reserving His deferred payments of rewards and punishments for a world to come. The silence of Mosaism on all these subjects struck a deistical age, such as Warburton's, with an uncomfortable feeling of omission. Clearly here was a blot on the system of this clever legislator Moses, who, with all the wisdom of the Egyptians to hand, seems to have omitted future rewards and punishments, which was the very pulse of the machine of State in all other politics. Warburton saw this defect, and, like a keen apologist for orthodoxy in an unspiritual and deistical age, he turned round and twisted an objection into an argument. "Surely," so argued this bishop, "the omission by Moses, as it could not be accidental, was intentional. What a mark of a miraculous orgin it must be that he could work the machine of State by appealing to temporal rewards and punishments only, when Egyptian priests could only hold the vulgar in awe by calling in the hereafter to back up the task-master's lash in time. The whips and scorpions of the shadowland beyond the river were called in to reinforce the terrorism of temporal rulers. Moses must have been a marvellously clever man, and had a whole apparatus of miracles to back him up, before he dared to keep that many-headed beast, the people, in order without the lash of remorse and the branding-iron of eternal punishment."

So argued Warburton in the age of Deism; but his apologetics have gone to the same oblivion as the sceptics against whom he sharpened his pen. Defence and attack are alike out of date. We now see, as last century apparently did not, that a scheme of rewards and punishments on a nicely-graduated scale of terrorism is obsolete in jurisprudence, and for theology to furbish up such blunted arms is to show a stupid indifference to the best thoughts of the age. Ever since Beccaria replaced severity by certainty as the governing principle of law, a silent revolution has passed over men's minds. Without thinking why they do so, they have dropped without discussion the *Jupiter tonans* theology of our grandfathers: they have gone to their Bibles, and began to re-read them in the light of the new thoughts of God as the loving Father whose long-suffering is salvation. They now see that eternity is the sphere which the Eternal alone inhabits; and as for things created, from the angel to the amœba, they live only in so far as they live in Him. Thou takest away their breath, and they die. So of the animal world, and it is also true of man in so far as he leads a soulless, selfish life; "in that day all their thoughts perish," and so we render intellectual life and being together. Immortality is nowhere predicated save of the Eternal, and of those whose life here or hereafter is drawn from the fountain of life. Such was David's hope that his soul should not be left in Hades, or his flesh see corruption. There was a path of life even out of the Sheol of oblivion, and on this hope men lived and died from Moses to the Maccabees, trusting that the God of Abraham, Isaac, and Jacob, the God who is not the

God of the dead, but of the living, would be their God even for ever and ever.

Turning to the New Testament, we find at first, to our surprise, that it strikes the same note, and apparently does not lift the subject into a higher plane. The error, that the Jews knew nothing, is balanced off against an opposite error, that we latter-day saints know all about eschatology. We smile at the conceit of both dogmatisms. Martha at the grave of Lazarus was quietly disabused of her Pharisaic theology, the tradition of a Maccabean age, as to a resurrection of the last day. Christ cuts short her ratiocinations with a peremptory "I am"—the emphasis of which we seem to have overlooked, if we may judge by the language of the after-thinkers of theology, who are often Pharisees of the Martha type. As for "Resurrection," Christ would say, "I know of none" but in me: "I am the head of the new humanity, and the first-fruits of the dead." With one little word He seals up all the old fountains of Pharisaism,—would they had never been opened again!—and lays down the new law of the life eternal. It is a new law, which is, in truth, only the old which was from the beginning, that life is in Christ only, and that if He be the head of humanity, then it follows that "as in Adam all die, so in Christ shall all be made alive." There seems to be no limitations, unless of our own making; and here it is that the afterthoughts of theology come in. The heart of God is too large, His fatherly pity too profound, for His erring, ignorant, younger children, for the elder brother, the elect of our day, to understand it at all. He is angry, and will not come in on these terms, and so theology, with the aid of Augustine and other famous doctors, has drawn up a traditional scheme of theology, with all its provisions and safeguards, its limitations and conditions, some subjective, others objective, here of faith, there of the sacraments, which are so ingenious, but at the same time so perplexing to the minds of untrained theologians, that the poor vexed layman often dies like Nelson, hoping he has not been a great sinner, and that perhaps Christ's mercies may reach unto him, at least as a makeweight.

The criterion, then, as to what are and what are not mere afterthoughts of theology turns on this point. All outside "theology proper," limiting the term to its strict meaning, the doctrine of the love of the Father, the grace of the Son, and the fellowship of the Holy Ghost, are mere afterthoughts. They belong to that outside region in which the perspective is hazy, and theologians can make affirmations do for argument. There is no term so much misused as that of "grace," which the New Testament brims over with, and to which the awakened spiritual heart leaps up, as the bride in the song, to the voice of her beloved. Who would have thought that this term, which has

> "a charming sound, melodious to the ear,
> Heaven at the echo shall resound, and all the earth shall hear,"

could have become the key to lead us into another house of bondage—a legalism as bitter as the old legality which the Christian Pilgrim supposes he has got quit of? But so it is. It is impossible to glance at the long-standing old disputes of Jansenists and Jesuits, without feeling that truth does not lie so wholly on the Jansenist side as the inimitable wit of Pascal, backed by the fervour and austerity of Port Royal, would have us suppose. On the *victrix causa diis* principle, the world has judged that the Jansenists were right because Louis XIV., cajoled by the Jesuits, took the Pelagian side, and stamped out the Augustinianism of the half-reformed Gallican Church, thus crippling her religious together with her civil liberties at one rude touch of arbitrary power. The world has sat in judgment on the Jesuits, and dearly have they paid for their treacherous act of calling on the State to stamp out theological differences in the Church, which was to be Catholic, but only on their terms.

On the other hand, it must be said that the Jansenist sense of the term grace was almost as wide of the apostolic meaning as the Jesuit. It has been said with some justice, that Jansenists made of grace a kind of fourth Person of the Trinity. The taunt is not so wide of the mark as it seems. The old realist trick of taking a Biblical term, and then importing into it all sorts of derivative meanings, and so setting it up as a kind of entity to keep house for itself, has been the making of technical theology. It is the one parent source of all its "afterthoughts." As soon as we depolarise an expression, as the "Autocrat of the breakfast table" urges us to do, much of the mystification of scholastic theology in such phrases as Church, sacraments, grace, condignity, congruity, and what not, all go off. Realism is the one magician's wand which turns these rods into serpents, or serpents into rods, according as we take the primitive or the technical and after sense of the term grace. By itself the term grace simply means God's distinguishing favour to men, the beaming forth of His love in such a golden shower of warmth and light that it is able to pierce the mists of unbelief. Grace is described in the text: "God, who commandeth the light to shine out of darkness, hath shined in our hearts to give the light of the knowledge of God in the face of Jesus Christ."

But as soon as we thus think of grace, there steals into the mind this first afterthought on which theology begins to build. Why is grace efficacious in some and not efficacious in the case of others? To the term "grace," so simple by itself, we add an appellative, "efficacious;" and in trying to explain this we end, as too many interpreters do, by making simple things difficult. Every step we advance on the road of making religion easy, we only get farther into the tangle, and so lose ourselves, as the divines of the seventeenth century did, in interminable strifes between Remonstrants who Pelagianise, and the school of Free Grace. The criterion, then, here comes in. Theology is to be tested in this way as to whether it is pure or applied theology. Applied theology is the Shibboleth which may be slain at the brook—pure theology can render up but one meaning, that the Father loved the world, and sent His Son to be its Saviour. We are painfully conscious how meagre this aspect of God must seem to the trained theologian.

This is the true note which theology in Cambridge has never failed to strike, and whose philosophy, ever since the reaction against Paley set in, has emphasised the same note of "strong-siding champion conscience." May I name two only among our worthies of the near past whose memories still echo in the ears of the elders among us? They shall be the names of Hare and Whewell. It is not so much for what they taught (though much of this is precious to many of us as the aroma of spiritual and self-verifying thought, emancipating us from the leaden yoke of dull tradition and blind authority) that we shall revere the names of Hare and Whewell. Behind Hare and Whewell lay, of course, Coleridge, that Titan who might have been a Prometheus, had not a fatal spell, accursed as that rabble rout of Comus and his crew, arrested his will and paralysed it in the endeavour to produce something which the age would not willingly let die. As it was, his followers, the Coleridgians of the type of the Cambridge men of the early Victorian era, have caught up some of his Sibylline leaves and woven them into something like a system. It has traced the outlines of a new theology on lines not unlike his own "confessions of an inquiring spirit," which startled the old orthodoxy by its free utterances on the subject not of the matter, but the form; of inspiration, critical, but reverend at the same time as to the contents of the sacred book. It is Coleridge who, more than any other professed divine, broke the yoke of our old Bibliolatry, and asked us to face, fair and square, certain theories of the atonement, and to ring out their meaning, fearless of the taunt of a crypto-Socinianism being hurled at us. We in this day enjoy all this liberty, but forget at what a price it has been gained. We have been born free, let us all the more reverence those who bought us that freedom with a great price, the Cambridge Platonists of the seventeenth century, the Coleridgian Platonists of the nineteenth. They have left us a legacy which it is for us to improve by putting it out to interest. Light and liberty should be our twofold claim — light with which to explore the hidden meaning of the record, and liberty to deal with its details as the results of criticism call us to do. That which stands of theology after this straining off its lees of traditionalism will then be new wine of theology proper, which Christ on His coming in His kingdom left to His apostles as the authentic depository of truth. Our theology, in a word, will undergo that process of gradual purification, by eliminating extraneous and redundant afterthoughts, described in Ruckert's fable of the king and his library—

> "Von einem König wird erzahlt dass im Palast
> Er hat sich gehauft, die grosste Bücherlast."

Setting out on a royal progress, he found that his library would amount to a hundred-and-one camel-loads of books; which, finding burdensome, he set a hundred-and-one sages to work to condense into a single mule's burden of books. Even this, at last, seemed so much useless baggage, and a further condensation brought the whole contents of this library into a single pocket volume, which became the king's library in a hand-book.

But let us not in a seat of learning even seem to pour contempt on letters, much less on sacred letters. There always was, and there always will be, a literature gathering around the one book which is itself a library: it is the best of all that ever has been said on the one subject of imperishable interest to mankind. A library has gathered around that library which is growing every day. It is a library partly of comment, partly of criticism on the records; so that we may describe as the lively oracles no longer dumb when intelligently interpreted. Since our oracle is lively, we are therefore bound to make it intelligible to living men, as a translation baldly literal fails to do. It asks and rewards all the labour of the student, whether of philology or philosophy. It has a system of its own, best understood when it is set side by side with the systems of men. Faith has her own philosophy; it has even a science, as we may call it, since it tracks all secondary causes into the abyss of first causes, and there lays bare the secret of the universe. It detects as the one ultimate fact of the problem that there is a Supreme Will, whose three expressions or names are Love, Wisdom, Power, and whom we adore as Father, Son, and Spirit.

Any theology of this type will bear both expansion and contraction. It is not too vast when the king's library swells out into a hundred-and-one camel-loads of books: it is not too contracted when it is condensed into the modest compass of a pocket Bible. But the criterion we have insisted on all through this chapter is, that the camel-load of books shall be no more, no less, than one continued comment on the one Book of books, which is a library in itself, the literature not of one race but of several, and whose record, like the title on the Cross, has been written in Hebrew, in Greek, and in Latin.

In one sense, Ruckert's fable seems to gain a fresh meaning as we glance at history. The king employed a hundred-and-one sages to reduce the hundred-and-one camel-loads of books into a pocket library or single mule's burden; this, too, was found to be mere surplusage, and the king at last settled down to the sober compromise that a traveller's library should consist of one book only—so Pilgrim on his progress carried a roll, and no more. But the Reformation theology fell back on a tame compromise, which failed, as all compromises usually do. The mule's burden was found too much or not enough,—too much for the unspeculative man of active benevolence, who, like the sailor, wants only chart and compass; not enough for the student and scholar, who must know all that other men have said, and who, of all states of mind, most distrusts a state of half knowledge. The most dangerous condition for theology to be in is to be charged with its mule's burden of books, and mistaking abridgments and common-places for the whole body of divinity. There may be a sense in which the half is more than the whole, but this Hesiod gnome is more often quoted than understood. Melancthon, Turretine, and, generally speaking, the Swiss and German Reformers after the Reformation, who brought in a new scholasticism, with Augustine for their one *doctor seraphicus,*—theirs was the theology which, like the condensed traveller's library, is at once too much or too little. In matters of learning we must have all or nothing. In law, searches for precedents done out of compends are worse than misleading. The real case lawyer sees an easy victory when he has to deal with an opponent who thus comes half-armed into the battle. David's sling, or a panoply from top to toe,—there is meaning in either of these extremes. It is the mean between the two, adopted from the new Schoolmen of the post-Reformation age, which makes us tremble for the faith, when it has flung away antiquity and authority, and then set up a new antiquity and a new authority of its own. It was the same with Anglican apologists of the Bishop Jewell order. They went too far or not far enough. In his discussion with Harding the Jesuit, all that could be alleged against the Roman supremacy is alleged, and from the historical point of view Jewell emerges the conqueror. But on the dogmatic-development ground Jewell comes off with divided honours. What right had he to stop at the fourth or fifth century, and to take up with the Byzantine type of royal supremacy as the primitive pattern of Church government, based as it is, not on Christian antiquity, but on a crude analogy from Hebrew history, when the true theocracy was debased, and when Samuel reluctantly, and against his better judgment, consecrated a soldier-chief, and so brought Mosaism down to the much lower standard of a military monarchy. Anglicans of the Caroline type argued in this uncritical way, and much of this has come down by tradition to the Anglican school of our day.

We have illustrated our meaning at sufficient length, that theology as a science must have no half-learning.

To avoid compends and digests is the only safe rule in any subject like case law or traditional theology, which rests on precedents. This is the reason why theological disputes are best left in the hands of case lawyers, who look at it in the *lumen siccum* of precedent. The so-called spiritual courts are the tribunals of half-trained lawyers, who import their prejudices, and try to pass their private opinions off for the verdicts of past ages. Again and again we say, let us have all or nothing,—let us be on sea or on land, afloat with tradition or on shore on the rock of personal conviction; but that one foot on land one foot on shore position of the Reformers after the Reformation — Anglican, Lutheran, and Calvinist alike—is the position which no man who respects his own judgment can take up. Let us add, in conclusion, that real learning is the last danger which a theology resting on the rock of conviction has to fear. Instead of *Dogmatik*, German professors now teach theology as a *Dogmengeschichte.* The distinction explains itself. Before the birth of criticism, in a word, before the age of Kant, Lutherans, and Reformed, the Evangelische and the Reformirte Churches of Germany wrapped their mail armour of *Dogmatik* around themselves and glared at each other, attack and defence being equally out of the question. But in our age of *Dogmengeschichte* all is changed—a new attitude comes over the Churches. The movement for some Unions-Kirche, though set up too much in the Prussian drill-sergeant style, has this to recommend it, that horses stalled together are expected not to kick out at each other. It is a step towards comprehension, and one step often leads on to another. The result of the critical method applied to theology, begun in Germany a century ago, and beginning in this country since Anglican and Evangelical have been compelled by certain Privy Council decisions to eat out of the same stall and manger, is already encouraging. It will bring together things new and old, the past and the future, on a basis which, if apparently sceptical and subversive of old dogmas, is in the best sense restorative of that which is the oldest of all. God, it has been said, wants neither our learning nor our ignorance, but we can get on better with either extreme than with the dangerous mean of half-learning. A hundred-and-one camel-loads of learning seems a large order for the theology of the past; but when we condense, let us do so thoroughly, and not put up with a mule's-load of compends. Let us then turn back to the compacted form of certain prophets and apostles who taught as having authority, and not as the scribes, and who wrote, as we are told by one of themselves, "not of their own private interpretation, but as they were moved by the Holy Ghost." The criterion of theology, then, is simple—all that is taken first-hand out of these records is theology, the true doctrine of God; all that is merely derivative is among these afterthoughts which dogmatism asks us to spare, but which criticism lays bare with a knife and scalpel as destructive as Kant's *Kritik* was, only that, like Kant, it may become constructive again of something better and more enduring, as Clough's lines express it—

"The souls of now two thousand years
Have laid up here their toils and fears;
And all the earnings of their pain,
Ah, yet consider it again."

CHAPTER V.

EXCUSE FOR AFTERTHOUGHTS.

BUT let us be just to these afterthoughts of theology, this sub-apostolic type of teaching in which doctrine passed into dogma, and religion became a cult, with its ritual and ceremonies, its holy places and holy days, and with its priests and its sacraments. The transformation was complete in Augustine's day, whose two widely contrasted sayings—*ubi Christus ibi ecclesia* and *habere Caput Christum nemo poterit nisi qui in ejus corpore fuit*—may be said to measure the whole diameter of Christian thought from extreme individualism to extreme collectivism. Let us be just, then, to these "afterthoughts," and instead of condemning them unheard as apostasies from the primitive standard of διδαχή, let us see what needs in human nature sacramentalism and sacerdotalism represent. Perhaps we shall then come to the wise conclusion of the truly charitable, because far-seeing, apostle, that "circumcision is nothing," and that also "uncircumcision is nothing." Those who see far, as St. Paul did, into the mind of God, see that the mind of Christ, as we may call the pure gospel, must be an attainment only to be reached at the end of a lifetime; it is not seen at a glance at the beginning. To be baptized into Christ as a formulary is one thing; to drink of the cup which He drank of, and to be baptized with the baptism which He was baptized with, is quite another thing. All Church history and all Christian experience alike confirm this. On the one hand, we find the instinct for collectivism too strong for that of individualism. We find the *cœtus fidelium* agglomerating into Churches under impulses quite irresistible—we find those Churches presided over each by its own presbyter-episcopos. This clerical office develops in two directions, under that law of differentiation, in which Herbert Spencer has found the key to all physiological and ultimately of all sociological processes. The presbyter and the episcopos differentiate, and so the elder of elders becomes ruling elder, and to him the style and title of episcopos exclusively attaches. He presides over the Church planted in every city; for as yet Christ has not left His mark in the open country. Rustics are pagans, and the chorepiscopos is a kind of deputy-bishop, his functions corresponding to those of a rural dean among ourselves in this day. Into the details of the other stages of differentiation we need not enter. The late lamented Dr. Hatch, whose loss Oxford still regrets, had opened up fresh lines of thought on this subject, and had worked out the Baur theory of the defensive dogmatic attitude of the Latin Church, in face of the Gnostic heresies, on lines which showed both research and original thought. In any case, without pursuing details further, we may say that these afterthoughts, by which *didaché* grew into dogma and faith fixed itself on form, represent a true instinct. It was this conservatism which carried Christianity in the corporate form of a Church through the cataclysm of the break-up of the old Roman world, and presided over the birth of a new world after the long night of the

Middle Ages was over. A thousand years had to pass over between the death of one type of thought and the birth of another—between the geometry, for instance, of Ptolemy and the geometry of Descartes and Newton. As if to prepare an ark against that deluge, God had provided the Church, which, with her ascetic clericalism, was so unlike the mind of Christ; it was nevertheless better prepared to do the rough work required of her, than if she had grown into a philosophical school like that of the Alexandrian catechists, or had lost herself in dreams of saintly piety like the hermits of the East or the mystics of the West. Ecclesiasticism is, we admit, a debased copy of an ideal much "too good for human nature's daily food." In this sense individualism comes nearer that ideal; when, for instance, the Friends at a meeting-house sit waiting for angel visits, and the stirring the waters, which are rare in this age of mammon worship, we seem nearer the primitive type than with any of the more ceremonial forms of worship. But ideals may be unworkable, *ἐρᾶν βελτίστων νόσος τῆς ψυχῆς*—the desire for idealisms is a disease of the soul. This is Aristotle's wise way of clipping the wings of young idealists, more Platonist than Plato. Man is a social animal in worship as in other respects. The governmental tendency in religion may be carried too far, but it may easily be neglected so entirely that the spirit evaporates with the form. Doctrine may wear away, as coins do, when a certain alloy of dogma is not put in to harden it. We may come to see, after considering all the conditions of the problem, that Judaism, if we must call it so, is a phase of religious thought which the world has not outgrown, or is likely to do so as long as it remains as it is, while the enmity between flesh and spirit continues. What confirms this view of the case is the distressing fact, which idealists have never explained away, that as soon as one type of Judaism had been thrown off by large sections of Northern Europe, the Reformers lost no time in settling down to another type of Judaism. It was like the revolt of ten tribes against two under Jeroboam. We do not say that it was calf worship against temple services—that comparison is unjust and question-begging. But it certainly was the setting of Rabbinism in place of Sacerdotalism, and it is a question whether the young Rabbi was not a spiritual despot as harsh as the old priest. New presbyter was old priest writ large. So Milton thought, who dreamed of an independency which should comprehend all types, but which in its turn degenerated into a new type which we may call "Pastorism," since Congregationalism is quite as much a thing of traditions and tenets as stiff and unyielding as Presbyterianism, against which it was the same revolt that Presbyterianism had been against Prelatism. Thus sects come and go, and God fulfils Himself in many ways, lest one good custom should corrupt the world.

But the moral of the whole is this, that for wise reasons God has willed it so, that "faith should fix itself in form." There are some who are of a philosophical temper, and who are tempted to stand off from the hurly-burly of life: like Saturn, which sleeps on its luminous ring, they should "leave their sister where she prays her early heaven her happy views;" since if they are real philosophers, and not merely wearing the cloak, they must know that difformity is a worse evil than conformity. In joining a Church and accepting its limitations, both of doctrine and discipline, there is more true humility than in "remaining single and talking of population." Isolation is no sign of strength, though it seems so. We may belong to a dogmatic body but escape the dogmatic temper, as conversely we may become ultra-dogmatists while our standpoint is the dissidence of dissent and the Protestantism of the Protestant religion.

> "And spite of praise or scorn,
> As one who feels the immeasurable world,
> Attain the wise indifference of the wise."

It was not accidental that the gospel should grow into a "cult" with a "creed," and with custodians of that creed, as it did soon after in the sub-apostolic age. We must see in this something more than God's bare permission of a degeneracy. Much as Ahijah saw that the revolt of the Ten Tribes was of the Lord, so we may go on to say that this regulative religion was providential, since, but for this hard Roman type of Church, the barbarians would never have been beaten into shape. Those hard Romans, whose very games were cruel, and who butchered their prizes of war to make a Roman holiday, were not a lovely type of humanity, but they did for the world what neither talking Greeks nor mystic Syrians could do. Even in passing away they left a legacy of strength, mixed with severity and dashed with cruelty, on which the Church entered, and which has carried on Christianity down to our day.

Whether the Roman type of haughty unbending dogmatism has not also had its day, and may now cease to be, is an anticipation which we make with many reserves. Dogmatic Christianity, including in that phrase all that we mean by the afterthoughts of theology, still lives on, and seems likely to continue to live. The reaction Romewards has partly spent its strength; but then the age has ceased to rail at it. Popular Protestantism has forgotten its fears of forty years ago, and going over to Rome "verting," as it is now gaily described, is one of these swings of the pendulum which we look for and balance off against "verting" in the contrary direction. The conclusion seems to be, that in our present imperfect state of being, and with flesh and spirit so opposed, the flesh so strong, the spirit so weak, some "regulative" type of religion, with its stiffness, its inexorable dogmatism, is needed to right the balance. That it is so, we infer from the rise of Protestantism, with its infallible Book, to oppose Romanism, with its infallible Church, and between the two dividing the pale of professing Christendom. The admission made on both sides seems to be that religion, unless in some corporate form, will never be accepted by the mass of mankind. There must be a need for these afterthoughts, which run out either on inspiration or on Church authority—in other words, which set up some regulative principle outside conscience. It lies in this, that the average ill-instructed and nominal Christian has some vague dread of something after death which he can neither explain nor explain away. He believes in God and the devil in that sort of divided way, that .the Samaritan remnant, being plagued with lions, "feared the Lord and served their own gods." It is conscience which makes cowards of us all; but this, instead of inducing us to silence conscience, or smother it with lies, should lead us on to read its whispers aright, as St. John teaches us to do, 1 John iii. 20, 21. In the one case, he supposes that the heart, the seat of self-consciousness, condemns us, and for that he points, not to some scholastic fiction, but to the spiritual truth that God is greater than our hearts, and knoweth all things. Repentance towards God and faith in the Lord Jesus Christ, not priestly theology of any kind, is the only salve for a sore and sick conscience. In the next place, he goes on to deal with the happy case of those whose hearts condemn them not, and who, accordingly, have confidence toward God.

This is the only true remedy for the sense of sin which

is distance from God; it is that of direct dealing with God as the Father of our spirits. But the mass of mankind, the baptized as much as the unbaptized, seem to have such a feeble sense of God's fatherly relation to them, and of their original sonship, which only waits the spirit of adoption to become a full fruition, that they are all their lifetime subject to bondage. The misleading direction of Pauline teaching, for which Augustine is chiefly responsible, has set up a new and false relation between God and men. They are told they are children of wrath, and that He is an angry God. The old devil-worship of our past heathenism had scarcely been driven out when it came back with seven other devils, more wicked than the first. Men, mistaught by divines themselves scarce escaped from Manichæanism, went on to represent the Blessed One who hates sin only because He loves the sinner, as if His wrath passed on from the act to the person. Since, in our half Pharisaic dread of contagion, we hate the garment spotted by the flesh, we go on to regard Christ like another Aaron, as standing between the living and the dead till the plague is stayed. Too often have we thus limited God's mercies, and measured His compassion by our poor stint of pity. This lies at the root of our religionism, and will continue to do so as long as Augustinian conceptions of election and particular redemption reign as they do under one modification or another.

The painful truth is, as Pascal long ago suspected, but did not himself see the remedy, that man needs the gospel, and will have it; but as soon as he gets it he finds it too strong meat, and sets about mixing it with his own seasonings. He makes it into a religion with cult and creed. He takes over the terms of the old classic world — parishes, dioceses, liturgies are all phrases to hand, they have a well-known secular sense;

he now fits into them a new theological meaning. His very church clothes—dalmatics, copes, surplices, and what not—were all once secular garments, and he is offended to be told that his Aaron's wardrobe is only everyday Roman dress under a new name, as the late Dean Stanley took pleasure in impressing on him. All this is true; but it does not shake the fact that since man must have a religion, that of Christ's is the only religion which can walk abreast of the age; but it must at the same time be accommodated to the age. *Il faut des spectacles pour les grandes villes: il faut des romans pour les mœurs corrompus.* This opening sentence of Rousseau's *Emile* explains other things besides Rousseau's excuse for dressing up his moral reforms in a garb of sentimentality. The grand simplicity of the gospel, that God so loved the world, is too much for men in the full flash of life; it may sustain us on our dying beds, it will carry us into the haunts of sin and vice, but for summer-weather religionism there must be a certain Ethos and Œsthesis,—terms best left untranslated,—that flavour of Patristic lore, which, whether East or West, early or late, alike carries respect. In a word, tradition reigns in religion with a rod of iron. Human nature, timid in proportion to its ignorance, and with a thick curtain lying before the unknown hereafter, distrusts novelties. It is enough to say that a theology is new to condemn it. Prescription, a phrase first coined by Tertullian, has reigned ever since, and, like all long settled dynasties, has become an intolerable tyrant. The average of mankind who hear with complacency of the new chemistry, or of the new jurisprudence, regard with something more than suspicion the use of the phrase the "new theology." They never trouble to ask whether the so-called old Augustinianism was not once a novelty against which Vincent of Lerins drew up his canon *quod semper*, etc. Tried by these three tests of constancy, ubiquity, universality, in all three directions Augustine was the innovator, and Pelagius of the two was the one who, in the opinion of the whole East, stood in the old ways.

The foolish world, whose *forte* is not criticism, has forgotten all this; and as we must take human nature as we find it, we have to say with Rousseau, "There must be spectacles for great cities, and romances for an age which likes to be cheated with a mixture of truth and fiction." On these grounds the old Roman conception of religion as *civilis* and *licita* must be adhered to. We must drop our ideals, which only land us in a type of transcendental Quietism, like the Friends and the Cambridge Platonists, who both alike felt themselves very much out of harmony with the theological strifes of the seventeenth century. It must be said for the two dogmatic types, against which Friends and Platonists entered a feeble protest, that both Calvinists and Anglicans understood the age they lived in much better than these well-meaning mystics. "What must I *do* to be saved?" is the first cry of the awakened soul, and it lays all the stress it possibly can on the word doing. To be told to *do* nothing, and "only believe," sounds senseless, almost mocking; for even those who say "only believe," as all strong Protestants do, mean a good deal more. Their "belief" is in reality a "salvation of works," though they do not think it such. The fallacy of solifidianism was long ago detected by the late Thomas Erskine, who bluntly put it, that of the two he preferred the extreme Arminian to the extreme Calvinist as the less insincere of the two. The one understood by good works, such as were good and useful to men in the ordinary sense of the term; while the other turned his solifidian creed into a new title to salvation, as if a mere apprehension with the intellect of a plan of substitution and vicarious merit could transfer merit to the one who so apprehended it. Can we wonder that as *chimæra chimæram parit*, so the solifidians of fifty years ago are now the chief champions of what are known as "holiness" meetings, in which the same one-sided stress is laid on entire consecration of heart and life as was formerly laid on the bare apprehension of the forensic transfer of merit. So true is it that narrow minds can only take in one truth at a time, and, like children, must drop one pebble before they can pick up another.

All this impresses us with the conviction that there must be a religion for the people, and the more sober, grave, and unsentimental it is the better. For this reason, if a college of philosophers instead of a chapter of divines were to sit down and draw up a good working religion for the average mass of men and women, they would alight on some such happy compromise as the English Church has dropped on, though scarcely owing it to her clerical guides. It has been the large, roundabout common sense, as Locke calls it, of the average Englishman that has done it all. As for the sacerdotal spirit, whether in its Calvinist type as Whitgift, or its Anglican type as Laud, it has been sour, severe, and Augustinian, with all the faults of the master exaggerated in the disciple. It is to Englishmen at large that we owe that type of theology of which the English Prayer Book is a happy example. It is ever old and new and receptive of what is good, even without formal revision. For instance, it omitted a hymnal, which, considering how archaic the music of the sixteenth century would sound to-day, was a happy omission. But it is supplemented by the unauthorised printing of hymnal companions as an appendix to the Prayer Book. Taken thus as a whole, our prayers and hymns together make up a model of offices, which, when controlled by sanctified common sense in the preacher, makes up a type of worship which few Dissenters would dissent from. The proof of this is that in most cases, when on the Continent or on shipboard, Nonconformists of all but one or two extreme types prize the services of the chaplain, especially if he is not very young and very "one idea'd" about his own sacerdotal importance as a dispenser of the sacrament. In that case the liturgy suffers, because the liturgist forgets that the leitourgos is the ministering servant of the community, whether in Church or State; he belongs to it, not it to him. It is this half-educated type of mind, filled with some small theological cram and little else, which has brought the good old Church of England into a place where two seas meet, and where she is in danger of going to pieces unless skilfully piloted out again into the open of a new and broad theology.

These are the grounds which make us patient of afterthoughts since the age asks for them; and since there must be a religion for the people, it is of all types the least unreasonable. All that men of thought with something of the Promethean mind have to ask themselves is, what is the type which will best prepare us for the Church of the future? Now that the world is open to us, the study of comparative religions goes on even among those who are not students. It is impossible for a young officer to be quartered in India, for a young lieutenant or surgeon-assistant to sail round the world, without learning that lesson of Peter's great sheet let down out of heaven full of all beasts, clean and unclean. General Gordon's religion, so Christ-like in its grand simplicity of dogma, so unlike the Scotch creed of his forefathers, is a sample of what is going on everywhere. It is not exactly syncretism—that is too philosophical a method for the average Englishman, who above everything abhors formulating his ideas. But it is that conservatism of the old joined to an open-mindedness towards anything new, which at the same time seems true, and, on the whole, leads to a fair temper of mind. It is the same in the working of our old British Constitution, in which changes are readily made in proportion as they do not go down too deep. To unsettle the Union Settlement of 1800 will take, not one or two, but three or more wrenches of the old oak, and so more than one Milesian Milo has learned to his cost—

> "Beware of Milo's end,
> Wedged in the timbers which he strove to rend."

Our only excuse for an incursion into politics is to point out that the same temper of mind governs the average Englishman all through his thinking. The late Mr. Buckle, who wrote loosely about inductive and deductive types of mind, generalised hastily that all Scotchmen were "deductive," Englishmen "inductive" only. What he should have said was that the Scotch intellect is *perfervidum.* The wheels take fire with their swift rotation, and the result is that they see principles in their extremest form. Scotch Toryism and Scotch Radicalism are both full flavoured. It is the same with their theology. It was more Augustinian than Augustine, and for this very reason, when waking up to see that Augustine's version of Paulinism was too subjective, while his grasp of St. John's teaching was wholly defective, they are seeing it with a distinctness which few Englishmen can attain to. The leader of most progressive minds in Scotland was a layman, the late Thomas Erskine, who with little more critical apparatus than an acute legal intellect joined to a saintlike devout spirit, in which, in his later years, he bettered the example of Augustine's earlier years, has become the latter-day prophet of Scotland. Englishmen, as a rule, knew little and cared less for this anti-Augustinian reaction, for the best of all reasons, that they have never been in bondage to any man or any system of theology. Their innocence of systematic thinking of any kind has been at once their strength and weakness. It is three Scotchmen, Adam Smith, M'Culloch, and James Mill, who built up that deductive system of political economy, based on *laissez faire*, which like the chain armour of one age is not found to fit another. Englishmen of the new democracy feel where the shoe pinches, but do not know how to remake it. The same lesson meets us in theology. Its "afterthoughts" are many of them felt to be out of date, and sorely to need revision; but who is to do it, and how is he to be listened to? As for councils for the revision of theological formularies, to name them is to show we must put no trust in princes, much less in the Pharisees of tradition. Even in so small a matter as textual revision we see what trusting the broth to too many cooks has cost us. Professors, again, with the weight of official responsibility on them, are the last to lead in a movement on which they may smile silent approval. They are experts, and their testimony is invaluable as experts; just as case law comes in when a new judgment has to fit in with the precedents of leading lawyers of the past. It is only once in a generation that the judicial bench rises to the dictum, *fiat justitia ruat cœlum*, as it did in the case of O'Connell's release from Richmond Prison in 1846. Even then it was a great Whig lawyer commenting on the decisions of great Conservative judges who reversed their sentence on appeal. This teaches us how rare, how exceedingly rare, is judgment in its purest form in professional circles. To the trained mind, whether advocate or divine, precedent is too strong, and the fear of "unsettling men's minds" haunts them to a degree which they can neither describe nor account for.

Knowing, then, the springs of action in human nature, we take men as we find them, and accept their adjustments and compromises on religion as the best possible under the circumstances. We know that "perfect love casteth out fear," but the majority of mankind think it presumptuous to dream of perfect love in this imperfect state of being. Fear then enters in to fill the vacuum. "The fear of hell's the hangman's whip;" this is not a noble motive for soul-saving. But it exists; it can be replaced only at a cost which no one is prepared to pay. As for that jerky, jaunty thing known as American universalism, it is the old theology without its solemn sanctions, its vista of infinite hopes and fears; and the watch is expected to go without its mainspring. We do not judge human nature in this way. Mankind is not at all likely to put off Augustinianism as a whole unless it is given something much better to put in its place. But to get at this, the whole superstructure of Latin theology must be taken down and the building renovated from its foundation. A new psychology must precede a new theology, and the age has not as yet awakened to this thought. A few mystics as they are considered of the school of Maurice, have tried to assure us that we are the sons of God by nature, and not merely by "adoption" and grace, as the old orthodox teach. The age is so puzzled by statements of this kind that they put Maurice and his school on one side as mystifiers, who make broad assertions on a slender basis of fact. So it is if we go to textual theology and try and piece it out with Paulinism, into which we presume to put a new meaning of our own, much in the same way as Swedenborg first put into the Athanasian Creed all sorts of Swedenborgian senses, and then produced it as the pattern of the theology of the New Church.

It is precisely the same with the "Broad Church" school, which asks us to take up with a new theology, but does not make clear to the public mind whence it is getting it, and from what wells it is drawing its water. Again, we insist that a new psychology must be the *prodromus* or forerunner of the Christ which is to be. We must not take up the story of man at the "Fall," as old theology usually does. The story of the contrasted doom of mankind, if Augustine is to be our teacher, represents God as acting as Pharaoh did when the chief butler and the chief baker were in prison, hanging the one and giving the cup of confidence back to the other. It is no use patching up this old theology by filtering new meanings into it.

A new psychology must lead the way to a new theology. It will not be content to open Genesis at chap. iii. It will open at chap. i., which describes man in his ideal state as seen in Christ, who is the Logos or archetypal man before the worlds were. As for the story of the so-called "Fall," and of God's dealing with Adam and the rest of the covenant race, it is a part, not the whole of our story; we never understand the whole till we see that it is headed up in Christ, who is also its fountainhead—the Alpha and the Omega of all history, which, like these rivers of Eden, parted into four heads, never meet till they mingle at last and for ever in the ocean of God's love. Man is thus made in the image of God; he is a child or emanation—God's image in flesh and blood. This, like God's "image in ebony," seems far below the ideal, and so it is.

We are much lower than the angels, but only for a little while; and to judge of the whole of humanity from its behaviour in a body of corruption, is to judge of a Newton from the babe which was so tiny that it was put—so the story goes—into a quart pot. Theology has been far too rash in overlooking the second birth of death and the baptism of blood which we must all pass through, saint and sinner alike. This opens up possibilities on which it is best to be silent; but at least it suggests that as the education of the human race is not limited to the covenant people, so the education of every man is not finally closed when he passes out of the school of life.

Psychical—pneumatical—here are two contrasts which the word of God is said to pierce and divide between, as it certainly does in the case of those who reach the deeper self-consciousness which becomes mingled and lost with that of God-consciousness. But how of those who scarcely attain self-consciousness in this life, and who, with regard to God-consciousness, are entire Agnostics? What are we to say, for instance, of three of the world's leading minds, Confucius, Aristotle, and Goethe, to name no others? Is their existence here a mistake, a huge blot on the copy of God's book of remembrance? This short and easy way of reading the world's history as if it were a monk's chronicle, or, as Bossuet's, miscalled universal history, which meant Palestine and the lands adjacent, is now, too, out of date, even for censure. It is part of the childhood of man when he understood as a child. We now think thoughts more worthy to be called thoughts of God, who does not regard man as a thing of naught because his time here passes away so soon.

All history is prophecy—it is travailing with the birth of the Christ that is to be, and who already is the desire of all nations. We are accustomed to speak of a Messianic people, it is very true, though also true that the elect race is the one race which has nationally rejected its Messiah. But in strictness all progressive races have been Messianic; to have no future of promise is to perish as Azteks and many of the red and black races have perished, leaving nothing behind them. But who can say that Greek and Roman races were not Messianic, seeing that their geometry and law remain ours to this day? Greece and Rome have between them helped Palestine to build up all that we call our culture, which is the one permanent element, wanting which mere material greatness, like that of Nineveh and Babylon, becomes only civilised barbarism. We conclude, then, that the world's history is one long preparation for Christ, and the whole of man's education here, the beginning of his education in æons yet to come. This notion, if taken in in all its bearings, must transform theology. This was beyond the thinking of all but a few great names in the past of theology. It was impossible to all but a few Promethean minds who saw beyond their age.

But how are we to rescue it from seeming to be the dream of a few mystics, who took a too optimist view of the future of the race as redeemed in its totality in Christ? The answer is one which theology by itself cannot give, though we must not build too much on the general silence of Sacred Scripture. "Then cometh τὸ τέλος," as we translate it,—the end,—but as it should be rendered, not *finis*, but *eventus*, the goal up to which we are tending. What that goal is the heart of man cannot conceive, for God is greater than our heart: He is far more benign to us than we are to Him. But we are not to allow the silence of Scripture to imply tacit approval of an eschatology which the heart of man rebels at, and which made Wesley (half a universalist, as those who know affirm) say that "Whitfield's God was his devil." We may say with a secular poet—

> "Then at the judgment let's be mute,
> We never can adjust it."

But, turning from the silence of the lively oracles, let us consult another living oracle, our own deep self-consciousness. Its longings for immortality are the theme alike of poets and divines, and those very longings have been twisted into strange forms of pre-existence, as also of arguments for the necessary existence of the soul as a thinking principle, and other foundations of natural religion, latterly very much shaken, and crumbling since Kant's pulverising criticism. Enough of this: there are august anticipations, as we should call them, of a yet unborn faculty in man, which in exact language we call the Pneuma. It is only rudimentary at present, like the lungs in a bird still in the ovum stage. How much embryology has to teach theology if theologians were only modest enough to learn, we dare not say. But the "learned ignorance" of divines is appalling. What is worse, it is an ignorant ignorance. It forgets that side lights are the best lights in which to see new truths. If Darwin and Newton had not spent their twenty years of brooding over difficulties, do we suppose we should have heard an *Eureka* at the end of all? Theology has long since acknowledged its debt to Newton, and in the pretty rhetoric of Pope we write on his tomb, "God said, Let Newton be: and all was light." Are we prepared to see that Darwin may have done more for theology than even Newton? The one rolled back the curtain to show the vastness of the universe all under control of three simple laws of motion; but the other has carried us much farther; he has shown that, instead of several successive creations, there has been only one; and though some of his followers have been rash enough to infer that thus we can do without a presiding intelligence, Darwin has never said so, nor do his lessons lean that way. The old Aristotle school of fixed types led us to think we could get on very well without God, except when we came to the end[1] of a series, when a miracle of new creation must be slipped in, as in Babbage's argument for miracles, which makes God a kind of mill-hand, half-asleep over a power-loom. But Darwin's teaching leads up to that *creatio continua* (John v. 17) where "*hitherto*" is mistranslated for "*up to the present.*" Translators with a deistical notion of creation do not seem to have understood the passage which teaches that the Eternal Will and the Eternal Logos have been ever in the world, and are to this day "creating," notwithstanding the symbolical conception of God entering on His Sabbath, not to be taken too literally.

This being so, and taking "evolution" as the keynote of the universe, why not suppose that man is on a spiral of evolution ever working upward? We should not dare to affirm this of man, if he were only another "quadrumanus." If he were not a worshipping animal; if his aspirations and his adorations akin to love, but much more lofty, are not to be considered "magnetic mockeries,"

[1] Very much to the point on this subject are Wallace's remarks in his new edition of *Natural Selection*, v. p. 212: "If, therefore, we have traced our force, however minute, to its origin in our own *will*, while we have no other knowledge of any other primary cause of force, it does not seem an improbable conclusion that all force may be will force, and thus that the whole universe is not merely dependent on, but altogether is the *will* of, higher intelligence, or of one supreme intelligence." If this is what evolution is working up, who can say but the Theism of the future will look back on Darwin and his school as suspected enemies who were allies in disguise.

the disease of a soul which, Narcissus-like, is in love with his own image, this cannot be the last stage. Those who affirm this, are themselves diseased. They are like deaf men denouncing music, or the blind who bemoan not their fate, but ours, who are entranced with art. It is on these august anticipations of spiritual existence hereafter that we build up our reconstructed theology. The new psychology, as we affirm it, has observed the Pneuma, and placed it as Adams and Leverrier placed Neptune. That this new planet does not swim before our eyes, and give us ocular demonstration, as Galileo gave of the moons of Jupiter, does not disturb the scientific astronomer, who, reasoning deductively, had placed Neptune, before the eye, assisted by the magic glass, had come to the aid of deduction. So with objections to the Pneuma, they may be many, and valid from the side of sense experience, but what of that? Need it disturb the deductive theologian, who argues in psychology as much as in physiology, that function implies organ as much as organ suggests function? The terms are reciprocal, the one unmeaning without the other. Is there, then, any spiritual function distinct from a mere intellectual act? Is there a bowing the will in prayer, an ecstasy of silent adoration which words and phrases, so far from helping, very much interfere with? The question turns on this; and if any one tells us that they never prayed in that sense, our reply is that the courtly flatterers of King Darius so reasoned when they decreed to shut heaven up for thirty days, leaving only one vent-pipe open, through the man-god Darius. Heaven, in a word, is easily closed to formalists, to whom it has never been really open. In this sense it is easy to deny the spiritual life which men have never felt. But to some the function is so distinct, so unique, that they feel compelled to predicate a special organ. If the old Scotch psychology does not help them for a type, they must invent one for themselves; and if the school psychologists object to this, we can only turn round and say, so much the worse for psychology. Happily, the day is over when man's tripartite nature needs to be contended for. The hints let fall up and down Scripture have been picked up by careful critics like Bishop Ellicott and Dean Goulburn, to name no others of less note. What we call pneumatical psychology, to coin an odd misnomer, is no longer on its trial, it is past that; but its application to reconstruct theology still lags on account of this ultra-conservatism which hangs around us under the shadow of Augustine's great name, as if whatever the African did not know is never worthy of notice. When this fit of somnolence is over, we shall first go back, then go forward, and so pick up those missing links in theology which, from Justin Martyr downward, are thick strewn in the East, but only escape us in the West.

Then a new theology will emerge, and this without effort or stress, as soon as a new psychology has made it imperative. So one invention or discovery leads to another. Faust's movable types moved the world—it discovered America, it made the German renascence of religion, and the Italian renascence of art and scholarship—it made monkery impossible; and so one by one the owls flew off because the sun had risen. In the same way a new theology will some day steal on us, and meanwhile we must put up with "afterthoughts," and make the best of them. He is a bad workman who quarrels with his tools; but he is a worse one who, if he can get better, does not fling away the old. As soon as man's true nature and his deep inalienable relationship to God is understood, the old make-shift arrangements of plans of salvation and conditions and terms, whether of subjective belief or objective use of sacraments, will be found to be only provisional, not permanent arrangements. They will take themselves off of themselves, for the same reason that Judaism faded away before the risen sun of Christ's coming: when that which is perfect is come, then that which is in part shall be done away.

But the new psychology would be a barren thing if it ended in itself. It may be interesting to know that man has a seed of a "deiform nature," to use Whichcote's phrase. We must go on to apply this to ethics and theology. Intuitive theology and immutable morality seem to be the two pillars of the temple of truth. It is sad to think how many there are who fail to see the connection between these two. Many refuse to recognise that a scheme of morality raised on the shifty foundations of the *utile* or the *dulce* is left dependent on custom or caprice. It is opportunism in morals, which, if it does not debauch the moral sense at once, goes a long way towards it. It is the same with theology, unless its truths are intuitive, and by that we mean resting on the conscience for their ultimate support, we are compelled to say that "the pillared firmament is rottenness, and earth's base built on stubble." We are aware, of course, that in describing theology as intuitive, we lay ourselves open to the retort that in that case there can be no need of revelation. The distinction between natural and revealed religion disappears of itself, and all that we mean by the mysteries of the faith, such as the Trinity, the atonement, and so forth, become mere evolutions of the moral consciousness, much as Hegel evolved them out of his logical consciousness, to his own satisfaction, and to the no small distress of devout souls.

We do not take intuition in this sense as the exclusive

source of the Christian consciousness. All we contend for is that no truth deserves to be called a revelation of God from heaven which is not so "commended" to the conscience. Here is its criterion—by this touchstone we test it. The old theology to a great extent overlooked this. It was authoritative because dogmatic: striking this one note of authority, in a Book as its charter and a corporate body of teachers to interpret that Book, it has stood before the world and claimed obedience. Ever since Augustine's day, if not before, this magnificent conception of the Church has imposed on men's minds, and all but a resolute few have bowed before its pretensions. Philosophy was forced to go into retreat, and scholarly men kept their doubts to themselves; and on this condition of silence were not molested. They were tolerated, as the phrase goes, because of two evils, to leave them alone was the least. But the age has assumed a new attitude to these questions ever since the advances of science have made the old traditional account of the origin of man simply impossible. The Church has not agreed on any new interpretation of the early chapters of Genesis to replace the Augustinian theology, which rests on this as a building does on its foundations. Till this is done, the whole subject of sin and its supposed derivation from one man's offence may be said to be unhistorical—the waters below are cut off from the waters above, and honest minds who wish to believe their Bibles, but who cannot evade the teachings of science, are in the utmost distress. They do not see, and no one has the courage to say so, that with Augustine's name and authority the literal interpretation of Gen. ii. iii. stands or falls. But for these Augustinian inferences of original sin, and its derivation from a single source, we might let go the literal interpretation, and read it, as Philo and the Jews did, as an allegory. Our whole point of view would then be changed, and this distress growing out of the conflict of reason and faith would pass off of itself. We should then take up the narrative and read it in a new light. We should see that the education of the race began from the beginning, when, in the early morning of history, a great while before day, the first of the primates awoke from a long sleep of animalism, and God breathed into his nostrils the breath of lives. As soon as man had passed (and this is the true creation point of the race) out of the anthropoid ape type, and became a rational and moral agent, with conscience as the centre point of his being, he must enter on the trial or testing stage. He is led to know good and evil by that which symbolically is called a tree of knowledge, and when he yields to the baser side of his nature, and so fails of true immortality, symbolised by the tree of life, then his education is entered on under sterner conditions. He is no longer allowed to dwell in a garden of delights, but is put to till the ground and eat bread by the sweat of his brow. There is a fall and a curse; but the fall is at the same time a step upward, in that man learns his weakness and its source in the strength of his animal desires, and the curse becomes a blessing disguised, since he learns to toil, and so to subdue and keep under the desires of the flesh. Then begins that long warfare of flesh and spirit which is the key to all man's long history from the dawn until now.

The key, then, to the new theology lies in a fresh exegesis of Genesis. The literal story as taken from Augustine will stand no longer. Unless we are to reject it altogether and relegate it back to the original Chaldæan legends, of which the Mosaic seems to be an expurgated and a spiritual version vitalised by the great truth of Monotheism, we must read the narrative as a spiritual allegory of the origin of man and his passage from the purely animal on to the moral stage. It is the story, not of one man, but of the race "ha-Adam"—humanity at large. Seen in this light, we see the stages of development. Man is at first of the earth earthy, an animal only, then he is "breathed into" and becomes soulish; but he has not yet reached the last term until he becomes a living spirit through the quickening presence of the Logos, who is the Lord from heaven. These are the three stages of man's development, two of which are attained on earth—the animal and the rational; but the third of which, the pneumatical, waits its full fruition when flesh and blood, which cannot attain the kingdom of heaven, are laid aside in the grave. Then the psyche-pneuma, emancipated from the flesh, shall attain a new stage of being; then as a formative principle it shall build around itself a new body, and that which was true of Christ, the first-fruits, shall be reached by all who are Christ's. "Destroy this temple, and in three days I will build it again;" we take this saying as exclusively true of Christ. But it may be, as Swedenborg taught, that this is typical of the transformation of the whole of redeemed humanity. This is very unlike the Augustinian doctrine of the resurrection of the old body of flesh, with hair and nails *quantum decet.* But the question occurs, may not Swedenborg be right and Augustine wrong; and if so, shall we not have to throw overboard this and a good deal more of the literalistic materialism which clings to traditional theology, and makes its reception a burden and a heartsore to many who in heart are with Christ, but who only come to Him by night and secretly, for fear of the Jews?

This Judaising gospel sums up all that we have said on the subject of afterthoughts in theology. It is better than blank unbelief; it is a provisional system in which the Church is kept at present shut up as in a kind of ark, till the fulness of the times has come. Of such a state we may say that it is bondage to the letter—it falls short of the liberty with which Christ would make us free. It is a faith which is neither robust nor abreast the best thoughts of an age, either in philosophy or science. It can attempt no concordat with either, for it lags behind in the crude and childish literalism of Augustine and his times. Still, as it is a faith, as it sets forth Christ in His full Godhead and manhood, and points to His cross and resurrection as the turning-point of the world's salvation, we have only to say of it, "Hold fast that which thou hast till I come." As a faith, mixed as the gold is with the clay of traditionalism, it may elevate the soul and purify the life. Judaism, to those under the covenant, was perfect freedom, as the writer of the 119th Psalm points out through twenty-two couples of acrostic verses on the law. May not our present Church theology be such a liberty to many devout souls? All that we desire to press is that it is not God's last word to men, and that there are many truths ready to break out of God's word, as old Robinson of Leyden taught, if we will "observingly distil them out."

But the difficulty of getting at a right interpretation of Genesis lies not only in the crude literalism of writers like Tertullian and Augustine. There is also another cause. It is an old remark, attributed to Selden, that the afterthoughts of theology are all explained as rhetoric turned into logic. If this is so, the lesson that it teaches us is sobriety of speech. We may not believe every spirit, but should try the spirits by this simple test—Did the so-called Fathers and doctors of the Church weigh their words; or did they anticipate, or even so much as suspect, what strange extensions of meaning would be put on their

Byzantinisms by those who came after? Would Chrysostom, for instance, have applied such phrases as the "dreadful sacrifice" to the oblation of the Eucharistic bread and wine, could he have foreseen that a new sacrificial sense would be put on the old act of oblation, and that, instead of a feast upon a sacrifice, the Eucharist would be turned back into a spectacular re-enactment of the sacrifice itself? In this way "Pelion on Ossa, error on error piled," the minister of a simple memorial act and love-feast has become the actual sacrificial priest of a renewed atoning death. As soon as rhetoric is thus turned into logic, it never stops there. Error, like the irruption of the barbarians, is not to be bought off by a single payment down. Having tasted Roman gold, Goths and Avars, Gepidæ and Huns, swarm on one after the other; and history shows us that, as wolf never preys on wolf, so Goths, like Stilicho, hired as mercenaries to defend the empire, did not turn against old comrades in arms like Alaric who were invading the empire. It was so under the great Theodosius, and still more signally under his two degenerate sons, Arcadius and Honorius. The development of doctrine into dogma, and dogma at last into distinct departure from primitive truth, is full of instruction to those who keep a cool head to see facts as they are, and do not let their imagination loose in a deluge of phrases. Heated "pulpiteering" was too often the atmosphere in which the Fathers of the fourth and fifth centuries lived. They were in many cases tribunes of the people, Mirabeaus of a mob of ignorant monks and women vowed to virginity. How could a Cyril, for instance, keep cool in Alexandria, when Hypatia was set on by a howling mob, led by Peter the Reader, and by parabolani or grave-diggers who were the scum of the people? The breath of popular applause was the theological hothouse in which they lived, and out of which they came fired with zeal to maintain against a rival Patriarch some new dogma, such as that of Theotokos, or to stamp out some old school like that of Antioch, which seemed to them to miss the precision of the new definitions of the dual Christ as of two natures inhering in one person. Cyril of Alexandria,[1] sainted on account of his resistance to Nestorius, may be said to have reached the high-water mark of that new orthodoxy, which only called out fresh heresies in resisting the old. If the East split asunder at last between Monophysites and Nestorians, and Churches once Catholic separated never to reunite together under any form of orthodoxy, who is so much to blame for this as those word-splitters who carried Greek subtlety of speech to the point that it seeks to enclose and hem in by a technical term conceptions which we cannot even shape in thought? The mode of indwelling of the divine in the human must be left at the point where Athanasius broke off in resisting the shallow rationalism of Arius; to carry it on into the second stage, where Cyril contended with Nestorius, was to open the door to endless definitions, meaning nothing but the separation of those who wanted a *casus belli*, and who found it in disputing over an inscrutable mystery. Such wranglers end in wrangling the life out of a divine truth.

[1] Tillemont, on this subject of the reputed saintship of Cyril of Alexandria, shows his usual discretion and good sense. He observes: "S. Cyrille est saint, mais on ne peut pas dire que toutes ses actions soient saintes," adding, with words of memorable significance, "les plus saintes ont beaucoup a craindre la tentation qui nous porte a régarder comme légitime ce qui semble nous pouvoir faire réussir dans les entreprises saintes. Il faut combuttre pour Dieu selon les loix de Dieu si l'on veut qu'il nous couronne."—Cf. Pusey's translation of *St. Athanasius*, p. 149. That we are not crowned unless we strive lawfully, is a test of saintship which theology has never looked square in the face.

It is melancholy to reflect how much hurt to souls has thus been caused by this strife of words, to no profit but for the subverting of the hearers. We have selected Cyril as the epoch-making man, who set theology in the East on the wrong track of dogmatic definition. It has been said in his defence by Canon Bright and others, who are the defenders of Conciliar Church teaching, that Cyril only came forward to defend the truth when first attacked, so that Nestorius was the innovator, Cyril only the champion of the old faith. Fairness compels us to admit that there is something in this remark, and the truth probably lies with Neander's summing up of the subject. He holds that Antioch and Alexandria represented contrasted conceptions of the Person of Christ, the one more clear and logical, the other more mystical, and fading away into a one-sided theosophical exaggeration, against which the humanitarian recoil was inevitable. All this is true enough; but the blame must rest with those who pushed theological *nuances,* or tendencies of thought in conceiving a mystery, into the fierce light of popular and passionate speech. Here Alexandria was most at fault, and Cyril was the chief offender. His claim to saintliness rests on precisely the same ground as that of Augustine: we may add that the two characters mark the same temper as dominant East and West at the same time and for the same reason. Both were ascetics and monks, who went into logic-chopping because cut off from the serious business of life, "to make a happy household chime to bairns and wife." If we overlook all this, as professional theologians are in the habit of doing, we shall miss the meaning of this Selden phrase, that rhetoric turned into logic has brought theology to its last crowning contradiction—the doctrine of the corporal presence in the Eucharist. This is seen in Cyril's case: one error of exaggeration opened the door to another. As we have seen, Goths never fought against Goths: the mercenary, paid to guard the frontier, let in the new invader, who was of the same race, and so Church and Empire went down together, and from the same cause. From the admitted truth, that the flesh of Christ was received in the Eucharist as life-giving, Cyril argued that it must be in some sense the flesh of God, and so that the Nestorian error of Mary being the mother only of His manhood could be stopped by appealing to sound Eucharistic doctrine. This is an illustration of the way in which one dogma leads on to another, and reminds us that rhetorical phrases are not so innocent as they seem. We forget the "fetichism" that ignorant human nature is too prone to. There is a sensual side to which a spiritual truth invariably falls over, the instant that we forget that the "words which I say unto you, they are spirit, and they are life." Alas for the fact that erring men and women are too prone to the idolatry of sense, and that, in certain stages of low development, a spiritual truth cannot reach them at all unless under symbolisms which are revolting when too literally taken! To eat His flesh and drink His blood must be symbolical. No Jew could have been listened to by Jews even for an instant unless he were assumed to be speaking symbolically. So far all are agreed—Romanists included—as to the strict meaning of the Lord's words in John vi. But when these same theologians turn to the Eucharist and attempt its interpretation, then they drop their own conception, and interpret the Lord's words in a literal sense, which would have been revolting to those who first heard them. Instead of taking John vi. as a well-known

[1] See Smith's *Dictionary of Christian Biography*, "Cyril," by Dr. Bright.

Eastern symbolism of "eating," for "reading, marking, learning, and inwardly digesting," they run away from this, its true primary, and to an Oriental its natural sense, and set up a crude cannibal sense which is unbearable applied to the original flesh and blood of the Lord, and therefore must be equally unbearable of any transmuted bread which, under the magic of consecration, is said to become "flesh."

We are not here discussing "transubstantiation," or any other such afterthought of inventive dogmatism. All we are discussing is the state of mind out of which this trick of loose speech governing loose thought, instead of clear thought controlling accurate speech, has grown up. It has arisen, as Selden has remarked, from bad rhetoric passing into worse logic; but who are to blame most, the "rhetoricians," who escape rebuke, or the logicians, who are so severely scolded by all Reformation divines, and by Anglicans most of all? To do Anglicans justice, especially the Caroline divines of Laud and his school, they are extremely opposed to the doctrine of the "corporal" presence. In this they are honourably distinguished from their later copyists, who follow Keble in his lapse into what is substantial Romanism on this point, when he struck out the line, "not in the hand, but in the heart," and altered it, in his old days, so as to admit Eucharistic adoration of the corporal presence. On this subject the old Laudian Anglicans stand stiffly on the Protestant side of the controversy, as their degenerate descendants seem to forget. But let this pass; our point is that Anglicans, old and new, who oppose twelfth-century scholasticism for defining the nature of the change, and so rounding off the dogma logically, have not a word to say against the rhetoric out of which all this twelfth-century logic grew. For our part, we hold that the Schoolmen were the more innocent of the two. They took from the Fathers such phrases as the "dreadful sacrifice," and rendered it into intelligible terms of the understanding. They rationalised, if it must be so said, concerning a mystery, that of the "presence," whatever that ultra-scriptural phrase may mean; but they only rationalised as men must do, who, given three terms of a proportional, go on to find the fourth. In this "rule of three" way the Schoolmen reasoned as they were bound to do. A priest implies a sacrifice, as conversely a sacrifice suggests a priest,—the terms are reciprocal. Granted, then, the priesthood and the altar service, what is so natural as to suppose that the Eucharist is such a sacrifice? We are already a long way on the road,—we have got as far as the "unbloody sacrifice," which soon is seen to be a verbal contradiction. Where is the fault of their logic? We fail to see a single flaw, unless it be, as Anglicans say, in jumping the gap and erasing the term "unbloody." As for the term "transubstantiation," it is a long word for what meant very little in the twelfth century, and which we now see grew out of muddy metaphysics and still muddier conceptions of physics. That bread had a certain *substantia* or entity apart from its phenomena, was part of the prevailing realism. This, when it got mixed with the reigning notion in chemistry, that base metals could pass into noble as soon as a certain flux was introduced into a cupel signed with the sign of the cross, and so called a crucible, explains what seems to us a monstrosity of thought. It did not seem such a monstrosity to the twelfth century. To this day it is no monstrosity to the devout Romanist, and to men of at least as keen logical acumen as any Anglican or ultra-Protestant. How can we account for this divergence of thought, assuming, as we are bound to do, perfect honesty on both sides? It is explained, as we have seen, by the trend of thought in the human mind. Started on one line of rhetoric by theologians enamoured of their own self-importance as an order of "priests," all then follows, since the laws of logic are inexorable. The decline is smooth, but it is the torrent's smoothness ere the torrents fall. Terms meant to be only rhetorical are taken only two literally, and who is to blame but those who gave currency to such phrases? To recall them, as Anglicans ask us to do, to their primitive Patristic sense, is to ask us, too late, to cork up again these Genii of an afterthinking theology; we must go back altogether, or not at all. If we go back, we get up to the first thoughts of the *didaché* of the apostle's age; but if we go forward into the sacerdotal age of theology, we may as well go on, and take development, as Dr. Newman has insisted on, as our guiding star. If it leads to the Roman obedience with Corpus Christi Day for our second Christmas Day, when the mystery of the Incarnation is explained by the mystery of the Mass, let us not complain, let us not say we have been carried farther than we wanted to go. This is the penalty of afterthoughts, that they are weak in themselves. They have no root in the moral sense, without which religion is only a form of words, and God becomes a mode of explaining second causes by inventing a first cause. Thus we have to go on piling, as we have seen, hypothesis on hypothesis, dogma on dogma, till "Pius IX. last" has become a byword for that inept Jesuit way of silencing doubt. To be religious we must be manly, and face the consequences of our own beliefs. If these come out ugly fetichisms, wanting all support in the moral sense, we have only ourselves to blame for putting out the eyes of the mind, and then complaining that we are scared with doubts. On the other hand, if we make the first sense of awe and mystery our last, if with Moses and the elders we go up into the mount, and there eat and drink with God, in the grand metaphor of the old Book, all other mysteries will then melt off of themselves, and we shall certainly never again be led away by the mystification of juggling priests. God, let us add, God in Christ, will be intuitively seen reflected in the light of the awakened spiritual faculty. The pneumatical man judges all things, yea, the deep things of God. For why ?—he has a God-consciousness; he has seen God, if not face to face, at least in the Son of His love. He can trust those who report that they have "handled of the word of life;" and though ours is at present only second-hand, yet, being authenticated by credible witnesses, we reach forth spiritual hands into the unseen, and instead of merely groping after, we now grasp God, as Jacob did on that memorable night when he was named no longer Jacob, but Israel, because as a prince he had prevailed.

We have, in a word, one remedy, and only one, against that pullulation of dogma which has gone on unchecked from the fourth century to the sixteenth; and which, even then, was wounded with a deadly wound, like the "serpent scotched, not killed." This is to have done with afterthoughts, one and all, and to hark back to first thoughts. The two schools, of intuitional theology, and of immutable morality, stand hard by each other. The great but now forgotten Cudworth, who, if the last, was also the greatest of the Cambridge Platonists, laid the basis of morality deep in our intuitive sense of right. His ethics are substantially those of the Kant school, who reject utilitarianism as a misnomer when applied to questions of right and wrong. He is with Kant in planting his feet on the rock of an eternal inherent contrast between right and wrong. The heavens may fall, and God Himself fade out of consciousness, before right can ever be confused with wrong. The voice of Duty is awful, her imperative is categorical. Such is Kant's ethics, such were Cudworth's. But where Kant halted (for after all he was a *terræ filius*, a child of the age of Deism) Cudworth went on, and took up, as all his school did, the standpoint of an intuitional theology, the only worthy sequel of an immutable morality. In proportion, let me add, as Cambridge is true to these two positions, which none of her sons have so nobly asserted as the little Emmanuel school of divines, who stood aloof from Puritans and Prelatists alike, and their strife of tongues, —in that proportion will Cambridge hold its own as the light-bearer in the race of the *Lampadophoroi.* We may conclude in the favourite phrase of the late Dr. Whewell, himself a distinguished Platonist and Christian—

"Λαμπαδια εχοντες διαδωσουσιν αλληλοις."

CHAPTER VI.

NOT TO PREMEDITATE.

In the direction of Christ to His disciples as to their line of defence when brought before kings and rulers for His name's sake, this remarkable injunction is added, "Settle it therefore in your hearts, not to meditate before what ye shall answer." The expression, "Settle it in your hearts," like all of Christ's injunctions, seems forth-reaching and prophetic. It anticipates the very state of things which occurred, and condemns it by anticipation. There are apologetics of the Christ-like type and apologetics which offend against this canon. Those of the early sub-apostolic age are to be contrasted with apologetics of the later post-apostolic age. We may say, speaking roughly, that Justin Martyr was the last of the first type and Tertullian the first of the second. In an age of first thoughts, it is the simple message of Christ's love which is proclaimed, and His followers are a little flock who follow His steps like sheep on a sheep-track, walking one by one. In an age of afterthoughts it is Christianity as a whole, and the Church as the keeper of God's word, which is defended, which is quite another matter.

This injunction not to premeditate, *i.e.* not to give anxious thought to the nature of their defence, seems to touch by anticipation at the root of all these mistakes of defensive dogmatic theology. As errors arise, let the error be met. A frank reply to a frankly-faced difficulty is sure to do good on both sides. Would that the Church of Christ had acted in this way, and that her apologists of later ages had followed the admirable example set by the apologists of the second century. Instead of that, we can trace a steady deterioration in the tone of the apologists in proportion as the Church approached her hour of triumph and began to change places with the world. We can speak of a golden, a silver, and at last, by Augustine's time, of an iron age of Church defence. Such we may describe Augustine's tone in dealing with the Donatists, when he perversely, and in the teeth of all sound criticism, misquoted the text, "Compel them to come in." In this respect the contrast between the second and fourth centuries is the contrast between the iron and the golden age. Even the fierce Tertullian, forerunner as he was of much of the defective method of later dogmatism, starts back with horror from persecution: "God has not hangmen for priests; Christ teaches us to bear wrong, not to revenge it" (*Ad Scap.* 2). In his *Apology* he says, in his antithetical way, "Take care lest it redound to the cause of irreligion that we take away the liberty of religious worship." Nor is the silver age, as we may call the beginning of Conciliar Church authority, from Cyprian to Athanasius, deaf to the same note as understood by the heathen, that *Deorum injuriæ Dis curæ.* This was the ground of Athanasius, who suffered much wrong, but never requited it in return. "Nothing," he says, "more forcibly marks the weakness of a bad cause than persecution."[1] When Ambrose and Martin of Tours indignantly exclaimed against shedding the blood of heretics, and refused to communicate with

[1] Archdeacon Farrar, *Lives of Fathers*, vol. ii. p. 537.

those who had ordered the execution of the Priscillianists; they were only continuing the traditions of the early Church. They shuddered at those who were champions in name only, but in reality were the mere mercenaries of the faith. "It belongs," said Tertullian, "to the human right and natural power of every man to worship what he thinks right, and the religion of one is no advantage or injury to another." Gregory of Nazianzen had always expressed his abhorrence of persecution, and his determination to employ no methods but those of moral suasion. Even under Constantine, Lactantius had written that "religion cannot be enforced: we must act with words rather than blows, that the will may be with us. Nothing is so voluntary as religion." Even Augustine in his earlier days had repeatedly insisted on the true method of dealing with heretics, which was by reasoning and forbearance.

But alas, the fine gold had become dim! By the time of Theodosius, when the last pagan reaction under Julian had spent itself, and the orthodox Catholic faith had ceased to tremble at the possibility of another Arian Cæsar, too soon the note was changed, and we must add with regret, that it is in Augustine's lifetime the strange transition began, when persecuted and persecutors changed places—the persecuted Church became the persecuting. Nor have we far to seek the explanation. As soon as a creed fossilises into dogmas, what before was conviction passes away into conformity. It calls for no inward act of spiritual verification; it sets up no struggle, such as that indicated by the expression, "Lord, I believe, help Thou mine unbelief." All these strivings within—the desire to believe, attended with difficulties, intellectual or moral—the travailing in birth till Christ be formed in you, as an apostle describes it,—these are phases of faith unknown to an age of mere dogmatic belief. Hence it is to an age of afterthoughts that intolerance itself is transformed into an angel of light. To rescue from hell becomes the first duty to the mere dogmatist. He has himself bolted his own opinions, why should others then stand off in mere squeamishness of conscience? Such scruples as these should be whipped out of men. There is a short and easy method of drilling men into conformity. The state of mind which calls in the sword to cut the knot of controversies can only be understood when we have seized some of the deep contrasts which faith suggests.

Faith is, in truth, a complex state of mind, the result, as it has been well said, of a consent of the will following on an assent of the understanding. But to rest the whole of our faith on a single support is to require too much of human nature. Authority is, we admit, of use in the first instance to raise initial presumption in favour of religion; then follows reason, or the orderly marshalling of proofs, on which the divines of last century laid if anything too much stress. Lastly, there is the concurrence of conscience, since, unless it is seen to be right by the best lights which God has given us, how can we pretend that it comes from God. The result of this is that the supports of our faith are these three—(1) antecedent testimony or authority; (2) reason, or the harmony of these proofs with each other; and (3) and lastly, conscience, or the correspondence of the revelation without with the interior light of that candle of the Lord lighted in every man's breast. There are thus, in the language of St. John, three that bear record on earth, tradition, the written word, and the interior word; and when these three are found to agree in one, then we reach the state of assurance—our heart condemns us not, and we have confidence with God.

Men have unfortunately failed to see this composite character of faith, and that it rests, not on a single strand of private persuasion, but on a threefold cord of authority, argument, and private conviction, which is not easily broken. Hence the desire has arisen for a theology of safeguards, and we fall back on dogmatisms as defensive outworks of truth. In the good old days of the evangelical revival, marked by such works as Scott's *Force of Truth,* the note of all true religion was that it was "experimental;" men believed because they knew what they believed in. Accepting it first as a pious tradition, a deposit of truth found in the Church, they at once went on to test it for themselves, using the usual evidential tests, historical and internal, and only settling down to a belief in the deep and true sense of the term when Faith had seated herself firm on her tripod of the Church, Bible, and conscience, and was able to say, "These three agree in one." This was the experimental religion of those Samaritan converts who said, "Now we believe, not because of thy saying, for we have heard Him ourselves, and know that this is indeed the Saviour of the world."

This leads us to notice the strange oversight made by the Evangelicals of last century, as indeed by the whole Augustinian school, with its right and left wing of Bible and Church authority. Such has been their narrow distrust and suspicion of the school of interior light, that they have almost gone as far as deliberately to put out one of the eyes of faith. They then expect it to see plainly, forgetting that the eye is single only when there is the one picture painted on the brain, and that from two distinct camera views are two separate retinas. Binocular vision is so well understood in our day, that we fail to see spiritual things unless there are also two eyeholes. Without this provision there must be want of perspective; man becomes an intellectual Cyclops; and sometimes, sadder still, on his discovery of this requirement of the self-verifying power of truth, he starts back in amaze at his seeing things in some distorted form, and punctures out his eyes, like another Œdipus, in horror at this discovery. Far better is it to act on the line—

> "He fought his doubts, he gathered strength,
> He would not make his judgment blind,
> But faced the spectres of the mind
> And laid them: thus he came at length
> To find a Higher Power his own;
> And Power was with him in the night,
> That makes the darkness and the light,
> And dwells not in the light alone."

It was the glory of the Cambridge Platonists to have restored the truth of the verifying power of the spiritual consciousness, which later Augustinianism had departed from, if he never expressly denied it. Augustine in his early and better days was not averse to this type of Christian Platonism, which he unhappily threw aside for the dogmatic theology of his later life, and which lost itself in the sands and shallows of controversy against Manichees, Donatists, and Pelagians. The overwhelming authority of Augustine, overshadowing every other teacher, left the faith impoverished by the deliberate exclusion of one of its three factors. Tradition and the Bible between them helped to bolster up a religion of authority. But such a religion, with one afterthought brought in after another to supply the missing link of the spiritual consciousness, only prepared the way for scepticism. It is a case like that of our food—exclude one of the three essentials, the albuminous, nitrogenous, and the heat-supporting hydrocarbon element, the result is slow decline. The soul may be starved in the same way as the body;

and it is not without significance that just as the body, denied one of its three constituents of food, flies to it and gorges on it with greediness; so in the spiritual world the discovery of the neglected truth of the inner light, by seekers like George Fox and other uneducated men, was attended in its first stages with all sorts of extravagances which brought this type of early Quakerism into contempt. Happily the Cambridge school of Platonists, with their calm and almost too philosophical way of putting things, restored the doctrine of the inner light to its true supremacy without that senseless recoil against steeple religion or Book religion, such as the early Quakers fell into. Well would it have been for the age if this sweet reasonableness,[1] which Cudworth, Whichcote, and More showed, had spread out into wider circles, and had been better understood by the following age. This was unfortunately not the case. After Tillotson, who was the last expiring echo in public of this cloistered type of thought, there began a sterile age of external formalism, in which the Church lost itself in dull discussions with the Deists as to the reasonableness of revelation. It set out with cutting Scripture in two, and divided between

[1] On this neglected chapter of Church history the late Principal Tulloch's work is still our chief guide; but the subject is one well deserving fuller consideration; and if Augustinianism is ever to be dethroned, it can only be by recalling the memory of these worthies, who in an age steeped in dogmatism dared to appeal to the counter principle of the spiritual light of the Logos born in every man. "The days," Dr. Tulloch remarks, "of Augustinian dominance are for ever ended. It can only come by the slow elaboration of Christian reason looking before and after, and gathering into its ample thoughtfulness the experience of past as well as the larger aspirations of the present." Of Hales of Eton, Dr. Tulloch sensibly remarks that he did not pass, as too many of that day, out of dogmatic Calvinism into dogmatic Arminianism. When he wished John Calvin good night, it was not to say good morning to Arminius. This probably is the true ground why the Cambridge Platonists took no root. Their calm philosophical temper was not understood.

what it called the internal and the external evidences for its truth; but a truncated is never a living body, it is simply the limbs of Osiris collected in the chest of Isis; and we know what impression this piecing together of the mangled remains of truth must produce on the age.

Wesley, under Moravian teaching, came to a clear conception of the subjective side of religion; but, like too many revivalists, he ended in turning his subjectivity of conversion into a new objectivity of a dogma binding on all on pain of damnation. The Church Evangelicals then took up the task, and began well; only it has ended ignobly in tame and meaningless compromises between the Church and the Bible, in which the supremacy is alternately shuffled from the one to the other, leading to panics and protests like that of the *Essays and Reviews* controversy, repeated again the other day. The true remedy is to get back to the "three witnesses" theory of faith which we have glanced at, and which has never been held with the same distinctness by any body of Church teachers as by the Cambridge Platonists. In the reaction against Augustinianism and its afterthoughts, the best thinkers of our day have discovered to their deep satisfaction that in this comparatively obscure school of Reformers after the Reformation, they had met with the singular anticipation of their best thoughts. So the late Principal Tulloch of St. Andrews, Scotland, and many more whom it would be invidious to name in this honoured seat of learning, have looked back on them as in a sense their fathers in God, the spiritual progenitors of anything good and lasting in their teaching. Among such may I venture to class myself, as a follower of forty years' standing? To the merchantman seeking goodly pearls, it is always treasure-trove to come upon something in the past which anticipates his own best thoughts. It encourages him to feel that he is not a mere egoist and off the track, since he finds that he comes upon footsteps which show that others have traced the same solitary path of internal experience, and found that it leads to Christ. He who is the Way, the Truth, and the Life, will most certainly be found by us when we are on the same "way" which others have trodden before us; when we find that it is the "truth" which corresponds to our best intellectual apprehensions, and that it is the "life" which satisfies all our spiritual longings.

It strengthens us, then, and gives us a sense of security, to find that many, if not all the best minds of former ages, have taken the same road that we are journeying on. They rested their faith, as we do, provisionally on authority, only to ground it at last on the sure rock of an internal conviction from which we can never be shaken. Had others done the same, we should have had less of this base tradition of second-hand dogmatism to sweep, like last year's dead leaves, out of our path. But let us be just to this age of defensive dogmatic theology, the age which, in its fear of a general shipwreck, came to regard the Church as the Divine ark of a doomed and perishing age. Augustine's philosophy of history is the theory of two cities, a Babylon and a Jerusalem, out of the former of which we must escape to be saved in the other;—this may seem narrow, but it is the same conception which coloured Bunyan's vision. Both were bounded by the same horizon, and for the same reason could see nothing for the soul but to escape from the city of destruction. The larger thought of the world reclaimed to God, and of the progressive growth of the mustard seed, of the inward leavening of the whole lump—this sweeter aspect of Christ's work was as foreign to the thinking of the fourth as it was to the seventeenth century. The old Roman world was incurably corrupt, and, steeped in unutterable pollution past all remedy, it was dying and had to die. It was too late. The Church could not save the Empire; it could only save itself. It could only look on, sadly in some cases, exultingly in others; but it looked on like a loving nurse. It waited, as has been well said, with her gentlest and unwearied ministrations by the miserable death-bed of the ancient world.

So, again, the ascetic principle which came in early in the fourth century soon began to corrupt the simplicity which was in Christ. It had this excuse, that in no other way could men escape the corruptions that were in the world through lust. Finding it hard to conquer, they learned to fly. The nobler course, no doubt, would have been to follow the path of holiness in the quiet circle of the home life. But one error, as is always the case, led on to another. The dogma of sin as *ex generatione* had led, at least in the West, to a strange overestimate of virginity as such. It was not enough to observe purity of life in a home and hearth where no corruption was allowed to cross the threshold. It was a certain defilement even to be born. Instead of seeing, as they should, that the Son of God, by clothing Himself with our humanity, had dignified the passage into life, they read into it a new and strange meaning. "Thou didst not abhor the Virgin's womb," suggests a mode of thinking on the subject of the eternal order which would be revolting if it were not the too naturalistic sense which they took of the generation of evil, resting on a crude, uncritical interpretation of Psalm xxii., in which David declares he was shapen in wickedness.

The Gnostic and Oriental notion of the intrinsic evil of matter has travelled far, and lost nothing in its wanderings to the West. From India to Persia it had passed on, till it had infected the Latin Church of the West with its subtle misconception of the source of evil, not so much in the depraved will and conscience, as in the existence of matter and of our present subjection to matter, through our imprisonment in a corporeal frame. We all know how Sankya Muni began the struggle by seeking entire emancipation from all flesh environment. The pure love of wife and child were as much polluting as the actual defilements of sin; and the forsaking even of family life was regarded by this prince of ascetics as the first step upward and on to spiritual emancipation. Passing on to Persia, this ascetic principle took a deeper dye, if possible, when brought in contact with the theory of two rival deities of light and darkness. Dualism thus entered in to deepen and still further deprave the ascetic principle; and the two errors, when combined, first the Buddhist conception of the inherent evil of matter, and, secondly, the Persian dualism of rival deities of good and evil, poured in one tide into the Christian Church. The Christian doctrine of sin was thus distorted by two corruptions which depraved its original meaning. Sin, as it is understood in the Hebrew Scriptures, is a form of lawlessness. Amartia is defined as Anomia: hence without the law, sin might exist, but only as a peccant humour, some latent inability to do good; but the law entering in, to follow the vigorous Pauline metaphor, a marriage takes place between the law and the flesh, so that flesh now quickened by the law conceives lust and brings forth sin—the end of which is, and must be, death, or the destruction of a progeny so unnaturally gendered.

But the afterthinkers of theological systems in the fourth century were not content to pause here with this simple scriptural theory of the genesis of evil, gendered by the irritation and clash of two opposite principles, the law of right and the desire for wrong. They went as far as to Persia to fetch thence a dualistic theory of evil arising from the eternal discord between the all-good and the all-evil. They wandererd even farther East—they went to India to import thence a theory of the inherent evil of matter as such. Sin had thus two fresh factors in the Augustinian theology which are wanting in the Pauline, or at least are glanced at in the lightest way possible. Sin arises from the malice of the devil, the Ahriman of the East; and sin also is produced from this flesh of ours, which is inherently evil, and from which there is no escape but by the ascetic discipline, not merely of keeping the body under, but more than this, of so mortifying it that the spirit may become a pure and passionless image of the Divine perfection.

Thus asceticism in its two types, the Hindu and the Persian, laid hold of the Church of the fourth century. It must be said that at first its wildest excesses were more Eastern than Western. It was only slowly that the West followed the East into its excesses of monachism. The good sense and stern self-restraint of the Roman mind was too averse for better or worse from that type of dreamy abstraction which is more Eastern than Western, and more germane even to the speculative Greek than to the Roman training of lawyers and soldiers. Nothing but the overshadowing name of Augustine could have fixed such a type as the favourite one in the West, where, singularly enough, it was a reaction against one type of monachism, that of Pelagius, which impelled Augustine into another. The Pelagian theory of perfectability had so impaired the sense of original sin, that in his anti-Pelagian zeal Augustine struck out an exaggeration in the contrary direction. The race had been tainted at the fountainhead. Evil, not mere *vitium*, but *peccatum*, had entered in with Adam and descended to the whole race, who accordingly became guilty, according to the strange distortion of this African Father, not of temporal consequences only, but of eternal. Instead of a mere privation of good, there enters at birth (whether *per traduceum* or not, Augustine will not decide) an active principle of evil, which makes every man born in the world, not a member of Christ,—a child of God and an inheritor of the kingdom of heaven,—but the opposite of all these. He is a child of wrath,—a child of the devil, and doomed to the same everlasting exclusion from God's presence unless sacramentally sealed in the laver of regeneration.

Is it strange, with these conceptions of the genesis of evil *ex propagatione*, that the ascetic principle rooted already in the East sprang up in fresh and rank luxuriance in the West? If men were born children of the devil, the less of this serpent's brood brought to the birth the better. Virginity thus got a new sacredness as such strangely foreign to the whole texture of Old Testament thought. Marriage had been honourable in all, and the bed undefiled, but at last marriage was barely permitted, for the curious reason glanced at in the marriage ritual as a "remedy against sin," and for those who, as mere tertiaries, made up the rank and file of lay religionists. For all the higher ranks there was only one rule, viz. that of absolute undeviating continence. Pelagius the monk was now "hoist with his own petard." Here was Augustine, the rival monk, with an ascetic theory more terribly consistent than his own, not resting on a half-Manichean, half-Buddhist theory of evil which Pelagius would have started back from with horror. It was not easy to bring the East round from the Pelagian to the Augustinian view of evil as inherent in the flesh. For some time the Pelagian was the orthodox view. Not in the East only, but even in Gaul and other Churches whose traditions were those of the East, Augustine's was considered to be the novelty; and even Jerome, that prince of theological trimmers, was slow in coming round to the Augustinian view of the question. We may ask what induced him to do so, and the whole East after him, since Jerome in his day was the one living bridge between East and West? The explanation is that the poison of the ascetic system had so eaten into the sounder mind of the Greek Fathers, that they reluctantly gave up their sounder traditions and followed the Latins into theories of the descent of evil *ex traduce*, which but for this they would have treated with contempt. These supporters of the doctrine of free will and man's responsibility turned round and changed sides under the darkening superstition of monkery. It was an evil day for the Church and for truth when celibates and ascetics became her theologians, as was the rule after Augustine. In Ambrose and Cyprian's case, with all their hierarchical pretensions, there is lingering on a common-sense element of moderation, at least in cases where their own private prejudices were not rudely crossed. But in your genuine ascetic all this moderatism disappears. The price which human nature pays for trampling out a whole class of instincts and desires, is that passions dammed up in one direction break out in another. If it is not good that man should dwell alone, the reason is more than a mere sensual one. It is because, as a fact of rude experience, neither his ethical nor his intellectual unfolding is possible in absolute solitude. Shut in to himself, shut out from society, and, above all, from that best of all training grounds of the will, in the innocent, expansive play of the family affections, man's egotism runs wild. He becomes arrogant, self-sufficient—in a word, an "intellectual all-in-all." Nay, his very zeal for the glory of God, or what he considers such, distorts his perspective. He sees errors of opinion, not in the large lenient way of the great All-Father, but as a kind of *lèse-majesté*; it is a slight on a great Supreme, whose viziers and avengers the clerical order consider themselves to be. The companionship of woman is something more to man than he at first supposes: as long as he regards her solely as the half-savage does, either as his nurse at one age, or his concubine in another. Woman is more than this, or she has failed of her mission, as she had failed in that corrupt age which marked the decay of the Roman Empire, and when the ascetic system sprang up. Woman trained in the home has leisure to see life under those softer side-lights which escape man. Life is not seen by woman in the white light of some abstract theory, whether political or religious, but broken and melted in its many hues of home charities, of personal pities, of likes and dislikes, sympathies and antipathies, for which she can give no other reason but a woman's.

All this seems to strike man as sentimental and illogical; but is it the logic of real life—not the logic which rules in cloisters and within chancels—not the logic of Church Councils and Assemblies, but the logic which, like that of the poet of spiritual insight, regards man as a tangled chain of good and evil?

We do not know what broader and more general type the fierce African doctor might have developed into had his mother Monica remained by his side, or had he carried out his first intentions of an honourable marriage hastily come to in Milan after his conversion, and as hastily abandoned. The truth must be told, which Augustinian critics have strangely overlooked. There were two Augustines, the early and the later; and our attachment to the author of the *Confessions*, the early Augustine, has blinded us to the defects of the Bishop of Hippo, who spent the latter years of a long life as red-handed with perpetual battle; or, to use a milder metaphor, he clasped in strife so often, that, like the dyer's hand, his very style acquired a brand.

No one forgets to rake up against Tertullian the falling off into heresy of his later Montanist writings. But Churchmen, carried away by the letter of traditional orthodoxy, seem to forget that there is a Montanism or spiritual pride and rigorism quite as hateful in the later Augustine as in the later Tertullian. The one, it is true, cut himself off from external Church fellowship, as the other did not, and it tells to his advantage. But let us not forget that Augustine was a champion for the Church only when the Church was on the side of Augustine. He was not provoked as Tertullian, the mere layman and lawyer, was to wander off into the by-paths of sectarian separatism. But the same temper was there, and we have misread all Augustine's later polemical treatises if we do not see the same temper of unyielding and arrogant dogmatism as in the seventeenth century Calvinists, who stamped on the pride of the Prelatists with a greater pride, and who soon showed how it would fare with religious liberty under a yoke as bitter as that which they rebelled against.

We shall never deal fairly, then, with these afterthoughts of theology unless we set them down principally, if not entirely, to one school, the Carthaginian, and to one man, the latest and greatest of the three dogmatists who have darkened theology with their type of diseased egotism. Human nature only too readily takes a wrong bias under its idols of the den, its subjective colourings of truth; but when to these are added the idols of the theatre, when the *zeit geist*, or spirit of the age, has taken up a popular delusion, such as asceticism, and works the delusion to death, the results are disastrous. As a monk, Augustine came to look on original sin in a new light. It started out in new distinctness, like a letter in invisible ink when held before the fire. Then he began to see and teach for the first time that mere generation genders sin. The simple, self-evident truth that "like produces like," the law of heredity, in a word, which is a law as much of science as of Scripture, got a twist in the cell of an ascetic, who, in renouncing carnal lusts, forgot that lust is only one out of many forms of evil. Augustine succeeded, though not without many protests, in forcing on the West a dogma of original sin. It was *peccatum*, not merely *vitium*, out of which grew that amazing superstructure of covenant theology, which in Witsius stands out like one of those old houses on London Bridge,[1] storey over storey, and each arching over the other, till the wonder begins why it had not toppled whole over long ago into the river. Adam was a supposed covenant head of humanity. The race germinally lived in the loins of their first parent. In his sin there was the sin, not the mere misfortune, of all of him born. His responsibility was direly aggravated by this consequence, which he was assumed to be conscious of. There was a Titanic presumptuous revolt of our first parent, who, more like Milton's Satan than the Adam of Genesis,

[1] Fuller, I find, has forestalled me in this simile, which I should quote to clear myself of unconscious plagiarism: "As such who live in London and like populous places, having but little ground for their foundations to build houses on, may be said to enlarge the breadth of their houses by height; so the Schoolmen in this age, lacking the latitude of general learning and languages, thought to enlarge their active minds by mounting up, so improving their small bottom with towering speculations;" cf. his *Holy and Profane State.*

dragged after him millions of his unborn posterity into the same hell-deserving Titanic attitude of God defiance. That we are not found lying on the fiery marl, but laid helpless babes in a mother's arms, is the only exception to this gloomy mythological afterthought, this travesty of the myth of the fall of the Titans transferred to the story of the first man. Let us not follow out this now forgotten theory of the theology of the covenants into the details of these Augustinian afterthoughts. It is, from first to last, one long *petitio principii.* It has been riddled through and through with criticism, and the average layman lays it on the shelf with the easy remark, "Thank God, we are out of our baby-clothes, or grave-clothes rather, of seventeenth-century Calvinism!" But this so-called Calvinism is in reality Aquinism in the first stage, and in the second it is Augustinianism; and we must break, not with Thomists only, but also the whole traditions of the Latin Church, before we get into light again. Our half-Reformation of the sixteenth century must begin again where it left off; it must aim at a mark which Calvin, Luther, and Cranmer alike miserably missed, and for reasons which no one so well set out as the late Bishop Hampden in his Bampton Lectures of 1833. It must rise above that type of Protestant scholasticism, the evil of which no one so well understood as Dr. Hampden, who was probably one of the two or three men of his day competent even to say what scholasticism really meant. The theology which is to substitute something better than Augustinianism, filtered through Anselm and Aquinas, and so passed on through Augsburg and Geneva into Anglican channels, must be at once more primitive and more progressive. As primitive, it will never stop short of the Greek type of theology, which was Christo-centric, not anthropo-centric. As progressive, it will accept the best thoughts of our age as to an increasing purpose running through man's story, and elevating him by slow stages, as geology reminds us that the evolution upward of organic life has been slow, constant, and continuous. The crude theory of a "fall," out of harmony with all science, and quite as unreconcilable with sound conceptions of an unchangeable God, must be replaced by another account of the matter quite as orthodox, and incomparably more reasonable. The half-Manichean, half-mythical conception of a Satan who is a rebel from a previous order of things, and who is found stealing into the young earth to draw the race after him, must give way to some simpler account of man's origin, and of his slow evolution upward from the anthropoid ape up to his ultimate destiny, as equal with the angels. It is a libel on true science to represent it as if instinctively averse to a spiritual view of the origin of all things, and of a cause behind causes which we can only adore with a "Thrice Holy" whisper. But science also, like true faith, insists that this "*causa causarum*" should never be described as arbitrary only; He is also holy, and just, and good. It is this taint of arbitrariness, in a word, that worst of all anthropomorphisms, which exalts God into another Pharaoh, or Cyrus, or Cæsar, whom He wills He slays, and whom He wills He keeps alive, which lies at the root of the recoil against religion of so many scientific men. Simple souls, who never analyse their own thoughts, ask us do we dare to deny God's "sovereignty"? as if the use of the phrase "sovereign" covers the question. People of this class forget the connotation of terms, and that the most august and ancient titles of Deity may for that reason have become semi-profane through the clustering around it of conceptions which repeat the Gnostic theories of the beginnings of evil. For, let it be known, the objections of educated men to the popular theology do not lie any longer in the direction that they once lay. It is, in our day, no longer a question of detail and of criticism, more or less verbal, as to the book and its contents. This might be the case in days when the Puritans debated points in dispute with lawyers like Selden: "Perhaps in your little pocket Bibles, with gilt leaves, which they would often pull out and read, the translation may be thus and thus, but in the Greek and Hebrew it signifies the other;" and his opponents had to bow to his superior knowledge. The difference lies deeper now. It is not even natural and revealed religion which have to be harmonised with the course of nature, as in Butler's day. The roots of dissent with the popular theology go down deeper still. What men want to know is the character of the God they are asked to adore. Is He intrinsic goodness, or only an angry God, conciliated by an amazing sacrifice. At least, in the Hindu Triads, Vishnu and Siva are not equally benign emanations from Brahm; evil is not eternal, it is the mere shadow of goodness. It is a dream which is to pass away when Brahm awakens. But the popular theology, mainly, if not entirely, under Augustine's leading, has starved down our conception of the All-good, until sovereignty becomes the oppressive vision of God. All other rays but the red rays are cut off in the prism, and with it light loses all its sweet actinic property of fostering life. We ask, in our ignorance of all this, why the scientific mind inclines to Atheism? but we forget that to ask the question is to answer it. Doubt is never natural to any mind, it is too tormenting for that; it is the noblest intellects that, as a rule, crave for God; but the scientist cannot accept such conceptions so coarse that they only adapt themselves to the savage stage of mind.

There must be no crude terrorism, no thunderbolt in the background, to frighten souls whom love fails to persuade.

We are at this point at last set on the true track of all, or nearly all, the objections to evangelical religion, not of men of taste merely, such as John Foster tried to reply to in his day, but of men of intellect and candour, who would believe if they could. The day has gone by when a few texts of the Bible uncritically interpreted are to decide the question, and those who reject them are told to stand back and consider themselves infidels if not Atheists. We want to turn the flank of the class who rather exult in the phrase "Agnostic," forgetting as they do that but for certain types of Gnosticism among the orthodox, their phrase would lose all its point. But for the recoil against the peremptory conclusions of Augustinian theology shutting up the whole of man's destiny to the few short years of his spiritual infancy on earth, there would have been no room for Agnosticism. To say that a man is indifferent, and sneers at the three tremendous verities which awoke Kant out of his sleep of dogmatism, the law of duty or personal lawgiver, and our accountability to Him here or hereafter, would be for a man to write himself down a fool. No man in his heart of hearts ever went so far as that, however he may brazen out his infidelity, more to shock simple souls than really to deceive those who detect the false note in Iconoclasm of this kind. Let us say, and say it with satisfaction, that the declining tone of dogmatism of the old type brings with it a corresponding decline of that contemptuous tone which regards all religions alike as mere survivals, the prolonging into an historical age of a class of conceptions which went out with the first dawnings of a conception of the reign of law.

How to clear true religion from these superfetations which we have described as afterthoughts, is not so easy as it is to denounce them. But it is something to have traced them to their root in certain misconceptions of God and man, dualism and asceticism, the Persian and Hindu distortions of what God is in Himself, and the relations of spirit to matter,—these are the prolific source of all the corruptions of Christianity. That they entered in together, and about the fourth century, has never been disputed; but the working out of the two has been somewhat different according as we turn from East to West. In the East, where asceticism ran to extremes even more revolting than in the West, it resulted in that petrifaction of faith in mere orthoxody which we recognise as the true note of the East. On the other hand, the West, if less extravagantly ascetic, only escaped this error to fall into a worse. It failed to purge the conception of God from that dualism which Augustine shook off in name only, to return to it in a disguised form. Augustinian dualism was no longer like that of Manes, two distinct deities struggling together. The scission now was in the attributes themselves of the Divine Being. His justice and love were turned from abstractions into concrete entities by the Realists, who make theology. God's good will to men, which none disputed, was barred by the prior demands of justice. There was thus a variance between the very perfections of God, a dead-lock, so to speak, in His administration, until by a covenant of the Trinity, which approaches perilously near Tritheism, the Son and Spirit covenanted with the Eternal Father to cancel the claims of justice by a satisfaction and equivalence of punishment. Out of this grew, as we know, the whole Latin theory of the atonement so foreign to the East, that we are not aware of a single theologian of the

East who has ever approached the subject from the Anselmian point of view. To the East the theory of satisfaction suggested compensation to Satan, the slave-holder, before the ransom of the sinner was complete. But the East never intruded into the council-chamber of the Most High, there to view His attributes of mercy and justice at variance, and to ask itself the way in which the Father's wrath against sin could be slaked by the sword of justice being plunged into the heart of His own dear Son. "Awake, O sword, against my shepherd, against the man that is my fellow," was uncritically taken from one of the old prophets to mean, that Deity could be satisfied with nothing less than the sacrifice of the Shepherd who was God's fellow and equal. Exegesis of this kind carries its own refutation, and it would lead us into a new field if we were to turn aside to discuss it. Here we confine ourselves to the single remark that East and West differed in nothing so much as their distinct senses of the term theology. To the theology of the West such discussions as distracted the East, the mode of the incarnation, and as to whether the Divine will replaced the human or merely energised it, the Monothelite and Duothelite controversies were, so to speak, non-existent. Nestorian and Eutychian controversies ruffled not the hard metallic temper of the Latin mind. Here we see the advantage of their non-metaphysical, unpsychological turn of thought. But reverse the picture —regard man as part of a scheme of the Divine government, as a moral agent and a defaulter to the law of duty—then theology in the West opens up fields of controversy which the East regards with blank indifference. Pelagian and Augustinian are to the West battle-cries, the same as Nestorian and Eutychian are to the East.

As long as we regard these contrasts with a mere

critical eye, we may be disposed to say a plague on both your houses. We may regard both as the mere scuffling of kites and crows. In this sense the history of theology is the history of battles in the air, or rather of school metaphysics, all the more absurd because not fought out in the schools, but brought into pulpits to disturb the thoughts and perplex the minds of simple laymen. But is this a fair account of the whole matter? May we set aside Homoousion and Homoiousion alike with a solemn sneer as that of Gibbon? Is the whole subject of grace and its relation to nature a mere logomachy of two sophistical monks, Augustine and Pelagius?

Such a temper is unfair, and only too common among those who stamp on dogmatism with dogmatism. It is no use reviling theology, much less for its using dogmatic terms for its definitions. Every *δόξα*, it has been well said, is a *δόγμα* in the making. The subjective element of private opinion, inherent in the aoristic form *δόξα*, is eliminated in the preterperfect form. What was a Doxa grows soon after—too soon—into a dogma; and as soon as this transformation occurs, then begins the age of heterodoxy, then of heresy, last of schism and of ex-communication. All these results of religious rationalising grow with accelerating force as time goes on, and as men recede farther and farther from the fountainhead of truth. There is no check to the evil but one, to insist on what are and what are not afterthoughts. By bringing back theology, as we have seen, to the strict sense of the term, the character of God in His dealings with men, some check may be set to afterthinking. The doctrines of theology, passed through a prism, break into many hues, and as we see God through one of these or the other, do we fail to see Him in the white light of His perfection. The East failed in this way when it lost itself in Nestorian and Eutychian subtleties, against which the sublime Monotheism of Islam rose and swept it away as with a blast of Divine displeasure. Equally so the West failed when the Pelagian and Augustinian doctors tore nature and grace asunder, as if nature without grace or grace without nature were not as unmeaning as the Divine or human in Christ, apart from their union. Here we trace in both cases the dividing line between a theology of forethoughts and of afterthoughts. After Athanasius in the East, and after Augustine in the West, it lost itself in a quagmire of subtleties, and the only safe path for the theology of the future is to dissolve continuity by cutting out of the page of its record, and treating as a great dismal swamp, the ages after Nice almost down to the present. The conclusion sounds Philistine to some. They say this is nothing else than the position of the old Bible Protestant of the seventeenth century. But this is precisely what it is not, although the Bible Protestant, ignorant of his own ignorance, assumes that it is so. He is Pauline, as he supposes he is, because he stands true to the teachings of Luther and Calvin; he is only so in so far as early Protestantism was a true transcript of Pauline theology. But we have wasted words, unless we have shown cause for treating Augustinian with the same distrust as we do the entire post-Athanasian theology of the East. The dividing line between what are and what are not afterthoughts begins in the tenth century, and only deepens with the division of East and West, and the after division of the West into Reformed and Unreformed Churches. To repair these afterthoughts by agreeing to sink some of them while retaining others, is impossible—what is written is written—what is rent is the seamless robe of Christ, which is not to be patched up by hollow compromises. But it is something to know the mistakes of the past. It sets us on the right track to amend them, and so we are learning the right road of reunion in our day. A sweeter, more truly catholic, more conciliatory theology is growing up around us. Humanitarianism is not a name now of hate and fear among theologians. Rationalism is now admitted to have taken its beginnings, first, among the orthodox, then to spread outwards into heterodox circles. Agnostics are admitted to be the illegitimate offspring of Gnostic parents; there are heresies outside the Church regarded as truths which we failed to take the bearings of. In a word, the age of polemics has passed away with that of eirenics, and so a clear space is thus being made where we may ground our arms, proclaim a truce, and mark a new departure to unity, in the sincere endeavour to hold the unity of the spirit in the bond of peace. "Even so, Lord, hasten it in its time. Surely I come quickly. Even so, Lord Jesus, come quickly. Amen."

CHAPTER VII.

AUGUSTINE AND HIS SYSTEM.

It is not enough to point out the divergence between Paulinism and Augustinianism, unless we go on to trace the error to its true source in an entire misunderstanding of the purpose of the apostle's teaching. It has been often remarked that the letter of Pauline teaching seems to support the predestinarian system which Augustine first and Calvin afterwards laid stress on. But the source of this mistake has not been made quite so clear as it should be. It seems to have sprung from honest ignorance of the Pauline standpoint. The apostle set forth predestinarianism, not as an absolute, but only as a relative truth, and solely with a controversial purpose. What he had in his mind was to beat down the immoral predestinarianism of his countrymen. The Israel after the flesh maintained that God was bound by His promises given to the elect, and so their salvation was sealed and secure, no matter how evil their lives were. The Gentiles, on the other hand, were non-elect and reprobate, and the apostle had to beat down this presumptuous dogma, as he does in Romans iii. and ix. God must be true, though every man were a liar. The apostle thus wrests this weapon of predestinarianism out of their hands, and turns it against them. He is more Calvinist than Calvin, more Augustinian than Augustine, but with a very different aim in view than that of these doctors of a theological determinism as lurid as the teachings of modern pessimism. The tendency of the apostle's teaching is the very opposite to this narrow creed of despair. It is, that God has included all in unbelief, in order that He may have mercy on all. It is a Christian adaptation of the teaching of Hosea, that Ammi is Lo-ammi, and Ruhamah is Lo-ruhamah. He will call them His people who were not His people, and will have mercy on those on whom He had not mercy. This casting off of the Jew was to become the riches of the Gentiles. Here we may pause to note the deep contrast between Pauline predestination and that of those later doctors, who took the letter but missed the spirit of his teaching—by and by He might have mercy on all. At this point, when Jew and Gentile have been alternately elect and alternately reprobate, leading up to a universal salvation wide as the wide world, he can contain himself no longer. He bursts out into a rapture of praise, and "silent as on a peak of Darien" he looks out on this boundless ocean of God's love, and exclaims, *Oh altitudo.*

But it is when we turn to the Epistle to the Ephesians that we get the true key to the Pauline sense of predestination. It is here when we read that we begin to understand His knowledge in the mystery of Christ,—a knowledge, let us add, in which this less than the least of all saints surpassed all the older disciples. The Twelve were not mere narrow Judaisers; it was with no reserve on that *disciplina arcani,* which is polite for duplicity, that they gave the right hand of fellowship to Paul and Barnabas; but they never reached the same spiritual elevation as the apostle who, if younger in Christ, surpassed them all in spiritual insight into this mystery of the Gentiles being fellow-heirs, and one body in Christ. They went as far as this, that the Gentiles should be admitted into full fellowship, and on their own terms released from observing the mere ceremonial precepts of Mosaism. But, after all, it was admission only by a back door. It was the overflow of God's grace—crumbs from a rich man's table—that the Gentiles were entitled to; but they had a younger son's portion, never the birthright and blessing of the elder. This doling out God's mercies at the door of the synagogue did not content Paul as the apostle of the Gentiles. He magnified his office; he proclaimed that the admission of the Gentiles was no mere "afterthought" of God, a grace of superfluity. It was the eternal purpose of the eternal God. As the Lamb had been slain from the foundation of the world — so the Gentiles had been "predestinated" quite as much as the elect of Israel. Peter could address the Diaspora as elect, according to the foreknowledge of God the Father; and Paul is quite as emphatic as to the predestinating purpose of God towards the Gentiles.

This is the keynote to the predestinarian teaching of the Apostle Paul. It has no meaning unless to convince the Jews that there was no difference in this respect between Jew and Gentile. Now, every writer, as we know, must be taken in the sense that he sets out with. Unless we look at the subject from his own point of view, we are sure to miss his meaning. His statements are *ad hoc*, and to be taken no farther. The predestinarianism of later theology was an "afterthought" which would have staggered the apostle, and made him wonder how men could have wrested his words to get out of them so partial a sense of God's ultimate purpose. We may go on farther to say, that by anticipation he almost excludes the room for such an inference as that which Augustine and Calvin drew from his teaching. Instead of cutting the human race into two sections,—a small remnant of elect and saved souls, and a mass of rejected reprobates foredoomed in Adam's transgression and afterwards doomed through their actual sins,—he regards the race as drawing its first unity and last destiny from Christ; it is a case of a universal ruin met by a universal redemption. The only difference that he makes between the two universals is that, if possible, the race has gained in Christ more than it lost in Adam, and that not intensively only, as the old school hold, but extensively as well. It is not the case that the many are lost and the few saved, as Augustine taught, but the many or the *massa perditionis* becomes the many or multitude that no man can number, who stand before the throne all washed white in the blood of the Lamb.

The dark shadow of Augustine and Calvin's limitation of God's love will never be rolled away till the Church goes back to the apostle's own teaching, and takes his predestinarian phrases in their true sense. It is not an absolute transcendent truth, but a truth adversative to the narrow construction of the Jew—the elder brother who grudges the goodwill of the Father to the younger and prodigal son. Predestination, election, effectual calling, redemption, and final salvation—these are the same five points over which the elect Israel wrested, as later divines do, on the five points of the quinquarticular covenant and charter. These the apostle snatches out of their hands and passes them on to the Gentiles. It is a sorry abuse of language, when later theologians, repeating this Jewish mistake, also set up five points again by which to cut off the mass of the Gentiles and to disinherit them over again. More Jewish than the Jew is our verdict, then, on this theology of afterthoughts; and till this miserable perversion of Paulinism, in which the letter has killed the spirit, is quite got rid of, we shall never read the Pauline Epistles aright. These letters are, indeed, hard to be understood, and ignorant and unstable men wrest them as they do other scriptures; but who is to blame for this so much as our interpreters, who, microscope in hand, discuss datives and aorists, but seem blind to the broad bands of light which play over the whole page like sunshine on a silver sea? The Church which, with some conspicuous exceptions, has so twisted Paulinism into a groove of particularism, must repair her own mistakes, and get back as best she can to true Paulinism. But this she never can do until she has made a clean sweep, not of Calvin only, but Augustine as well. The compromises of the school of minute criticism will never help us to roll away the reproach on theology, that it has made a yoke heavy which was meant to be light, and so has driven from Christ souls whom He meant to draw. Predestination is a word which seen in one light is a cloud and a darkness; it becomes a pillar of fire when we get behind instead of before it, and so learn that it beckons us on to our Father's home out of the Egypt of bondage to sin and self.

The lesson, then, which "Augustinian afterthoughts" point to should never be lost to the Church. Truth distorted is no longer felt to be truth at all, but that mixture of a lie which repels conscience and raises a revulsion against the truth as it is in Jesus. It is a sad fact that many in their aversion to Augustinian narrowness include some of the Apostle Paul's writings, especially the three chapters in the Epistle to the Ephesians, in which he dwells on an eternal purpose of God which has been mistaken for predestination in the later adulterated sense of the term. It is known that Swedenborg conceived an intense aversion to Pauline teaching, because he was so uncritical as to confound Paulinism with later forms of Lutheranism. Finding imputed righteousness taught in Sweden, and assuming (which he had no right to do) that this must be Pauline because some kind of imputation is referred to in the fourth chapter to the Romans, Swedenborg went so far as to reject Paulinism because he rejected Lutheranism. Augustine and Calvin in the same way have brought up an evil report on Paulinism which it does not fairly deserve. Criticism is worth very little if it cannot rescue the blessed apostle's teachings from such debased after-thoughts as those of the Determinist doctors of later Christendom. Alas! how little our ordinary exegetical criticism has done to help us on to a higher standpoint, we may see from the prejudice still felt against Pauline predestination on account of its seeming to agree, verbally at least, with the narrow notion of the election of a small remnant, and of the reprobation of the many of later theology! To read the apostle as he should be read, and to see that he is a Jew among Jews, beating down their dogma by a counter dogma of Gentile race election, this is what criticism is bound to give us. The *Partikel-lehre* of Hartung and the minute critics may be useful in its way,—we are the last to make little of it,—but the broad comprehensive view of Paulinism as a whole, this is the true Augustinian counterblast, and till it has been done, as it will be some day, and on a scale worthy of the subject, we must continue to suffer from these unauthorised glosses on the apostle. It is this reading into St. Paul a particularism he never meant to teach, which has led to that revolt which in America is described as universalism. Like many American reactions, it is loose and uncritical; it is handled often in a sensational way which revolts sober minds. This drives timid natures back into a counter-reaction in which they cling close to the skirts of so-called Catholic teaching; and as Augustine is *facile princeps* among Catholic doctors, this free handling of Augustinianism seems to them only another symptom of the dissoluteness of an age which has broken from its moorings and is adrift on a sea of doubt.

Again, then, let us raise the note of true reform by getting back into a pre-Augustinian stratum of theology. To the fresh feelings of the apostle the wonder of God's grace as seen in His electing the Gentiles and predestinating them in love to full fellowship of privilege with the Jew, this was a subject of adoring joy. Could we see predestinarianism in that light, instead of its seeming a hard saying, a *horribile decretum*, it would be the new wine of the kingdom, the Saviour's joy in bringing many sons unto glory. That dreadful particularism, which was the nightmare of the Church in a sacerdotal form before the Reformation, and in a non-sacerdotal form since that so-called reform which so lamentably came short, would then melt off, and we should see the sun as when the morning mists disperse. Anglicans, Catholics, Calvinists, all shiver alike under the cold shade of Augustinianism; they all alike, but for this theological taskmaster, the *durus pater* of particularism, would go on to see the educational view of God's covenant purposes, and we should hear no more of probation in this life as the be-all and end-all of theology in its two schools, the Reformed and the Unreformed, which divide Christendom.

The strange part of all this confusion in the popular theology is, that the critical few who know better do not step forward and denounce this base determinism, by showing that it has no warrant either in God's word or even in Catholic antiquity down to Augustine. It is the outgrowth of a spasm of terrorism which afflicted mankind about the fifth century, when, at the break-up of the Western empire, men's hearts were failing them for fear, and the *dies iræ* seems to have rung a dirge in Church and empire alike. The Flagellants and the Black Death processions of the fourteenth century have left their mark in history; but we forget that when Augustine built up his narrow scheme of particularism, based on the *extra ecclesiam nulla salus* dogma, the human mind had sunk to its nadir of intellectual decline. The ascetic theory had taken the virile temper out of theology. Greek philosophy, alike with Roman law, it had closed their schools, and had become the tradition of a dead past. The age was folding itself up for the long chrysalis-sleep of the seven centuries from Augustine to Dante,—a sleep so deep, though not quite dreamless, that we may pass it over like that legend of the Sleepers of Ephesus. To take our type of theology, then, from its most tainted source, as we hold Augustine's age to be, is no mark of criticism, but the reverse. How long we have submitted to this, and for what ignoble reasons, it is unnecessary here to repeat. Scholarly men, who have long ago shaken off the yoke of traditionalism, do not know and do not seem to feel for those who cling to Anglican or Calvinist theology, under fear that without these guides they would lose touch of the apostle. Even so-called Bible Christians, ignorant of their having read into Paul much that they have read out of him, go on confirming this false traditionalism. Out of all this confusion nothing but confusion worse confounded can emerge. There is "no night but of ignorance;" and this double night of ages and of her "night's daughter, ignorance," has gathered thick around the Church, chiefly resulting from its superstitious reverence for one great name. "The whole world is Jansenist," was once said by a Jesuit opponent; and as he added sarcastically, without knowing why or wherefore, the same unreasoning fit of Augustine worship is repeated as in the Jesuit-Jansenist scuffle of the Gallican Church. Five propositions which Bishop Jansen had picked out of Augustine's writings are condemned in Jansen, but declared not to be in Augustine. The poor Jansenists pleaded in reply that, as a matter of fact, these five points were all verbatim taken out of the writings of the African saint. But no, the Jesuits urged in reply, Augustine was a saint, and for this reason no such taint of heresy could be supposed to come from so saintly a source. Facts were against this Jesuit gloss; but so much the worse for the facts. The Pope's infallibility scarcely extends to making the facts, as the Jansenists urged; but all the same the Jesuits triumphed, and the weaker went to the wall. All the wit of Pascal, and all the piety of the Port Royalists, could not make the Pope budge from the absurd position, that what was heresy in the Bishop of Ypres was only orthodoxy in the Bishop of Hippo. Circumstances, we all know, alter cases, and so it has fared with Augustine more than once. He has escaped criticism, and, like Manlius in sight of the capitol, it has been impossible to censure him. For his extraordinary merits as the great sacerdotalist of one school and the great pietist of another, he has wrung absolution from both sects. Anglicans cannot, or rather will not, see his predestinarianism, and Calvinists do not pretend to see his sacramentalism; and so he is wafted off, as on a net of swans' wings, high out of the reach of criticism, like that sweet gossamer spirit in Rosetti's picture, which is seen as a sort of exhalation of earth above and beyond all criticism.

But the end of all this sentimentality is a stern demand of history to pass judgment on traditions which do not bear the light of common day. A gospel which is no gospel, but only a provision for a few out of many who are in a state of probation apparently, but in reality hanging like miners on a chain over the pit's mouth,—this conception will not conquer the world or reach and pierce the heart of humanity. That God so loved the world that He sent His Son to save only the elect few, this is not exactly the message to melt the heart and subdue the stubborn will. It wants a more powerful magnet than this appeal to the most subtle form of self-interest. Love which is death to self does not understand such a gospel. "My sheep hear my voice." They know self-sacrificing and disinterested love—the love that would die for a friend—the love which in losing its life finds it. This is not the soul-saving gospel of provisions and plans all based on the eudæmonism of popular theology, whose keynote is to make the best of both worlds, and whose latter-day prophets are those popular preachers whom the world has begun to turn from with something more than Carlylese contempt.

A reaction has set in; but where is it drifting us on to, unless to the sands of a shallow Deism, whether of the Unitarian or other defective drafts of the mind of Christ. The doctrine of sin as selfhood is overlooked, on account of the horrible distortion describing sin as an infinite offence against an infinite Being, and so deserving an infinite punishment. No one seemed to see that such a statement of sin, as qualified by the Being sinned against, cuts the other way. It is quite as certain that sin is finite because the act of a finite being. More than that, we define sin as the outcome of man's emptiness and lack of all true centre of being. Sin, as such, is as the chaff which the wind drives away, or, if collected at all, it is to be burnt up once for all in an unquenchable fire. This the popular Augustinianism failed to teach, and so has driven men to other teachers than Christ. It set up a crude terrorism, and threw the mind off its balance by appeals to flee from the wrath to come, never caring to define whether this wrath were temporal or eternal, either a judgment on the Jews of the Baptist's day, or the judgment of the last great day of assize. It was under the weight of one strong personality that these strange distortions of Christ's original message took permanent form, and at last were fixed as the standard theology, at first of the West, and finally of the East as well.

It is not easy to measure the slow encroachments of error on truth. To explain the rise of adulterated Christianity, we must go into history much more critically than the majority of Church historians do. It is easy, on the pragmatic side, to draw up lists of schisms and heresies, to fix their date and name their author. But this kind of pragmatism helps us but a little way when all is said: truth and error do not separate like two compounds not in chemical union, one of which is sublimated and the other precipitated. If it were so, the Christianity of our day would be apostolic and primitive; and there are ingenuous minds, who have not broken the shell of their dogmatism, who dream that it is so. But such a *sancta simplicitas* does not become the true student, who knows that life is not quite the same as a child's drawing on a transparent slate—a tame copy of a tame pattern behind. Many things happen with or without God's approval, though certainly not without His appointment. Whether we own to the phrase "evolution" as adequate to explain the laws of history, much more of Church history, in any case all will admit that the

Christian Church of to-day has taken shapes and developed tendencies which seem foreign to what its founder designed it to be. By the two parables of the Mustard Seed and the Leaven, Christ marked out the two sides or aspects of His truth—its external growth from the least to the greatest, and its internal action on society at large—as setting up a ferment, and making a new lump out of the unkneaded mass of the old humanity. With these two symbols in view, we may gauge what the gospel was designed to be and to do. It was to grow into a great outward society—the tree of the Church; but it was also to do a work on secular society, as such, corresponding to the action of leaven on flour.

The history of Christianity has been the carrying out of these two distinct and contrasted conceptions; but how imperfectly, and under what drawbacks! The seed, least of all seeds, has become a mighty tree; but then the birds of the air have lodged in the branches, and there, as from a perch, ungodly ambitions and pretensions to secular sovereignty have been screamed out from priestly lips. The leaven has leavened, it is true, the lump of the old pagan world; but the sad result has been that the reagent itself, the gospel leaven, has been reacted on, and if the faith has built up a philosophy of its own, that philosophy in its turn has moulded our faith into types distinct from the original. So much has this been the case, that some devout critics have turned the parable right round, and interpreted the leaven as the evil elements of the old heathenism which mixed with the gospel, instead of the new elements of Divine truth which were designed to infuse the old with a new spirit.

The truth probably is that both interpretations are correct. The gospel has leavened society for good; but then, on the other hand, society has leavened the gospel for evil. There is no reaction without a reagent; but, on the other hand, the reaction so destroys the reagent, that it passes by a kind of sea change into something rare and strange. Church historians, too often mere apologists, with too much of the advocate, too little of the judge, overlook all this. They are often uncritical in the last degree, and drop their judgment when they have to deal with a "saint," or one who passes for such. The injustice to Origen, for instance, who happens to pass down unstarred, undecorated, into the page of Church history, is only surpassed by injustice in the opposite extreme to Augustine, whom all sections of the Church compete for as their patron "saint." The one is too little of a saint, and the other too saintly by far. It is too late to rewrite Church history, or appeal for a rehearsing in both cases; but loyalty to truth compels us to say that all the mistakes of Origen were the mistakes of callow youth. His zealotry for sanctity by cutting off one of the external occasions for sin, marked the immature Christian. That he saw his mistake in later years is admitted by all, who fail to remark that he never fell into that very fault too common to the ascetic type of character, harsh uncharitable judgments of others. He was gentle even to the ungentle, and certainly did not render back railing for railing, as Jerome, Epiphanius, and other clerical scolds were in the habit of doing. But when we turn to Augustine, we meet with a character strangely contrasted with that of Origen. Both have need to exclaim, "Oh, remember not the sins of my youth!" and both purged these youthful follies in his own characteristic way. Origen matured into the student and devout thinker, "in labours more abundant," and, we may add, "in stripes above measure." He was Pauline in his width of sympathy and in his grasp of God's educational purpose in history. He saw with the apostle that the law was the pedagogue, and he also classed Plato with Moses as one of the preparations for the gospel. But he was also Pauline in his stirring up the enmity of the Judaisers of his day. He was the "mark for episcopal envy," and especially at the time when the episcopate was beginning to display that prelatical temper, the only issue of which must be the Papacy. No sound thinker, who can see effects or their causes, can withhold sympathy from Origen as the last type of that noble Alexandrian theology of which we may say in a memorable Butler phrase, "If it had the might as it has the right, it would have conquered the world."

Now, contrast with this the saintly Bishop of Hippo. All are agreed as "to the sins of his youth," but too many have stepped unguardedly into the sophism, "The greater the sinner, the greater the saint." If this is spoken without reserve, it may become more than a sophism—there may be the serpent's hiss in it. There are sins which are *φθαρτικὸς τῶν ἠθῶν*, so destructive of the basis of character which is truth, that if repentance is possible, it is the repentance of a man who has strained his spine, or who limps to the grave, like Jacob the supplanter. There are too many signs that Augustine passed out of the sinner into the saint class under stress of one of those sudden conversions which the Christian Church has accepted as normal, because it is assumed that they are cases in which the Apostle St. Paul was a "pattern to them that should hereafter believe." We must not turn aside to discuss St. Paul's conversion; all we wish to insist on here is that it does not justify, or indeed throw any light on, that mischievous sophism, "The greater the sinner, the greater the saint." In the case of Saul of Tarsus, it was the sudden discovery of one who had walked in all good conscience before God, that he had made a huge mistake, and had been kicking against the pricks. Jesus of Nazareth, whom he had regarded as the ringleader of a pestilent sect, was the Lord of glory. It was sudden conversion to learn that this Jesus of Nazareth was the Lord's Christ, and so far Saul of Tarsus was suddenly turned from darkness to light. In all other details his spiritual education follows the law of growth, extending over years, and was not a whit more precipitate than any of the other apostles'. On the contrary, measured by lapse of years, he was less of an ἔκτρωμα, one whom we should call an untimely birth, than any of the rest of the apostles of the circumcision. But let that pass.

Turning to the case of Augustine's conversion, whose genuineness we have not a thought of throwing a suspicion on, it has features in sharp contrast with that of St. Paul. It lacks, we are compelled to say, the same inner harmony. It has a jerky, impulsive air of a man torn between conflicting emotions, the slave of his sensuality, the most ape-like of sins, yet with a hearty desire to escape and be free. The majestic calm of the Catholic Church under such a ruler as Ambrose, its order, its self-consistency, its unbroken antiquity, its firm front to a rabble of warring outside sects seething in the filth of Eastern philosophies and mythologies, now out of date—all this brought him to the crisis in which the *tolle lege* echo of boys chanting seemed like a voice from heaven. His conversion, in a word, has a certain mystical element, not unlike that of Colonel Gardiner and other men of pleasure, who learn the Byron lesson that the "soul begirt with guilty woes, is like the scorpion girt by fire." That these men find in the crucified Jesus the very death they desire to the dominion of lust, is, we know, a glad truth, and we magnify the grace of God which can snatch them out of the fire, hating even the garment spotted by the flesh.

But we have to note in each case their after career, to see that they bring forth fruits meet for repentance. Their very way of extricating themselves from the mire of their old evil acts has to be jealously watched. We have never, for instance, understood the indifferent way in which Augustine flung off that concubine, the mother of his dear boy Adeodatus, and who, to all purposes and in God's sight, who hates putting away, was his lawful wife. The easy morality of the age may have condoned it, and a mother's fondness may have seen no sin in his annulling this left-handed marriage to contract one with an honourable maiden of his own class in Milan. So much of morality is conventional, that the "immutable" element, which is not for "an age, but for all time," is in danger of being overlooked even in saintly circles. But we must add that Church historians have been lax to a degree in slipping over this transition stage of Augustine's life, and never even hinting that eternal and immutable morality calls for some sterner judgment than theirs on such lax conduct. What became of his cast-off wife, the mother of his dear boy, not a hint is given. If sent back to Carthage, flung off into the whirlpool of unfortunates in that city of sin, we are sorry for the saint's memory. One so effusive as to his own secret thoughts and private vices, which he castigated Rousseau-like in public, might have said something on the subject. The world has not spared Rousseau for canting about virtue while casting his children off to sink or swim in a Foundling Hospital. Augustine was not such an unnatural father. Adeodatus was his acknowledged son, and shared his after life as a cœnobite in Tagaste and at Hippo. But what of her, the mother, but unacknowledged wife, who was "torn from his side as a hindrance to my marriage; my heart, which clave unto her, was also torn and bleeding"? Of her he adds (*Conf.* vi. 15), "she returned to Africa vowing unto thee never to know any other man, leaving with me my son by her. But unhappy I, who could not imitate a very woman, impatient of delay, inasmuch as not till after two years was I to obtain her word, not so much being a lover of marriage as a slave to lust, procured another." Is it strange that he adds that all this incontinence left its sting in his character? "Nor was that my wound cured which had been made by the cutting away of the former, but after inflammation and most acute pain it mollified, and my pains became benumbed, and more desperate."

The saint's own admission is more manly, and nearer the mark, than that of his too indulgent biographers. *Putrescebat et quasi frigidius sed desperatius dolebat*—his wounds were benumbed, but more desperate. So the Psalmist speaks of sensual sins—sin probably the same type of intemperate lust—"My wounds stink, and are corrupt through my foolishness." But the worst evil of sensual indulgence lies behind, "Oh, it hardens all within, and petrifies the feeling." This is the real sting of sin. It may be repented of, the lust may be subdued, but the unclean spirit has been known to return with seven other spirits more wicked than the first. So it is often with these sudden changes of sinners into saints. They become ascetics, and turn that same severity on others with which they stamped out their own lusts. In this Augustine is contrasted with Origen, who was never the slave to violent sin, and so his life was "gentle, and the elements so mixed, that nature might stand up and say, That was a man." Augustine, on the other hand, grew severer in his asceticism as Origen became gentler. He sold all his possessions at Tagaste, and so literally cast himself on God. Happily for him, he fell in with the cœnobite type, and so escaped the hermit folly, then at its height in the far East, but which never penetrated to the West till two centuries later, when Benedict of Nursia began to outrage nature by intruding as a "solitary" into her solitudes. As for Augustine, there was enough Roman good sense left in the fourth century to save the West from the folly of Eastern "anchorets." To what a degraded level these hermits brought down the religion of the Eastern Church in the fifth and sixth centuries, is known to history, though passed over far too indulgently by Church historians, afraid to be thought "illiberal" in judging the dead past.

But though Augustine was no monk, in the hermit sense of the term, he was a cœnobite, and with all the faults of his class emphasised in his case by his episcopal dignity. A prelate who is also an ascetic is thus exposed to a double danger. He is a monk of monks, and, like Dunstan or St. Thomas of Canterbury, it is hard to see how he can escape being a tyrant. "Spiritual despotism" is the sin of Churchmen. "How can ye escape the damnation of hell?" is the Master's warning to the Pharisees of His day. In Dunstan's, as probably in that of Anselm and à Becket, there was the excuse that a bad king called for a domineering priest. In the world's roundabout way of reaching right through wrong, one injustice is called out to check another. So Schiller's phrase rings out its rhyming meaning, that the *Welt-geschichte* is the *Welt-gericht*. To this excuse the Dunstans and Anselms are fully entitled, and Augustine may be included in the same amnesty of "pardon for praise." But here we must draw the line. As a monk he wrangled with monks, and Jeremy Taylor's verdict on the scuffle of Augustine with Pelagius is all that need be said on that subject. But the same contentious temper that seems to haunt the monk's cell, that "other worldliness" which is nature's way of paying off these unworldly men, is seen in Augustine in its most marked form. He scarcely rivalled Jerome in acerbity of temper; but in morbid egotism, and that desire to be *ego et rex meus* with God Himself, he is almost unique in Church history. Like all the "three Carthaginians" who gave theology a fatal twist, he was an intrepid asserter of his own notions of truth, as if they were God's own truth, not the shadows on the wall of his own mind, idols of the den. But where Augustine left Tertullian and Cyprian far behind was in the calm, bloodless way in which he looked down into the abyss of the hereafter, and waved souls into the fire-world of God's wrath for ever and ever, in a way which perhaps excused Dante for dealing out the same measure to his enemies, the Guelphs of Florence and the neighbourhood. Dante was an "artist," and is absolved by the easy code of art morals. But Augustine was a serious theologian, and has been taken only too seriously, as Calvin afterwards was for the same reason. The strangest part of it is that the Carlyle school, to whom "purpose" instead of charity covers a multitude of sins, have absolved Calvin, and also absolved Augustine, both for darkening Christianity and distressing souls. "Earnest," no doubt, he was; but what an earnestness, that earns a harvest of warring dogmatism and scepticism for all after ages! Men are sometimes said to be "intrepid," because callous to suffering. Such was Napoleon's intrepidity, when he turned cannon on the retreating Russians at Austerlitz, and broke the ice on the frozen lake across which they were passing. Such was Goethe's "intrepidity," which earned for him from his blind worshippers the distinction that he was a "demonic" man, superior to patriotism and other prejudices.

> "He took the suffering human race,
> He read each wound, each weakness, clear;
> And struck his finger on the place,
> And said, *Thou ailest here and here.*"

Such, let us add, was Augustine's "intrepidity;" and if we are to be Stoics of a new type of Carlyle's Christianity, we shall leave the aureole of saintship around Augustine now. But if not, we shall ask why he may not be "free handled," as poor John Calvin has been by Romanists and Anglicans at least. The Bishop of Derry has described one of Calvin's followers "with something of a narrow brow and something of a narrow heart;" will this eloquent Irishman, who has idealised Augustine in a graceful poem, now turn on the search-light of his critical faculty? Let us see how Augustine comes out in the fierce light of real criticism. We know only too little of our saint's after life, except from his own letters, which are not likely to be accusing documents. We have spoken of his *Confessions*, which, like those of Rousseau, set self in a sickly light of sentimentality. But we should wish that a prophet would turn on him the same light that Nathan did on David—"Thou art the man." We may then ask what he would shrivel up into. Women, who are always keener judges than men, passed the sharpest judgment on Augustine, and we wait for a life of the saint written from the woman's point of view. Who remembers, or cares to ask, whether Calvin was married? who, on the other hand, does not love Luther all the more for his home life, his Kate, the honest, perhaps too homely, German *Haus-Frau*, and his little George, to whom he talked, perhaps, the best table-talk that ever came from a theologian? We could give up a good many volumes of anti-Pelagian and anti-Donatist divinity for such touches of humanity as we find in Luther and Zwingli, the only two men of that age who were too great to muffle up their personality in sham Greek, like Melancthon, Œcolampadius, and others, who remind us of great schoolboys in comparison to these two men of men.

Till the critical method has put a knife into the hands of Church historians, we shall still cling to the traditional Augustine, with Calvinists and Catholics processioning from opposite sides to lay wreaths on his bust till the marble is not seen for the flowers. But truth is above charity, as charity is above rubrics. The rights of truth demand the deposal of the usurper of the West, if the West is not to sink into the same slough of superstition as the East. The honest verdict of history is that there is little to choose between East and West in their downward descent to superstition after the great age of the three Cappadocians. But the three Carthaginians, whom we set off against the three Cappadocians, all helped to push on the Church over the fatal descent into dogmatic hierarchy and spiritual despotism. Chiefest of the three was Augustine, without whom neither Tertullian nor Cyprian would have done much to fix that severe celibate type for which "priestliness" is the only phrase. But we cannot measure the depth of the descent which began only as yet with Augustine, and which we are at last working out of, unless we contrast Alexandria with Carthage, and limit our contrast to the Alexandria of Athanasius. To the Alexandria of Cyril's day we have nothing to say in stay of judgment. It was then given over to the same reprobate mind as the West, and we may drop the veil over both. The Goth was at the gates of Rome, as the Visigoth was in Carthage, and the Saracen soon coming on in the East to wave his scimitar and close the Church, as the Church had closed the schools of Athens under Theodosius. But truth compels us to add that, if Augustinianism corrupted the Church, early Alexandrianism, if adhered to as a type of anti-sacerdotalism, might have saved it. It was a premature type of philosophical Protestantism (to use popular language), doomed to perish, as all premature growths are. It failed as the iconoclasm of the Isaurian Leo failed in the eighth century, and for the same reason. The man and the hour must come together; if he steps on the scene one hour before his time, he will fail, as Arnold of Brescia, as Rienzi did, as Masaniello, as Mirabeau, and many other stage heroes. The world was not ripe for the revival of the larger hope school, so Origen has been made the scape-goat, and on his innocent head has been heaped all that fifth-century monks could fling out of the rinsings of the theological wash-pot. The strangest part is, that the heresies of the East were not the same as the heresies of the West. Origen's universalism was not the true ground for which degenerate Alexandrians reviled him. That they left to Augustinians. To the East his "heresy" lay in ambiguous phrases, which made it open to Arius as much as to Athanasius to claim him as on their side. Then, again, some fancies of his on the subject of the spiritual resurrection, and of pre-existence and the peopling of the stars, gave excuse to those who wanted an excuse for putting his name out of the hagiology. In the West, however, the heresies of Origen were of a deeper dye. If Origen were a theologian, what would become of Augustine, Anselm, and all the scholastics of the West, the mystics only excepted? It is clear that such a "pestilent" fellow must be made away with. "As for this sect, we know that it is everywhere spoken against." So Paulinism struck the Jews of Rome, and so early Alexandrianism has passed down into the traditional theology of the West as a sect everywhere spoken against. Catholic consent, whatever that is worth, has gone against it, and it seems foolhardy to try an *Athanasius contra mundum* in favour of Origen. So we should regard it if Origen were a single name, with a solitary set of opinions which were not as "Catholic" in the East as Augustine is Catholic in the West. But no scholar deserving the name can forget that in saying, with Luther, *Origenem diris devovi*, we are devoting *diris* the whole Alexandrian school, and that of Antioch and the whole East. But for Jerome, whose petty egotism deserves more pity than blame, the East would never have taken in that leaven of Augustinianism which in the end leavened the lump, and made Origen's name to pale before that of the Carthaginian school and its leader.

Criticism owes a deep debt of reparation for these misleading judgments of Church history. After all, professors are but men, and men too compromised by Church traditions to say out to their classes their real thoughts as to the names which have infected theology. But the time has come for plain speaking, especially since larger hope theologies are coming in by back doors, and men are asking, Is it prudent any longer for professorial chairs to keep silent when the ground is giving way beneath them? If it is rash to waken sleeping dogs, what shall we say of the rashness which goes on sleeping when watch-dogs are barking alarm? The age calls for a new theology, and will have it. For want of it, it flies to a hundred novelties, from old Deism to young Theosophy. But it is "God in Christ" which only can stay the soul' hunger; but it must be a whole God and a whole Christ. It is no God of "attributes" only, such as Western theologians teach us of, which will suffice. St. John the theologian has taught us not "about" God, of which we have heard only too much. He has taught us that God *is* light, God *is* spirit, God *is* love. Critics have often remarked that in all three cases the term is anarthritic. God is not the spirit, or *a* spirit, but spirit in the sense that spirit must to spirit in sympathy move before we can approach God at all. It is the same of God as light and of God as love. Till we walk in the light, till we learn to love, God must be an unknown God. Morality and religion are thus two sides of the same truth. This is the lesson of the early East which the West, since Augustine's day at least, has largely overlooked. The result is a deep schism between morality and religion. The two have gone each on its own course, and theology has stagnated because it has become "antinomian" under one form or another. The antinomianism of popular Protestantism is of one type, that of ceremonial sacerdotalism of another, but both traceable to the same roots in Augustine.

Let us then cut the cords which tie us to the traditionalism of one Church Father. The age asks for a new theology, and we can offer it one both new and old, if they will be old Catholics of an Alexandrian, not of a Carthaginian type. To timid minds who dread the new merely because it is new, it may be some solace to know that the new is in truth the old which was from the beginning, but which sacerdotalism, East and West alike, has overlaid with base traditions and afterthoughts which are unworthy of Christ's gospel. When that gospel is seen again in its true beauty, we shall wonder that we ever listened to that poor, debased copy by which, under prudential motives, we sought to save our souls, as Paley taught, because a mighty despot might send us to hell unless we accepted his terms. That this travesty of truth has lived so long, is owing to one name more than any other; and till that name is sent into the background to exchange places with Origen, we shall go on deploring the doubt and the dogma, which remain warring elements like the waves of the sea when driven by the wind.

Let us then see that our theology is a theology in the strict sense of the term, not that mere theanthropology which is neither one thing nor the other, but is a base syncretism of school philosophy and Hebrew faith in God. Both are set to the wrong note of a prudential scheme of soul-saving and providing for against an indefinite future. All our best and most spiritual intuitions cry out against the theology of bargain and barter, which is like Jacob at Bethel, but unlike Israel at Peniel. The strange part of Augustine's career is that, unlike other eminent names, he was Israel in his early years at Milan, and Jacob only in his later years at Hippo. If we have to overturn the St. Austin of tradition, we can best do it out of the teachings of the St. Austin of the *Confessions.* It is not often that a writer lends weapons out of his own armoury. Let us add in justice that his own *Retractations* were written at the close of his life. They harmonise so much better with the teachings of his conversion stage, that we may piece the first draft and the last draft together out of which to answer the Augustine of the middle or controversial epoch of his life. It has been his misfortune—one of those penalties of greatness—to leave behind him a quarry of hewn stones, out of which lesser divines of later ages helped themselves uncritically and without question. Just as the Coliseum was the ready resort of the palace builders of the Renaissance age in Rome, so Augustine left behind him a mass of polemical writings, out of which the system makers of a scholastic age had nothing to do but to pull out and pile up stones after their own fashion. It was a sorry result, as we know, for which after Augustinians are even more responsible than the original author. If theology ever since his day has been little more than a tasteless conglomerate of after-thoughts, bodies of divinity lacking the constructive spirit, let us at least divide the blame of this. Even to-day the saying is true in other places more enlightened than Spain, *Sin Agostino nul predigo.* This is the garlic which enters every dish, and wanting which no savoury meat is supposed to be served. An Augustine collection of commonplaces makes up the small library of a Spanish priest, who cuts into the master of sentences much as popular divines with us make up sermons "wholly Biblical" chiefly by the aid of a Concordance and the English Version. The sorry result is the same in both cases. This verbal knowledge of the letter of Augustine keeps up his authority, and the Roman Church is wise in its generation. As long as "salvationism" on the narrow basis of external authority and sacramental ordinances is the key to theology, so long the doctor of the West must reign without a rival. But the day of criticism has begun. The light of intuitional spiritual religion, self-evidencing to the awakened conscience, has been let in, and the New Reformation will make short work of the one doctor on whom the Old Reformation looked on too indulgently.

CHAPTER VIII.

AUGUSTINE, HIS MERITS AND DEFECTS.

BUT let us not be ungrateful to Augustine. There are excesses of certain thinkers of one-sided genius which are more helpful to a final settlement than the moderation of better balanced but less adventurous thinkers. The hardy dogmatism which pushes a theory to its extreme conclusions in which it breaks down *in foro conscientiæ*, comes to our help when we wish to hark back. Jonathan Edwards, for instance, rendered that service to New England theology. An intense one-sided nature such as Edwards', whose theology of God all in all almost bordered on Pantheism, was necessary in order to stir its consciousness of the counter truth which popular Calvinism had taken little or no account of. A reaction against the theology of mere sovereignty was only possible when sovereignty had been elaborated into a system on which to build up a final account of God's dealings with men, as it was held for the first time by St. Augustine. Till his theology had laid hold of the entire West, and moulded the thoughts of the Latin Fathers in one fixed type, there could be devoloped no counter theory of God's fatherly relation to men deserving the name. "Theories of the Fall" and of the "Headship of the first Adam" had not deepened as yet into that dogma of original sin which

Augustine affirmed in reply to Pelagius' too facile assertion of the indifference of the will, and the sufficiency of human nature to stand in its own strength apart from grace. It was this graceless Pelagianism which drove Augustine into contradictions quite as passionate in the opposite extreme. The indulgent decision of the Church between the two controversalists has been fair. It is that which Dr. Mozley inclines to. He holds that Pelagianism was an error which deepens into heresy, and therefore must be expelled or put down; while Augustinianism is only an exaggeration of a truth which lies at the root of all religious feeling, the truth "that without Me ye can do nothing." Hence this exaggerated sense of the need of grace even in the field of nature is a one-sided truth rather than an actual error, much less a heresy. This is, no doubt, a just summary as between Augustine and Pelagius. But though Augustine has been often opposed, and his great authority set aside, even in the West, it has been left for thinkers in our day to strike at the true root of his error, and so to lead the way into a sweeter, simpler conception of God.

One of the best results of modern philosophy is to remind us of the length of our tether, to use Locke's phrase; we never can know the absolute and unconditioned. The very personality of God, His thoughts, His decrees, and so forth, are only taken on trust. Language fails to describe how God thinks and acts, and hence the very term predestination starts a paralogism, something which can neither be thought as thought nor described in language. To Augustine and the Schoolmen it seems never to have occurred that this "magnified man" way of thinking of God was worse than presumptuous: it bordered on blasphemy. It represented the All-good as Absolute Will, and whose Omnipotence was the attribute which overshadowed every other. Wisdom, Love, Power, it is in this order that our conceptions of the Great Supreme should take shape. To put Power or Will first, and let the other attributes of Wisdom and Love follow after as contingent qualities not so primary as the thought of Absolute Sovereignty, is to freeze the heart [1] and to set up a type of Monothelite Monotheism, out of which it is not easy to lead on to the thought of a God in Christ reconciling the world unto Himself. The result of this passing of the Divine attributes through a prism, in which He is seen as a God of wrath out of Christ and a God of love in Christ, and only to the elect, must be presented in this fashion before its direct tendency to lead on to Atheism is understood. It is well for human nature that it is not quite the slave to its logical conceptions, or else this theology of afterthoughts would have made the world even darker than it has been owing to perversions of Christ's gospel. The three worlds of Dante's "Divine Comedy" strike a chill on the heart which we have scarcely recovered from when popular Protestantism takes up the same echo of Augustianism, with additions of its own still more lugubrious. Slowly we have worked through this *selva oscura*, and are emerging out of the horrible shadow of a God of terror into the sweetness and light of the General Fatherhood of God and the education of the human race. It has been the fear of Deism, with its dim defective views of sin, which has thrown this shadow of Augustinianism like an

[1] It is perhaps not without significance that it is in this order the three attributes of Power, Wisdom, Love are seen by Dante on the portal of hell—

"Fecemi la divina Potestade
La somma Sapienza e'l Primo Amore."

The vision Divine sees that God is Love, but devils, who believe and tremble, are fixed on the sight of God's sovereignty.

eclipse over the whole West, and we have not yet passed out of its penumbra. But it will soon be past; and when criticism shall have done its work of disengaging the truth from the error, we shall trace this misconception of grace to its true source in the under-current of dualism which steeped Augustine's thoughts long after he had shaken off his early Manichæism. This externalising the conception of grace in one of its two aspects, objective or subjective, never would have grown up in Augustine's mind but for the dualism of God and nature between which man was suspended, which was the fibre of all his thoughts. God was external to His works, the transcendent Lord of the universe, and could only act on the finite through some medium or channel which He chose to personify as "Grace." The old Gnostics had their Demiurge; and this new Gnosticism, for such it unconsciously was, could not conceive of any influx of the Divine into the human but through a medium which they described as "Grace." How much simpler our Western theology would have been had Augustine thought of God as an immanent Deity, and gone on to teach an immanent Christ as the Logos or light which lighted every man in through that candle of the Lord which we call conscience. Mystics and Cambridge Platonists held this concept of grace as Divine influx, the entering of light to the eye or of sound to the ear. But Augustinians, all misled by their master, could only see in grace something magical and external, so to speak, a "sixth sense," which only the regenerate have any faculty for. This is given in baptism, is fed by the sacraments, and, as the Reformed teach, came by faith, as faith by hearing, and hearing by the word of God; but both schools agree in externalising grace as a sense foreign to the New Testament.

When we turn to the old Book we find the grace of God is never dissociated from God Himself. All light streams from the sun, but we never use, unless as a playful metaphor, such a phrase as bottled sunshine. Science tells us that the carbon of coal is only fossilised heat, and that the sun gives us back in hydrocarbons the same light and heat which once lay stored up in plant life. Grace may be thus transmuted and pass into character and conduct, but still in its strictness all grace is of God, as all light is of the sun.

It will be some time before the Church is cured of her realism, and ceases to externalise grace in one of the two forms of popular Augustinianism. So great a change in the order of our theological conceptions is not to be wrought by one man and in one generation. But something is gained if we point out the source of the error. The science of epidemics leads on to demography, and therapeutics gain by not only naming a disease, but also its *habitat* and why it travels, as cholera, for instance, from India to Europe. We are no longer in the "Wandering Jew" stage of science so as to identify cholera with the curse of the impenitent thief. It will be the same growth to theology when the demography of the "ruling ideas" fixes this *habitat* of the "grace" notion in Augustine's too regulative mind. What was at first a subjective concept, at his conversion grew into a new objective concept in the grace of the sacraments, and there it fixed itself in form in the scholastic theology which the Reformation rose against and did battle to, and then itself broke down and fell away into new externalisms.

But we have not traced the error to its root until we go on to deal with another erroneous concept of the doctor of grace, the Divine sovereignty. That power belongs unto God is only an identical truth. It inheres in the very conception of God. But a great deal more than we suppose depends on our mode of first approach to God. Love, wisdom, power, this is the true order and subordination of God's three attributes which make up the Trinity of heaven. If we may be excused the expression, there is a Trinity of hell when we read his attributes backward, such as Dante read on the portals of that gate which opens inward only, and from which there is no return. Divine power, wisdom, love made me—can we wonder that it is added—

> "Lasciate ogni speranza voi ch'entrate,"

"Abandon all hope ye who enter here."

Sovereignty, in a word, is not the right concept with which to approach God. "If we being evil know how to give good gifts to our children;" we do not set out by training them to fear us, and to feel that the distance between us and them is vast and immeasurable. On the contrary, all true parentage on earth takes the opposite course. It first creates the sense of fondness by familiarity, and then goes on to chasten the child only in order to purge out those base qualities which hinder sonship. The Fatherhood of God, in a word, based on the analogy of earthly fatherhood, is the true key to any theology deserving the name. The comparison, it is true, between earthly and heavenly fatherhood halts, as we may expect it would, on account of fathers of our flesh correcting us for their own pleasure, *i.e.* arbitrarily, and sometimes with cruelty; whereas our true Father, the Father of our spirit, corrects us with a loving correction which makes us great; it is for our profit, that we may be partakers of His holiness.

Augustine, it must be said, in common with the whole West, overlooked this essential truth of Fatherhood. He never denied it, that would have been heresy; and he is entitled to the benefit of his own quibble, "*Errare possum hæreticus esse nolo.*" But his theology sets out with the wrong note of sovereignty. God is our Maker and Judge, but only our adoptive Father if we are brought in some way by faith and baptism into the covenant which He has made with His Son, and which is in all things ordered and sure. Nor is this a mere logomachy, a mere piece of transcendental reasoning, as shallow divines assume, whether we set out with sovereignty, and go on to love, or in the reverse order reason that the Blessed One must love, for that is His nature and property. God is love; and next to that being all-wise and all-mighty, He must love His creatures in that measure and proportion which infinite wisdom and measureless might dig channels for that love to flow in. His love, for instance, to all His lower works is in measure to their limitations. "Thou art good, and doest good," is the genuine voice of nature to its unknown author; and if we continue to stand beside the altar of the unknown God, we shall still think of the benevolence of the Deity, and thankfully adore an Almighty who might crush us as worms of the earth into nothingness, but who deigns to give us life and health and all things richly to enjoy.

But theology which sets out with this note of the old Deism, and then goes on to discourse on God in Christ as it already discoursed on God out of Christ, is a theology self-convicted of contradiction. That our Maker and our Judge is also our Redeemer, or at least of those who enter His covenant,—this is the reigning Augustinianism of the West. It sounds plausible; it has a pious ring; but it covers more errors and wraps up in reverend phrases more irreverence than even the flat blasphemies of the fool who says in his heart there is no God. Can we wonder that a theology of crude sovereignty which begins in Deism should run back into Deism? Unitarianism is the *lues theologica* of modern Calvinism, and few see or seem to see the *nexus* which is quite causal. When our keynote is sovereignty, we learn to tremble, we are before a mighty Allah—"Whom He wills He slays; whom He wills He keeps alive." When grafted on this we obtain an elective system, predestinating some to eternal life and the rest to eternal separation from the fountain of life; then a heart rising against this crude form of Deism begins. It is better, men say, and say it with reason, to get back to *le bon Dieu* of natural religion. This reaction against a theology of mere sovereignty explains all, or nearly all, these relapses into mere Deism, which under the name of Unitarianism were so common last century. What Rousseau says of Geneva in his day, was common to all Churches exactly in proportion as they set out from a mere Augustinian view of God as Judge first and Saviour afterwards. More than we think depends on the order in which we approach the Divine attributes. The Athanasian, which is true theology, as the Augustinian is not, is justly careful of the doctrine of subordination. In the Blessed Trinity, if no Person is before or after another with regard to dignity, there is an order of manifestation which never can be revised. The Father is ἀρχὴ θειότητος, the fountain of all Godhead; the Son is of the Father, who loveth the Son, and showeth Him all things that Himself doeth. The Spirit, the Person who proceeds from the Father (here the Greeks were justly jealous of the ἀρχὴ θειότητος), but who is sent by the Son to witness of the Son in the same way as the Son witnessed of the Father. This is the true doctrine of subordination, which Arius had so strangely misunderstood, because he took too anthropomorphic a conception of Sonship as suggesting some pre-existing Fatherhood; whereas, had he understood the Logos as Athanasius held, he never could have fallen into this fatal misconception.

Now second, and second only to this Arian mistake, was the error of Augustine in setting out with mere sovereignty or magistracy as ἀρχὴ θειότητος. Love is the fontal principle of Deity,—love which, as wisdom and power, proceeds forth into the finite there to lose itself in the finite, only to find itself again in moral and spiritual beings who reflect that love, and whose blessedness is like the seraphim to burn, and like the cherubim to blaze in the light of the eternal glory. God forbid that we should impair or diminish, even in thought, the goodness of God in showing mercy and pity! That we are rescued, redeemed, restored sinners, is a precious truth, the gospel of salvation and the first note of alarm as it reaches us when dead in trespasses and sins. But there is a deeper note than this which steals on the attuned ear when we come to the second stage of the gospel, and learn that behind the sending of the Son was God's infinite pity to men. As Law has put it,[1] what was love

[1] No one saw more clearly than the saintly William Law that God's wrath against sin is only another name for His love to the sinner, and that all punishment is remedial. It is the theme of his "humble, earnest, and affectionate address to the clergy," a tractate which has been often reprinted, but is still far too little known for its singular merits. The following extract contains the pith of his teaching:—

"Love, goodness, and communication of good is the immutable glory and perfection of the Divine nature, and nothing can have union with God but that which partakes of this goodness. The love that brought forth the existence of all things changes not through the fall of its creatures, but is continually at work to bring back all fallen nature and creature to their first state of goodness. All that passes for a time between God and His fallen creature is but one and the same thing working for one and the

in heaven became pity on earth. This is the heart of the gospel, which takes us at once beyond mere egotisms, such as saving our own soul, and a plan of salvation which we appropriate by faith, and through the sacra-

same end; and though this is called *wrath*, that called *punishment*, *curse*, and *death*, it is all, from the beginning to the end, nothing but the work of the first creating love, and means nothing else, does nothing else, but those works of purifying fire, which must and alone can burn away all that dark evil which separates the creature from its first created union with God."

Law is no stylist, but his dry, archaic prose rises almost to a Miltonic level, as in the following sketch of the ultimate end of redemption:—

"Amongst unfallen creatures in heaven, God's name and nature is Love, Light, and Glory. To the fallen sons of Adam, that which was *love*, *light*, *glory* in heaven becomes infinite 'pity' and 'compassion' on earth in a God clothed with the nature of His fallen creature, bearing all its infirmities, entering into all its troubles, and in the meek innocence of a Lamb of God living a life and dying a death of all the sufferings due to sin. Hence it was that when this Divine Pity suffered its own life-giving blood to be poured on the ground, all outward nature made full declaration of its atoning and redeeming power; the strength of the earth did quake, the hardness of rocks was forced to split, and long-covered graves to give up their dead—a certain presage that all that came by the curse into nature and creature must give up its power—that all kinds of hellish wrath, hardened malice, fiery pride, selfish wills, tormenting envy, and earthly passions which kept men under the power of Satan, must have their fulness of death and fulness of a new life from that all-powerful, all-purifying blood of the Lamb which will never cease washing *red* into *white* till the earth is washed into the crystal purity of that glassy sea which is before the throne of God, and all the sons of Adam clothed in *such white* as fits them for their several mansions in their heavenly Father's house."

This is, of course, pure Origenism, and should pass under the "Index" by those who have branded the greatest of the early Fathers' name with heresy, though, strangely enough, Epiphanius, who rakes together every charge of heresy he can think of against Origen, is prudently silent on this one reproach of Universalism, seeing that this was the orthodoxy of the East till long after Augustine's day. It was only in the West that punishment was vindictive and terroristic. There the *ignis sapiens* of Lactantius "salted" its victim with fire, and a class of gruesome conceptions grew up which at last brought their own relief, since purgatory came in a sense to put out of view the fires of an endless hell.

ments as channels *sine qua non.* Here Augustinianism begins, and here, we grieve to say, it ends. Unlike Origen, the saintly maligned Origen, who taught that all things are of God, and that sin being an abuse of free will springing up within and not without him, redemption must take this order in the restitution of man to his true selfhood, which is to be made, not in the image only, but also in the likeness of God (*De Prin.* iii. 6); in Augustine's mind, tainted to the last with a fatal taint of dualism, evil was something integral in a universe outside God, and man has to be rescued out of that outside world of matter, or the Demiurge, before he can enter into living union with God. The contrasts, in a word, between Alexandrian and Carthaginian theology are so deep and radical, that we are forced to say that if Origen and his school are deep theologians, Augustine and his school are defective. As a provisional scheme of pardon under concepts of God which stop short at mere magistracy, they may be well enough. But they go no farther. The "doctor of grace" soon saw his term "grace" turned into base equivocations, as χάρις ceased to be another name for love, and as such indistinguishable from God Himself. When grace began to flow in subjective channels, and, like the irrigating waters of the Nile, to be turned by the foot here and there, it did not stop till it went on to penances, pardons, indulgences, and all kinds of minor graces, the home charities of mother Church, which has *indulgenza plenaria* for all, because she has the key of Peter and a treasure-house full of the merit of Christ and His saints. Devout women have sometimes asked for the "sacrament on saint days," in order (to use their own strange phrase) that they might get the virtue of the blessed saints in the Eucharist, starlight and sunlight thus combined in one with the candle-light on the altar.

These Augustinianisms, as we describe them, would never have made their way to the front as "reigning ideas" in theology, but for the slavish concepts of God which it set out with. Beginning with sovereignty, we never get beyond it—our theology is a slave's theology, and genders to bondage. But when we set out with love, which is word, will, and work in one, and which what it doeth it doeth "for ever," all is changed. Our adoption into the family of God is grounded on the truth of original sonship defaced, not destroyed, by sin. We are Christ's by creation, and therefore much more Christ's by redemption. Every one of Adam born is also "Logos born," because he is a being breathing thoughtful breath, a traveller between life and death. These are some of the radical contrasts between early East and later Western theology which never have been given the emphasis they deserve, and which, when they are seen in their true importance, will put a new colour on our conceptions of God, and make "one thing of all theology," the theology of love, which we profess in name, but which we have smothered over with Roman magisterial conceptions of God, out of which a God in Christ emerges as the sun seen through a mist.

Errors in theology are like departures from the plumb-line in house building. The wall begins to bulge and lean out of the perpendicular, and it must be buttressed, and so an ingenious system of weights and counterweights goes on, till, like the construction of a cantilever bridge, the out-thrust and the back-thrust are exactly balanced, and a composition of forces is carried out often in a kind of haphazard way, which makes some mediæval buildings a wonder of the balance of statical forces. Augustinianism, to do it justice, as it came from its master's hand was one of these miracles of stability among decay. It balanced itself, no one exactly can say how, unless we throw in the explanation that one dogma had an out-thrust and the opposite dogma was accordingly given a back-thrust. Take, for instance, the doctrine of grace, that great master principle of Augustinianism. Happily for Augustine, so far from regarding "grace" exclusively from the subjective side, he went on to include in its action what are known as the material channels or vehicles of grace. Augustine thus escaped the narrowness which reduces grace to a single rill trickling into separate souls, according as God opens their heart in His inscrutable love and mercy, as the heart of Lydia was opened to attend to the things spoken of by Paul at Philippi. For Augustine grace thus had acquired two sides, the subjective and the corporate, and so he escaped that limitation dogma which seems to lead direct to predestinarianism and all its five points of Dort theology. Why Augustine did not push to the same one-sided extreme as Calvin, seeing his theology leads up straight to it, seems one of those puzzles which subtle minds, like the late Dr. Mozley, loved to ponder over, without, we must confess, throwing much light on it. The late professor of theology at Oxford, one of the most original thinkers the English Church has trained since Butler, was an Augustinian *pur sang*, and was misunderstood, therefore, by the popular theology alike of the dogmatic school of Anglicans and of ultra-Protestants. But so it was, because Mozley, like many other learned men, was familiar with his subject, but unable to familiarise others. He saw clearly enough, but has failed to impress others with the notion, that Augustine's theology touches the two extremes of sacerdotalism and spiritualism. Protestant and Catholic drink of the same water, and declare that the draught is as different as the buckets which hold it. They are both quite sincere in this, for they fail to see that Augustine the man is greater than the system which comes down to us by tradition as his. To return to our metaphor of a cantilever bridge, there is, in all Augustinianism, a back-thrust to balance an out-thrust, the grace of sacraments returns on us to sweeten and broaden the conception of a grace distilled into the separate soul. Thus the Augustinian conception of grace ran the usual course of all afterthoughts. It was first internal and subjective, then external and dependent on Church authority.

It may be said of every neglected truth of old and apostolic theology, that it is only excluded to come back in some distorted and menacing form. Heresies in this sense are like curses—they are the chickens which come home to roost, but they come in a fashion which the orthodox neither care for nor can control. The two truths of apostolic teaching, which have been passed over to the lasting hurt of the Church, are the Johannine doctrine of the Logos and the Pauline teaching of the election; neither has been denied, but both have been distorted. Till these truths are again seen in their own light, and not brought in as mere afterthoughts of man, but as the best and first thoughts of God to His Church, the present state of distress and confusion must continue, and even deeper divines will go on patching one afterthought on to another, like the piece of new cloth to the old garment, only making the rent worse. The remedy lies, of course, in a new theology; or if that term sounds too drastic to timid ears, dulled down to the droning note of traditionalism, let us at least point out that what sounds so new to some is, in truth, the old. What savours of heresy is instead Catholic, if we take that vague term in its simple first sense as the theology of the undivided Church down to Athanasius. To draw water at any lower point down the stream, either from Eastern or Western Fathers, is to go to a tainted source. If we are poisoned, or at least devitalised, as those would be who drink Thames water at London Bridge, we have no one to blame but ourselves. Let us see what it means to draw living water from these two fountainheads of all true theology, St. John and St. Paul, and we shall be able to measure the loss it was to theology when the key to the Logos doctrine of St. John, the election teaching of St. Paul, slipped out of her careless hands.

1. With regard to the Logos. For want of this key to true hermeneutics, faith and philosophy fell asunder, and look askance at each other to this day. The Logos is the true mediation doctrine, wanting which creation itself is an enigma, since between the finite and the infinite there is an impassable gulf, across which thought can throw no bridge. A transcendent Deity and a world hung in air, supported on nothing, like the tortoise in Hindu mythology, such is Creationism as conceived in the West, where the Logos doctrine soon became a dead letter. But with a Deity immanent in all His works in and through the Logos, the abyss of unthinkable Creationism is franchised, and all now proceeds in orderly evolution upwards from blind forces, such as light and heat, to life in its lowest plant and animal form up through life in all its stages, till the sentient becomes conscious, and self becomes a centre or seed-plot out of which love may dawn. Light, life, love, this Trinity, as Herder called it, is only conceivable under one class of conceptions, which are those of St. John's teaching of the Logos.

"Love took up the harp of life, and smote on all the chords with might,
Smote the chord of self, that trembling passed in music out of sight."

The bald Creationism of the West has raised more

difficulties than it can solve. Need we wonder that all mere Monotheistic systems, such as Islamism, are infected and honeycombed with Pantheistic mysticism. The abyss is too awful between creature and Creator; and bending over the chasm, peering into the darkness, fancy sees, or seems to see, a fairy world of its own of Peris and Jins and all those entities which swarm out of thought when the theological stage is over, and the positive stage of exact science not entered as yet.

Nothing meets this difficulty but the doctrine of the indwelling Logos, who is the light and the life of all that lower world in which man plants his feet before he begins to look up and to look out for something to love, some one to worship. At this stage, again, the Logos takes a new departure. "In Him was the life; and the life was the light of men;" and, he adds, "that was the true Light, which lighteth every man that cometh into the world." The Logos is thus the impersonal conscience, or the spermatic word, as Justin Martyr describes it, which in one way or other has been leading men on to God. The education of the human race, that best thought of the new theology, is thus the key to history as well as to philosophy. It at once bridges over that contrast between sacred and profane history, which to the Augustines and Bossuets of another school seems an abyss not to be crossed without a miracle. The prophets who taught within the covenant, and the sages of the East or of Greece, are not to be considered as distinct orders of men: they are the same order, only at a lower or a higher stage of enlightenment. No longer is book inspiration a dry dogma, as it became to the dull divines of the post-Reformation age — a miracle unproved and unprovable, which lays the Bible open to far more difficulties than it can solve. The magic of an infallible Book, only matched by the counter magic of an infallible Church, has been resorted to because the West had let go the true thread to the labyrinth in the doctrine of God immanent in the world through the Logos. It is the old story, a bare line thought of God let go—men have then to invent an afterthought, and so the Church or the Book religion was set up to fill the void which the light of God indwelling in and illuminating the conscience was intended to fill up. Whoever sets up a theory of book inspiration, convicts himself by the very statement of such a theory of not having the key to true God-consciousness.

> "God through Himself we then shall know,
> If Thou dost on us shine."

This is Charles Wesley's account of book inspiration, and the only one which, being subjective, does not impale itself on the horn of a contradiction, "Thou bearest witness of thyself; thy witness is not true." Such are all dogmas of inspiration—to name them is to expose their self-contradiction. But these afterthoughts of the West never occurred to the East as long as it held fast by the sense of an immanent Deity and an indwelling Logos. To have said to an Alexandrian that the word of God was all shut up in a roll of a book, would have seemed as simply unthinkable as that the word was in a wafer. Unless we drop plumb down into Pantheism, no Oriental would have understood what the West was bringing itself to, when one school of divines found their God in the host, another in the Bible. This bringing God down from heaven, or across from the sea, would have seemed as inept in its externalism as the Deuteronomist reminded Israel it was when they forgot in their idolatry that the Word was nigh them and in their heart. The Logos doctrine, to sum up all, was the one neglected truth which threw the whole theology of the West into confusion. To pick up the threads of this forgotten thought of God is to bring back order out of confusion. The psychology of the Bible alone explains its theology—they throw light on each other. Unless man's nature is interpreted aright, how can we approach the deeper mysteries of the Divine nature? So, again, the incarnation stands out in a certain bold externality as a dogma to be accepted, but for which there are no premonitions, no august anticipations in the deeper intuitions of our own nature as made in the image of God. All prophecy, all inspiration, whether of seer or sage, is a preparation of the gospel. It is God in history, as the *vox clamantis* crying out in the wilderness, and saying to the cities of Judah, "Behold your God."

2. If the Johannine doctrine of the Logos is one neglected thought of God which the West has let go, the Pauline doctrine of election is another which equally calls for a fresh restatement. How Augustine and Calvin misconstrued this truth, till it became an error, if not a lie, the history of predèstinarian controversies is one long comment. It was a dismal perversion of a spiritual truth, a blind afterthought, when election was understood in the later Jewish sense, not the early Abrahamic. To the Jew, perhaps even to the Twelve, election was regarded as the rescue and special salvation of the remnant. The Diaspora were the chosen few—the believing remnant left out of the mass of the perishing impenitent Israel after the flesh: this was the Petrine view of the subject, as we gather from his Epistle. The larger, more forthreaching view into the

future of the Apostle Paul was among those things "hard to be understood," on which "brother Peter" (assuming Second Peter to be genuine) seems not to have seen as far as "brother Paul." The very hesitation of the apostle of the circumcision perhaps throws light on the Apostle Paul's bold claim to have been given a distinctive knowledge of the mystery of election beyond any of the Twelve. They looked back, he looked forward. Their light was little more than that of Epimetheus, his of Prometheus. Instead of a remnant of a dead past, he saw in election the first-fruits of a future as yet unborn. To him predestinarianism was like Divine philosophy, not harsh and crabbed, as dull fools suppose, but the wisdom of God and the power of God calling out the Gentiles, and raising the elect of the Gentiles into the same place of privilege and responsibility which the Jews had been given, and forfeited through unbelief. The promise to Abraham was that he was to be the heir of the world—"In thee and thy seed shall all the families of the earth be blessed." What a distinction! what a privilege! It was the eldest born's birthright and blessing in one. But as soon as this birthright was made into a monopoly, a narrow claim to certain preferential blessings, it was at once forfeited, and instead of "Jacob have I loved, Esau have I hated," the word was reversed, and the left hand laid on the Jew and the right hand on the Gentiles.

Now, it is instructive and full of warning that Augustine and Calvin misunderstood election exactly in the same way as the Jew had done. They regarded the elect as separated to salvation by the favour of the one Father of all. That the election of a few implied the reprobation of the mass, seemed to these doctors of the

West too self-evident to be even questioned. That it was a hard saying, they never pretended to deny or palliate. Many men are better than their creed, as some are worse; but the hard fate of the reprobate did shock the conscience even of the *durus pater.* He tried to soften it down and mitigate the sentence of unending exclusion. The inarticulate wailing of *infanti perdidi* was hushed down to a simpler notion of purgatory, to soften down the dogma of an eternal hell and make it a little less incredible. In our age a great silence has fallen on the Church upon both issues into the unseen world. The old dogmas have not been expunged from our creeds, but a certain latitude of interpretation has been left us, and, thanks to Privy Council deliverances, the whole subject is left open either to "life in Christ" or to "larger hope" aspirations, which are tolerated on the one condition of being held as private opinions. In this state of suspense the age begins to breathe again, and much of the fierce invective of the negative school against popular theology is now dying out with the decline of much of the dogmatism of the old positive school. But this state of *interim* cannot go on for ever. Half beliefs in a theology of "afterthoughts" is a poor substitute for whole-hearted faith in a doctrine of God which can be "commended to every man's conscience." As soon as the age starts up, as it soon must do, and takes theology by the throat, requiring it to say out what it believes and what it disbelieves, there will be such a sifting and searching of heart as the sleepy old school of traditionalists have scarcely a suspicion of. Then, at last, the true Pauline doctrine of election will be seen to be the key of one class of difficulties of belief, as the Johannine doctrine of the Logos is the key to another. It will be a comforting conclusion to reach, when we find that election is not the same as selection, or the salvation of a mere remnant of Jews and Gentiles out of a *massa perditionis* is the only last thought of God to the race. We shall fling off those Jewish clouts, and rejoice in the liberty with which Christ has set us free. We shall see that it is by no back door that the Gentiles are admitted into the fold. The middle wall of partition between elect and non-elect will be broken down in the same way as that spirit of separatism between Jew and Gentile was in the apostle's day. Particularism and favouritism, that poor perversion of Pauline election, will be seen in their true light as "afterthoughts," and devout men will not be ashamed of election as at present, or of high doctrine, as they now apparently are. There will come a time, not so far distant, when the old-fashioned hyper-Calvinism will be seen to be nearer the truth, though not the whole truth of God, than free-will compromises. As for that Arminian explaining away of election as the mere passive foreknowledge of God of a certain contingent event, based on free-will, this will be seen to be the weak attempt to get rid of one "afterthought" by setting up another, if possible more illogical and less self-consistent. Arminianism and Calvinism are happily dying out together. They were not pleasant in their lives, and in death they will not be divided. But it is no use to dream of peace until something better than either starts up to take the place of both. Faith cannot live on mere negations or compromises. Our English instinct is to throw overboard both, and trust to "common sense," whatever that means, as if our fathers who fought for or against the "five points of Dort" were mere word babblers. The Quinquarticular controversy is looked down on in our day from a lofty point of view. We are such superior minds that we have settled, thanks to

Kant and his school, what is a theological "surd," which to name is to rule out of court. This is Dr. Mozley's verdict on Augustinianism. It is *ultra vires*, according to the Hamiltonian philosophy of the limitation of our faculties. But this saving of old dogmas by the new method of theology being "regulative" only, not "speculative," may last our day. But it will soon be seen that doctrines which we have to apologise for can be no longer considered integral truths of a gospel message which is good news to men. The latent error of these afterthoughts will have to be dragged to light; and the sooner our old theology, like the literature of the Bible, is passed through the fires of criticism, to test what is gold and what is hay, wood, stubble, the better it will be for all concerned. Who does not rejoice that a Regius Professor of Hebrew in Oxford can say out, as Dr. Driver has done, that the literature of the Hebrew canon is a fair field for free criticism. In spite of a timid protest, now forgotten, from a handful of reactionary divines, the right is established to take the traditional view of the canon to pieces, and to show what a patchwork it is of the Palestinian Masorites and of the Vulgate Revisionists, chiefly Jerome, who took the same liberties with the Hebrew canon that the Talmudist doctors had with the traditions of their fathers.

But enough of this. The parallel is at least instructive. We are approaching a day when the common conscience of lay Christendom will call on our theological lights to say out what they hold and how much they retain of the deposit of tradition locked up in Augustinian theology. To pass over one or two harsh dogmas, and to soften down the rest, will be to cry peace when there is no peace. A more thorough-going method will be called for, and those who see this, and say so, will be those whom the age will trust. The revision of popular theology, taken, as it is in too many cases, from tainted fifth-century sources, must go on till we again draw the water of life clear as crystal proceeding out of the throne of God and the Lamb. "Orthodoxy" has to borrow from "heresy" at present to eke out its slender stock of wholesome teaching. Why have we to go to learn, for instance, from Unitarians, of the general Fatherhood of God? Why, from Swedenborgians and other mystics, that the Lutheran doctrine of imputed righteousness is a mere scholastic figment? Why, from Christadelphians and other obscure sects, that the necessary immortality of the soul, and the unending misery of the lost, is a vain invention of a later theology. Would it not be simpler, more straightforward, to write off all these after-thoughts at once, and to begin afresh with theology drawn from the fountainhead? Instead of that thing of shreds and patches, the popular preacher's scheme of salvation, we might then be given a new seamless robe, woven from the top throughout. We have only to make a beginning, and in the right spirit, to succeed. We shall then shake off the nightmare of scepticism, which has squat hag-like on the sleeping Christian consciousness. The Church is afraid to face the thought of a new set of Articles of peace; and certainly no one would ask her to begin, as the sixteenth century did, by defining and drawing up *placets* on the safe but tame principle of "what divides the least." It will be time enough for Convocation to try "revision" of formularies when we see how revision of our English Bible has been accepted. If it is to be shuffled over as that revision task was got through, then a precious opportunity will be lost, and ten years be wasted on laborious trifling. Councils of war, we know, never fight; and so it has been with Conciliar attempts to attain Catholic consent.

Discarding, then, such methods, in which fussy officialism generally carries the day against the larger, calmer conclusions of scholars, let us strike out each on our voyage of adventure. The story of Napoleon when overtaken by the tide on the sands of Suez, is full of example on this subject. Standing still himself, he bid his staff strike out in all directions, with orders for the first who came to shoal water to signal to the rest that land lay in that direction. In the same hopeful attitude we may "stand on the old ways," and yet consider the new in the sense that Bacon employs that well-worn text. To sit down to compose a "new theology" would be to repeat the mistake of those Reformers who, ignorant of their own ignorance, sat down with intrepidity to sweep out as much of the past as they saw fit and to retain the rest. The result was a lame compromise, which at once went too far and not far enough, and which resulted in that recast of the old scholastic Augustinianism which we are asked to accept as primitive and Catholic, but which is in reality far from either. It is not contrary, we admit, to primitive truth, but it is far too steeped in Augustinian misconceptions of Pauline theology. It asserts predestinarian election, and then tones it down to mean almost nothing at all,—in a word, our popular Reformation theology is that diluted semi-Calvinism which satisfies no one, and which compels us to ask, why discuss the subject at all of God's purposes which the writer is afraid to carry to its legitimate conclusions? It is in no sense such as this that we desire to see a "new theology" replace the old. But we should desire to see those two truths of Pauline and Johannine teaching, "election" and the

"Logos" doctrine, set in their true light as "ruling ideas." The one is the key to God's purposely calling in the Gentiles, and points to the Abraham blessing, "In thee shall all the families of the earth be blessed." The other lays the basis for the larger hope in the education of the human race, and the true conception of "God in history" with the race as a whole, and not alone with the covenant people. These two truths, instead of "after-thoughts," are in fact God's first thoughts, but they are thoughts which were too deep for the age to grasp to which they were given. They have been laid by accordingly as seeds in the hands of a mummy, waiting the day when they could be planted out and germinate in a suitable soil. The time, as it seems to us, has come—yea, the set time, when this buried deposit of apostolic doctrine should be brought out to enrich the Church and enlarge its conceptions of what a goodly heritage lies before it as soon as it has courage to go in and possess the land.

What assures us that the set time is come, is when we glance at what is going on in India and the East. Missions on the old type of making "compound Christians" have gone on long enough. Young men trained up at home in theological hotbeds, some evangelical, some Anglican, but all of a narrow Augustinian school, have gone out by the hundred, and the impression made is as yet insignificant when we consider the masses of the East yet unevangelised. Acute minds at home see the defects of our "parochialising" India, and now even the Archbishop of Canterbury has thrown out suggestions which are meant to wake up our old missionary societies from the old drowsy delusion that we were to Europeanise the East first, and evangelise it afterwards. No one says this in so many terms; but this is the method which we set out with, and it will have to be abandoned, and the "leaven" principle, rather than that of the "mustard seed," resorted to more boldly. Japan already has slipped out of control of the homebred missionary, and a strange syncretism is beginning of Christian and Buddhist conceptions, not unlike the Gnostic stage of the second century, when the new faith and the old philosophy struggled for supremacy which should be the formative principle of the Church of the future. We are again face to face in the East with conditions which remind us of what occurred in the Alexandria of Clement and Origen, and in the Rome of Hippolytus and Irenæus. We shall have to meet it in the same way as the early Church did, by calling out a school of thinkers and teachers. The catechetical age must succeed that of evangelists; and though there are perils, no doubt, in the way of this syncretism, what path is there that is not perilous, and what is the promise of the Comforter given for but to guide us into the whole truth, if we will only go on believingly and step by step? It is to meet this case of Christianity in the East and on the mission field that we must go back to our muniments and see what they really teach us. God has more truth to break out of His word—of this we may be sure; but timid theologians assume that hermeneutics has said its last word, because the Greek of the New Testament is better understood than it has ever been before. But these grammarians forget that behind words there are thoughts, sometimes too deep for terms of precision to express. Not enough stress has been laid on the special standpoint which led St. John in his old age to take up the Alexandrian Logos doctrine as the keynote to his latter-day theology. Not enough has been made of St. Paul emphasising predestination in all his Epistles as part of the hidden wisdom of God which he was called on to unfold, and so magnify his office as the apostle of the Gentiles. We have looked at this subject too much in the light of later controversies, Arminian and Calvinist, and forgotten that before predestinarianism in the modern sense of determinism and free will was heard, there was a Pauline type of determinism unlike any that Augustine and Calvin ever suspected.

These are the outlines of the theology of the future far too hastily traced here. But the day is fast approaching for a settlement and revision of the old, by incorporating into it that which is so old that it is apostolic in the sense that Augustinian theology certainly is not. A grand impatience of hollow compromises is the certain mark of the strong mind. It is also a sign of true faith; for unless we can trust the living God and the guiding of the Holy Ghost of the future, what is our faith but the same clinging as that of the Jews to their dead deposit of Mosaism? The scribes and Pharisees of our Lord's day were sure that they had that deposit; nor does our Lord deny that in a sense it was so. But He goes on to warn them that faith in the past is not enough, or the claim to be Abraham's children of any value unless they did the works of Abraham. The far-seeing patriarch rejoiced to see my day, and he saw it and was glad,—let us then look forward in the same confident hope. The dry bones are stirring, the masses are evangelised at home as they never were before. India and the East are awaking out of the sleep of ages. To suppose that the Englishman's Prayer Book and Bible will go round the world, and in some translated but still traditional form awake the same echoes in the East as among homebred Englishmen—this is that simple view of missions which, as we have seen, we are outgrowing.

Let us be prepared, then, and for a new age set out in advance with a new theology. New heavens and new earth can only come when the time for both has arrived, as it seems to be in our day.

CHAPTER IX

DIDACHÉ AND DOGMA.

Church history has its stages of descent. To some, the conversion of Constantine and that fatal gift on which Dante laid such stress, marks the decline from primitive purity. Others go farther down the stream, and find in the schism of East from West the line of cleavage which marks the beginning of the apostasy, or at least the degeneration of later days. But both are wrong in going too far down the stream to mark where the true point of departure began, the first real descent from primitive and apostolic standards. Words are thus the records of things, and a change of a single term is a kind of signal to sceneshifters that we have closed one act and entered on another in the five act drama of Church history. During the whole of Act I., as we may call it, the keynote is always *διδαχή*; it is a doctrine, and those who preach or teach it are followers of the "way," witnesses of the "word," or stewards of the "mystery." Such is the apostolic keynote; and such it passed on unchanged into sub-apostolic times, and lasted on unchanged till the last of the "Confessors" of the Alexandrian school of catechists, Origen, died in exile at Tyre.

But a change came over the Church, which explains all her later "afterthoughts" in theology, as soon as the note διδαχή was dropped, and δόξα at first, and finally hardening into δόγμα, took the place of διδαχή. It is dogmatic theology in all its forms, early and later, which we indentify with that departure from the faith which the apostle (1 Tim. iv. 1) distinctly refers to as an apostasy. It has rent the Church ever since with heresies and schisms. No sooner has the Church cast out one form of error as a "heresy," than another has sprung up as a schism, fostered in the same way as a poison within for some time, and at last been cast off as a heresy, the Church in its simplicity supposing that as the apostle at Melita shook off the venomous viper and took no harm, so it should fare with them. But it is one thing when the viper comes out of a bundle of sticks, quite another thing when the venomous beast has been nursed in her own bosom. In apostolic times there were errors and oppositions, false apostles, deceitful workers; and none denounced them more vigorously than that Son of Thunder who had leaned on Jesus' bosom, and drank so deeply into His inner spirit. But to speak of the dogmatism of St. John as we do of the dogmatism of an Augustine, an Aquinas, or a Hildebrand, would be an absurd misnomer. "They went out from us because they were not of us;" this is the only anathema known in the age of preconciliar Church teaching. The same gospel which was attractive to some was a repulsive force to others, and, like electricity, its polar forces freely worked, and scattered or attracted to it those who were so prepared by inward discipline. In this free way the thoughts of many hearts were revealed. The noblest types of men, who beforehand were unconscious Christians, became instinctive Christians as soon as the cross was lifted up and began to draw all men unto it.

Well would it have been for the Church if it had not

gone beyond this rule, and sought to be wiser than those who were content with the foolishness of preaching the simple message. She had a magnet in her hand designed to attract all, and which in time would have attracted all, as in the ages to come it will, as soon as the Church unlearns her first folly, and drops the dogmatic note which becomes her so ill, and which makes her seem to this latter age like a silly sheep in wolves' clothing. She has long tried to frighten men like children into her fold, outside of which, as she declares, there is no salvation. But the mass of mankind looks on and smiles at this weak attempt to wield the thunders of the Almighty. They scoff at this modern version of the old Salmoneus of the *Æneid*, who presumed to imitate the unimitable thunderbolt with the mock thunder of his iron-hoofed steeds and the rattle of his brass chariots. It is dogmatic deductive theology, backed by Conciliar authority, which in the first stage has fomented schisms; it has then produced heresy, and at last filled the world with its moans over the divisions of Christendom which she has done nothing to allay. It is dogmatism which leads to separatism, certainly not separatism which forces the orthodox into a dogmatic attitude. The old fable of the wolf and the lamb is here applicable. The troubling of the waters invariably comes from the stronger side, from those cast out of communion, not from those who go out of communion. The Baur theory of orthodoxy and Church authority, springing up side by side in the second century, and out of a common instinct of the Latin mind, has never yet been confuted. Wearied with the endless confusions and vagaries of Gnostics, some Hebrew, some Hellenist, but all destructive alike of the true faith, the Latin Church in an evil hour for herself began to entrench and throw up external defences other than those of apology and argument. When an Irenæus in Gaul and a Tertullian in Carthage had shot their last arrow, then it seemed that the time was come to close the discussion. The Church under Cyprian argued no more, but acted. The primitive Episcopos developed into a monarchical type of Church authority, so that novelties could now be met and disposed of by bishops assembled in council. Constantine only acted on a precedent already set when he convened the entire episcopate to an œcumenical council. Then at last the development of dogma and discipline was complete. From this day on we may say that *διδαχή*, or a body of simple teaching, and *διδασκαλία*, or the method of teaching, ceased, and in its place *δόξα*, or private opinion, stiffening slowly and by tradition into *δόγμα*, became the catch-note of the Church catholic to this day.

It is precisely the same transition as passed over the covenant people as soon as prophecy ceased and the canon was closed. There arose as the result of this long silence of God, interpreters, self-authorised, who undertook to bind and loose like Hillel and Shammai, and so Rabbinism slowly developed out of the order of scribes and elders who carried on the traditions of Israel after the captivity. What Rabbinism made of Judaism we have Christ's own words to testify; but we must be blind indeed not to see that the same causes lead to the same effects everywhere. Instead of wondering, then, at the falling away from the primitive standard of a *διδαχή*, let us be thankful that the apostasy was not as utter as it easily might have been. Here let us notice how instructive is the parallel. The essence of Mosaism, the very keynote of its existence, was Monotheism. Wanting this, it was only one of many cults common to the East. All its rites, circumcisiom included, were seals and signs of the covenant;

but the heart of it lay in the word, "Hear, O Israel, Jehovah thy God is God alone," *i.e.* all other gods are vanity and lies. As long as this truth lay locked up in the ten words in the ark, all was safe. Priestism and sacrifices might all pass away, but the one deposit, the one διδαχή of Israel, was intact.

Now Israel, after coming a second time out of the captivity of Babylon, clung to Monotheism with all its mind and soul and strength. Corrupt in every other direction, here at least they have never blenched from the truth. So with the Church catholic. Its one deposit of truth has been the mystery of the Incarnation, and to this it has been faithful. In all other directions, like Mosaism depraved by Rabbinism, it has gone astray. It has departed from primitive simplicity in almost every direction. God has preserved His truth quite as often in spite of the Church as through the Church. Sometimes it was an Elijah alone stood up against the prophets of Baal, as it was an Athanasius against a world which was Arian, Church and State alike. All the same, through all its infidelities Mosaism never lost its hold of Monotheism, as the Catholic Church has clung on to the one truth, for the assertion of which alone she is Catholic. The sin of the Church has been the same sin as that of later Mosaism. She has let the Rabbis of theology lay down a new and second law for her. She has invented, as Rabbinism did, other terms of communion than those of confessing Christ. It was Lo here, lo there—the Catholic Church must be episcopal—it must claim apostolic succession—it must insist on certain sacramental rites, the validity of which depends on the *operator* and the *opus operatum.* It must lay claim to an infallible book, or, at least, its doctors must be infallible interpreters of that book. So one afterthought has been piled up on another, till we turn to the New Testament, and ask where is the authority for this mass of traditions. The answer is the same as in the case of Judaism, and we suppose the end is the same in both cases. Moses is read, but the veil is on the face; and so with this new Mosaism. Let us hope that in both cases the veil shall be taken away, and then we shall see when we turn to the Lord that same Jesus Christ who is the same "yesterday, and to-day, and for ever."

This contrast, then, between doctrine and dogma, and the gradual substitution of the one term for the other, may be said to mark the stages of descent into these afterthoughts of theology. Faith and doctrine, these are the two terms in frequent use in the New Testament, and invariably used in a single fixed and definite sense—the one as the spiritual, the other as the intellectual, organ of apprehension of things unseen and eternal. Faith is exercised on a person, and is only love in its inchoate form of trust—the trust in One whom not seeing we love, but whom when we see as He is we shall love as we ought. In this sense faith is invariably used in the New Testament as heart affiance, and to strengthen this weak faith of childhood there is given διδαχή, teaching,—certain object-lessons are set before us, such as the Gospel narrative of the life of Christ, and the wonders of love and mercy which He wrought, all of which attach us to Him, and compel us to say with our intelligence, "Is not this the Christ, the Saviour of the world?"

But as soon as we descend even into sub-apostolic times, faith develops, or degenerates rather, into "the faith," the deposit, that is, of *credenda*, which are to be taken on trust, because they are too high to be understood. But soon the intellect steps in and asks for some warrant of these things. Then διδαχή passes into δόξα, which soon hardens into δόγμα. Why, and for what stages, our opinion grows rigid as a dogma, it is impossible to explain, unless it be that men are impatient of opinions which continue long in a mere state of flux. They ask for something which, like law among the Medes, alters not—which is not here to-day and gone to-morrow. Stability, which is the very conception of a state, is even more importunately craved for in a cult. It is a just instinct in the mind that religious opinion should be rigid; hence, let philosophers complain of it as they do, this instinct for dogma is not quite so baseless as it seems. It is more than a mere relic of the superstitiousness of primitive times. But, unhappily, theologians have presumed too far on this craving for definiteness. Going beyond St Luke's modest endeavour to set forth in order an outline of the things most certainly believed among us, they have laid an interdict on free thought by confounding and mixing up together the intellectual and emotional sides of religion. Faith in a person, and doctrine or teaching concerning his work,—the former chiefly found in the Gospels, the latter exclusively in the Epistles,—have been made up into one conglomerate, until we are told we can have no faith in the person of Jesus unless we accept certain doctrines concerning His work. We will allow, of course, that the two regions interlap, as Epistles and Gospels dovetail into each other. But this is not enough for afterthinking theology. It reverses the natural order, and invites us to study the person in the work, not to see the work growing out of the person. In Anselm this inverted order reached its climax, who actually offered the atoning death as the explanation of the initial act of Incarnation, thus making the end explain the beginning, and reading the life backwards. The note, then, by which to detect the afterthoughts of theology is this, that it lays undue stress on dogma, and understands "faith" as "the faith." As soon as this stage is reached,—and it did not take long to reach it in the West,—the gospel has become a new law, and the bondage of the spirit to the letter has begun, from which Christ had once for all set us free. There is only one way of recovery from this decline, which is by insisting on "faith" in a person, and "teaching" concerning his work, to be laid stress on as the one thing needful. As long, then, as πίστις retained its primitive simplicity of meaning as trust or affiance in the living God, so long the term διδαχή was the equivalent phrase for those teachings which make up the body of revealed truth. The two terms together make up between them what we may describe as the subjective and objective sides of religion respectively. Only once, and metonymically, in one of the later and less authoritative letters, the Epistle of Jude, is "the faith once delivered to the saints" referred to as the *fides quæ creditur,* not the *fides quâ creditur.* It is a solecism, as all good critics allow, this use of πίστις for the body of doctrine. Elsewhere in the New Testament, with one or two insignificant exceptions, faith is always the subjective element of trust; it is the affiance of the heart, the unfolding of the flower to the sun, and in its integrity is less an intellectual than a moral act. Hence the close connection which St. Paul draws between faith and a good conscience,—a connection so intimate, that if the conscience is defiled, we shall make shipwreck concerning faith. Having thus fixed the meaning of faith as that subjective spiritual putting forth of trust as a response to God's truth, it is well to remark the balance of apostolic teaching. Our faith would be vain unless there was a "faithful saying," a body of teaching clear, consistent, and convincing, on which our faith may rest with unquestioning confidence, and feel like the Psalmist, "In Thee have I trusted, and shall never be confounded."

The primitive use of faith and doctrine as the two co-efficients of the gospel, as the subjective and objective sides respectively of Church truth, lingered on as a tradition far into sub-apostolic times. A precious testimony to that use of the true *διδαχή* is the recovery of that lost fragment of antiquity, the *διδαχὴ τῶν δώδεκα*, which critics agree is not to be assigned to a date later than between 120 and 160 A.D. To our thinking, the earlier date seems the most probable from the almost Essenistic character of its teaching, and the remarkable use of the Syriac watchword of the early Church, Maranatha, which indicates Antioch as the earliest home of the Gentile Church. "If any is holy," the writer observes, "let him come; if any is not, let him repent Maranatha. Amen."[1] The *Didaché* sets out with a scheme of moral precepts under the head of "The two ways of life and death," followed by ordinances relating to sacraments and the ministry of the Church, and concludes with a striking section on the judgment of the last day. That it should contain no statement or exposition of dogma, is in keeping with its early date; and, indeed, its reference to the sacramental cup as the vine of David is so peculiar, so half-Jewish, that it betrays its archaic style. It is admitted to be only a kind of skeleton outline of the fuller tradition referred to in the New Testament with *διδαχή*, or teaching (Acts ii. 42), which is described as one of the four marks of early discipleship, the other three being fellowship with the apostles and breaking of bread, or the sacramental commemoration of Christ's death, and, lastly, prayers, or some liturgical common service.

[1] *Teaching of the Twelve*, chap. x.

We have thus in διδαχή the primitive apostolic phrase, which was only slowly displaced as δόξα, the element of subjective opinion, stole into the Church from the schools of philosophy, and this in its turn hardened into δόγμα. The stages by which this transformation was completed were as follows:—In the schools of philosophy a private opinion was described as a δόξα,—δοκεῖ μοί, it seems to me, or "it seems good to me," was the usual *ad verecundiam* way of introducing some speculative novelty. But just as the resolutions of the will of the monarch were accepted by his subjects, that is, as it were, transmuted into resolutions of the will of other persons, so the affirmations of a thinker might be assented to by those who listened to him, that is, might become affirmations of other persons.[1] In the one case, as in the other, the one word *dogma* was employed. It came thus to express (1) a decree, (2) a dogma. The latter one tended to predominate. The word came ordinarily to express an affirmation made by a philosopher, which was accepted as true by those who, from the fact of accepting it, became his followers and formed his school. The acquiescence of a large number of men in the same affirmation gave to such an affirmation a high degree of probability; but it did not cause it to lose its original character of a personal conviction, nor did it afford any guarantee that the coincidence of expression was also a coincidence of ideas, either between the original thinker and his disciples, or between the disciples themselves.

The stages by which "dogmatism" in philosophy passed from the stage of a private judgment into that of a corporate, collective mode of thinking, which it was presumptuous even to challenge, are well known, and have been often traced. In the second and third centuries

[1] Hatch, *The Hibbert Lectures*, p. 120.

of our era there had come to be three main groups of schools. "Some men," writes Sextus Empiricus, "say that they have found the truth; some say it is impossible for truth to be apprehended; some still search for it." Philosophy was divided accordingly into three camps—the dogmatists, the sceptics, and the academics—or the philosophy of assertion, of denial, and of research or inquiry. But the first of these, as Dr. Hatch truly remarks, was in an overwhelming majority. The whole of the Stoics, and the larger section of the more enlightened Platonists, stood on the ground of dogma; *i.e.* that there were certain definite principles, landmarks of right and wrong, which could only be effaced by doing violence to our nature. It was because the empirics and sceptics took lower ground than this that they deservedly fell under a reproach.

But the philosophy of assertion, of denial, and of research alike lay outside the earliest types of Christian thought. To believers in a crucified and risen Christ the moral and spiritual elements of their faith were not only supreme, but also exclusive. They reflected the philosophy, not of Greece, but of Palestine. That philosophy was almost entirely ethical. It dealt with the problems, not of "being" in the abstract, but of human life. It was stated, for the most part, in short antithetical sentences, with a symbol or parable to enforce them. It was a philosophy of proverbs. It had no eye for the minute anatomy of thought. It had no system, for the sense of system was not yet awakened. But before the second century had quite passed away a new phase of thought passed over the Christian consciousness. Philosophy, at first distrusted and dreaded, began to be taken over, and to shape the thought of Christian teachers into a mould of its own. Two schools arose. The Eastern, which, generally speaking, through its doctrine of the Logos, held, as Justin Martyr did, that "the teachings of Plato are not alien to those of Christ, although not in all respects similar. For all the writers of antiquity were able to have a dim vision of realities by means of the indwelling seed of the implanted word."[1] On the other hand, the Western type of Church teachers held that philosophers had borrowed or stolen their doctrines from the Scriptures. As Minucius Felix observes, "From the Divine preachings of the prophets they imitated the shadow of holy truths."[2] "What poet or sophist," says Tertullian, "has not drunk at the fountain of the prophets? From thence it is, therefore, that the philosophers have quenched the thirst of their minds, so that it is the very things which they have of ours which bring us into comparison with them."[3]

But whether theologians maintained, as the Eastern Fathers generally did, that theology and philosophy were each independent springs derived from the same fountain of all inspiration, the Eternal Logos, or whether, in the opposite extreme, they set out as writers in the West did, by denouncing philosophy as stealing its treasures from the written word, in any case an approach of some kind was inevitable. The Church, perhaps unconsciously on her part, took over the methods and even the technical terms of philosophy. It had been alleged against Christians of the second century, that they still made it their boast, with the apostle, that not many wise men after the flesh, not many mighty, were called. Origen, from whose reply alone we learn all the taunts that had been flung against the gospel by Celsus, quotes the following: "Let no educated man enter, no wise man, no prudent man, for

[1] Justin Martyr, *Apol.* ii. 13. [2] Min. Felix, *Octav.* 34.
[3] Tertullian, *Apol.* xlvii.

such things we deem evil; but whoever is ignorant, whoever is unintelligent, whoever is uneducated, whoever is simple, let him come and be welcome." This state of things did not long outlive the second century. By the middle of the third century Christians were able to meet philosophers on their own ground, and to beat them with their own weapons. The faith was silently transformed into a philosophy, and the first sign that the transition was taking place was the use of the speculative method. In this way the δόξα of the one grew slowly and by degrees into the dogma of the many. Opinions which, in the making, were mere private judgments, soon gathered authority as they spread and became current, just as rivers deepen and broaden, and so make their own channel by the volume of water which they carry along with them.

In itself this is inevitable; and if it went no farther than this, the dogmas of theology would bring no more hurt to others than the dogmas of philosophy. But the formal end of the one is speculation only, the formal end of the other is certainty with regard to that one theme, our relation to God and the hereafter. Theology and philosophy deal with truth on quite a different footing. The same philosopher who is a dogmatist in one direction may be a sceptic in another. It is otherwise with theology; in this case scepticism is nowhere permissible. At every turn he is met with an affirmation, "Thus saith the Lord," and he is instantly challenged with a "Believest thou this?" In philosophy the end is not so much truth as the search for truth. Lessing has struck the right note for the true philosopher in the famous contrast, that if he were offered truth in one hand and the pursuit of truth in the other, he would take the casket which contained the search for truth, and exclaim,

"As for absolute truth, that belongs, O Eternal Father, only to Thee." This is in the true philosophical temper. Philosophy at its best is neither dogmatism nor scepticism, but the free play of both forces: it is the balance maintained between the two, of which the academics were the best examples. They held a middle position between extreme dogmatists and sceptics; they neither denied, with the sceptics, that truth was attainable, nor affirmed, with the dogmatists, that they had already attained it. They were on the search, and the position which they took up is the only attitude of mind which may be fairly described as philosophical, since if either truth is known, or in the other extreme is unknowable, what further use is there for that temper of mind which is that of the genuine sportsman, who pursues his game partly for the bag, but principally for the pleasure of the chase?

It is otherwise with theology; and as its ends are different, so its methods must differ from those of the schools. It is not so much the discovery of truth first hand, as its recovery out of the wrappings of tradition and the ravages of time. There is a body of doctrine or faith once, *i.e.* once for all, delivered to the saints. But how soon is that faith tarnished by tradition and covered by the cinder-heap of time, which soon swells into a heap of rubbish like that Monte Testorio outside Rome. The methods of theology are thus largely antiquarian. In this recovery our process is like treating refractory ores to extract the precious metal. All the helps of philology and sound exegesis, precious as these are in their place, is not enough, unless a fine critical faculty and an unerring spiritual instinct, that never mistakes metal for dross, does not govern the whole process. This is why the list of real theologians, in the strict sense of the term, is so small. The Fathers, with few exceptions, were uncritical in the last degree. With little science and no philology, how could they extract out of an ancient document, archaic even in their days, its true meaning, of which the official custodians, the Israel after the flesh, understood even less than they? Through ignorance of Greek, the later Latin Fathers could only grope their way through the New Testament, as only one or two of the Eastern Fathers could explore the meaning of the Old Testament. Both were workers in a dark mine, of which they had no ground-plan, no map of its galleries. Thus, as their methods were defective, so their conclusions are utterly untrustworthy. The day has gone by when we need either attack or defend the Fathers. The two dogmatic schools which a century ago fought over these old bones of theology, have both disappeared. Since the birth of criticism we hear less and less, both of attack and defence, of the study of the Fathers.

As for the Schoolmen, our interest in them is, if possible, even more antiquarian. In their case it may be said that the very ruins have perished, and for the best of all reasons. A comment on a comment is like a foil on a foil in heraldry. The Fathers are supposed to interpret the apostolic mind; and we bear with them, in the hope that we may catch echoes even second-hand of what those who had sat at the feet of Jesus, or had leaned on His bosom, knew and taught. But for Schoolmen we do not feel even that scant respect. In their case the tradition is so far off and unreal, so disguised by the later afterthoughts of an ascetic and superstitious age, that we have no patience with those who tell us that they have winnowed some truth from the times of St. Thomas, or the sentences of Peter the Lombard. It only raises a smile, when this second St. Thomas is set on a pedestal by the present Pope Leo XIII. as the guide out of the labyrinth into which modern Jesuit teaching has led that Latin Church over which the Pope is supreme vicegerent for Christ.

But if theology finds little help in Fathers and Schoolmen, what are we to say of the writings of those blessed Reformers whom the Parker Society tried to exhume and galvanise into the mimicry of life some forty years ago? The attempt was a ghastly failure, and the verdict of the public mind was decisively this, to let the dead bury their dead. The Anglo-Catholic theology fared no better; and we are shut in to the conclusion, which Beccaria's cynical saying abundantly verifies, that the history of progress is the history of error—it is the sight of wrecks, on which a few here and there emerge to the surface of truth. As for libraries, whether of law, physic, or divinity, they are the mere cemeteries of sleeping remains. The divining rod of the critic may touch dry bones here and there, and they may live. But in this case it is by reversing the sign of Elisha: it is the living man who puts life into the dead bones of the sleeping prophet. To assume that the prophet's bones touching a corpse will make it live, is to suppose a moral miracle out of analogy with all which we know of the action of mind on mind. The thoughts of dead authors may direct and even quicken the thoughts of living men, but only in the case where they are intelligently used, not read, that is, under blind authority; as some uncritical divines a century ago would go over a course of the Fathers in the original Greek and Latin, and come out of the course the same blind pedants as when they began it. A learned man exploring in the gallery of the Fathers and Schoolmen without the torch of the higher critcism in his hands, is as helpless as a tourist turned into the Catacombs of Rome to grope his way about, and then asked to interpret Christian antiquities.

What with the smoke of other torches, the broken letters are often at best undecipherable; and as to put a meaning into the whole, there is no such divination in the dull brain of an ordinary divine, that we can expect such miracles of the higher criticism in which a Niebuhr has failed. It is so much easier to say what early Roman history is not than to say what it is, that we have no right to complain because the Christian archæologist has not succeeded. Scientific theology is, like scientific history, still a desideratum. In Bacon's phrase, we have still to report it barren of fruit.

Bearing in mind, then, these contrasts between doctrine and dogma, let us not be too harsh on the dogmatists. Their mistake was the inevitable one arising out of the fragmentary nature of apostolic teaching. Evidently it has not been God's will to reveal His mind in a body of articulated truths, which the logical faculty could break up into syllogisms, and discourse on in dialectic form, as an Old Light, a Scotch professor, used to lecture to a body of students on the Westminster Confession. The Author and Finisher of our faith taught, like Socrates, in proverbs; His words were symbols; and His method, if not ironic as Socrates, had this in common with the irony of the sage of Athens, that He had to remind them that His words were only parables, but that by and by He would no more speak to them in parables, but show them plainly of the Father: "I have many things to tell you, but ye cannot bear them now; howbeit when He, the Spirit of truth, is come, He shall guide you into all the truth."

In the case of His twelve chosen followers, the authorised interpreters of His teaching, we find that it was *pede temptim*, step by step, that they were led on by that Guide. Slowly and cautiously they picked their steps out of Hebraism into Hellenism. One bolder than the rest, and who outran Peter, as John did when they both ran to the sepulchre, was first to emphasise the thought that election is not a narrow, arbitrary preference of one race over another, but that sovereign wisdom which sees, in the Jew at one time and in the Gentile at another, the fittest instrument for evangelising the earth. If this Pauline conception of election had been accepted from the first, we should have heard little of that hideous distortion of the doctrine which, under the shadow of two great names, has cast a blight on theology, and made some of its afterthoughts a strange caricature of its first thoughts.

Expecting to find all within the canon which could make up a body of divinity, they set to work putting fragments together, and turning incidental, *ad hominem*, kind of arguments thrown out by the way into propositions of general import. So it was in this uncritical way that Augustine, meeting with the Pauline expression, "Whom He will He hardeneth," went on under the iron logic of necessity, as Calvin also did, to extract reprobation as well as election out of the sweet message of mercy to mankind. This reminds us of those lines of the poet—

> "For, like those bees of Trebizond,
> Which from the sunniest flowers, that glad
> With their pure smile the gardens round,
> Draw venom forth which makes men mad."

The apostle in reality was stamping out the Jewish dogma of election by a counter dogma; *i.e.* that election was not an end in itself, but only the means to an end, and that in reaching that end, God, like the wise Father, often remade the clay, turning vessels of honour into vessels of dishonour, and *vice versâ*, the end being always the same, that He might have mercy on all. To read chap.

ix. without following on to chaps. x. and xi. of Romans, and never drawing breath till we reach the *Oh altitudo*, this is the only intelligent use of Sacred Scripture which seems to have been beyond those mere textuarians to whom we owe that which we call a body of divinity, and which, like the body without the soul, is dead.

Such is dogmatism which is the dogmatism of early doctrine. The first is apostolic, and lingered on far into sub-apostolic times. The use of the term *διδαχή* in connection with the teaching of the Twelve is a witness to the primitive standard. It is of the same value as a certain fossil in showing the Eocene age in geology.

The "teaching of the Twelve" clearly marks a state of transition in which the importance of a sacramental system and a sacerdotal order is beginning to dawn on the Christian consciousness; but as yet the new theology, as it was then considered, had not taken dogmatic form. It nestled behind the phrase *διδαχή*; it has not as yet been formulated. It is only a *δόξα*, or private opinion, which in the end, as a *δόγμα*, would put on the air of authority, and enforce itself under the threat of an Anathema. It is interesting here to note that the two expressions which St. Paul couples together (1 Cor. xvi. 22), "Let him be Anathema Maranatha," took two devious paths. The earlier Syriac watchword, "Maranatha, the Lord is coming," was the first to drop out of significance, and even of use. But at the time when the *Didaché* was written in the sub-apostolic age, it still floated on the ear of Eastern Christians; it had not quite gone out of use. On the other hand, the term Anathema had not yet acquired the conventional sense it was given when Conciliar authority came in to back up dogmatic teaching and give it is true ring. The solitary use of Maranatha would of itself decide as to the true date of the *Didaché*, as well as to the branch of the Church in which it was found. Such a writing, we conclude, could not have appeared later than the first half of the second century, or in any branch of the Church west of the Ægean. The phrase is a kind of water-mark on the sheet, fixing the date and place of its origin, and deciding for us, if we had any doubt, as to the meaning of its contents, both what it taught and what age of Church history it sprang from.

Only five times in the New Testament is the term dogma used, and in every case it has the same sense of a binding decree imposed by authority from without. In the first case, there went out a decree from Cæsar Augustus that all the world should be enrolled, we at once see its meaning. Cæsar's commands are dogmas in every sense of the term. In the same sense precisely the decrees of Cæsar (Acts xvii. 7) are referred to, and the decrees of the apostles after the first Council of Jerusalem are also described as *δόγματα*, Acts xvi. 4. In Eph. ii. 15 and Col. ii. 14 the Mosaic ritual is rightly described as contained *ἐν δόγμασι*, *i.e.* in positive external ordinances. They are right because commanded, and not so much commanded because right. In both these parallel passages the dogmatic teaching of the Mosaic ritual is contrasted with the higher liberty of the gospel. These dogmas of the ceremonial law have no intrinsic worth and no permanent value. They all are provisional, and replaced by a higher teaching which is not dogmatic, but which is written no longer on tables of stone, but instead, on the fleshy tables of the heart.

The general sense of dogmatism, taking all these passages together, is unmistakeable. Whether it is a decree of Cæsar or of Moses, or of the apostles even, it is a decree or ordinance extending only to external conduct. It begins and ends with the act of obedience. It strikes a lower note than that of διδαχή, and that the sub-apostolic Church was deeply conscious of, by clinging to the one term which recalled the one Master who taught as having authority, *i.e.* first-hand, and not as the scribes, by "base authority of other books." Now the decline of doctrine into dogma is a true note by which to measure the decline of the Church from her standard of primitive purity. It has been well observed that the criterion of the difference between the two phrases is this, that the keynote of doctrine is that it springs from life and its needs. It refers to our duty to God, ourselves, and our neighbour. Dogma, on the other hand, if not quite losing all ethical meaning, leaves that to fall into the background. It sets out by distinguishing between faith and conduct. It confines faith almost entirely to the intellectual side of our nature—we believe either because we understand, as one Schoolman taught, or we believe or alter that we may understand, as another and better Schoolman taught; but in any case *fides* and *intellectus* are so related that the one draws on to or presupposes the other. Having thus set up two sides of religion, the *credenda* and the *agenda*, the *amanda*, which in primitive times included both, quite falls into the background, and is left to those mystics and pietists who are in tacit revolt against the doctrinaires and dogmatists of Church discipline and Church authority.

We have referred to its ethical bearing as the key to the distinction between doctrine and dogma. There is this further test, doctrine never can be pushed too far, dogma easily can. Take the remarkable instance of Jonathan Edwards. He was one of that rare class of pulpit teachers who preached right out and without any reserve all that he held in his heart to be the whole counsel of God. He had no compromises, no reserves;

but, taking extreme Augustinianism to be the very truth of God, he flung it out among his people as fire from heaven to kindle where it might. The result was as we might expect. His enthusiasm rose almost to the point of insanity, and the people of Northampton rose at last in revolt against him, drove him from his pulpit and off into the wilderness, where he was prepared to wander off, like one of the prophets of old of whom the world was not worthy. The crisis in his case was happily tided over, and he ended his days in peace and honour as President of Princeton College. But the revolt against this gospel of terrorism, which drove Edwards out of his charge at Northampton, did not end there. It was the active principle of that remarkable and melancholy reaction which drove many of the best of the New England divines into that stunted draft of Christianity, that half-Deism, which we identify with Unitarianism. There is nothing more certain than this law of one extreme producing another *chimæra chimæram parit.* The semi-Deism of Boston was the natural necessary reaction from such an exhibition of the Divine Being as Jonathan Edwards and his school had twisted out of a few texts in the Romans uncritically put together. "Show us the Father, and it sufficeth us," was the cry of human nature at Northampton and elsewhere; and to that cry the response of Edwards was a doctrine of the Fatherhood such as wrung from Wesley the remark to Whitfield, "Your God is my devil."

Dogmas, when they reach this point that they not only revolt the conscience, but "compel worshippers to break windows in order to let in fresh air," as Oliver Wendell Holmes describes it, are preparing the way for their own removal. The ineradicable instinct of mankind teaches them that any ethical truth is more certain than a merely theological; or, to vary the thought, what we know of God by the voice within must be far more certain than the long-drawn deductions of a so-called logic in theology. Dogmas break down when brought to this test, and we are thankful to those who have the courage or the hardihood, as Edwards had, to test them up to the breaking point. The majority of divines, happily for their own peace of mind, hold their dogmatic theology as "regulative" truth only. They are thankful to Dean Mansel for inventing a phrase by which they can escape from their own conclusions. In the case of the lay-world, they dilute their theology with what they call common sense, and hold as much or as little of it as does not shock their instinct of right and wrong. But trained theologians have no such escape, so they have to invent one. Roman ecclesiastics, shut in to the dogma that out of the Church there is no salvation, have invented "invincible ignorance" as the loophole through which they may escape, consigning heretics and schismatics to eternal perdition. In the same way Anglicans, whose straight-laced orthodoxy admits of no deflection to the right hand or left, find a pious way of escape in this new regulative theory of religion. We are bound to hold our old dogmas whole and undefiled; but when criticism begins to tell on the dogma, we evade a decision as to its being true or false by the compromise that it may be speculatively false but regulatively true.

These are some of the pitfalls into which extreme dogmatism tempts its followers, and out of which ingenious apologists for dogmatism, like the late Dean Mansel, have invented escapes which want nothing but the sense that they are inventions. But as soon as we get back from dogma to doctrine, the difficulty disappears of itself, for the reason we have already seen. No doctrine, pushed however far, ever conflicts with our ethical sense of duty; with dogma it is otherwise. Here we enter at once a *mare clausum,* strewn with the wrecks of previous theological systems, and a conflict of duties at once begins. Dogmas, as Hobbes cynically puts it, are, like pills, best swallowed whole, and not chewed. Should we not, then, seriously ask ourselves, is this also the case with the *Didaché* of Christ and His apostles; since, if doctrine brings about the same conflict as theological dogma, mankind will have the same excuse for rejecting primitive Christianity which they have for refusing that amalgam of first thoughts and afterthoughts which we describe as dogmatic theology? It is no light matter which is here at stake. On Christ and His truth rests all the best hopes of mankind for the future. But the Church has, almost without exception, corrupted the simplicity of the gospel with additaments of its own, these afterthoughts brought in to strengthen men's faith, and which in the end have so weakened it that they scarcely know what to believe. Like overdriven sheep, they faint by the way, and instead of the voice, "Come unto me," they feel themselves driven into some Calvinist or Catholic sheepfold, where they hear too much of threatening dogma to catch the sweet, low notes of Him who is meek and gentle in heart. To put it plainly and bluntly, the question turns on this, whether infidelity, in one form or another, whether as high, polite Agnosticism or coarse Iconoclasm, is not to overshadow the age and veil the Saviour from our eyes? Are we prepared to discard dogma, and to return to primitive doctrine? Are we prepared to allow that theology, ever since the fourth century, took a wrong turn, and, in the West especially, has since gone from bad to worse, until dogmatism wrought its own overthrow at the revolt of Luther. Then, in a fit of short-sighted panic, the Reformers became more scholastic than the Schoolmen, and so it has come down to our day, in which the extreme peril of the situation is at last opening thoughtful men's eyes to see where the real danger lies. It is in a divorce of morality and religion. As soon as ethical teachers tell the age that they can get on better with such sanctions as satisfied Confucius than with those which Christ holds out in His Sermon on the Mount, men are in extreme danger of saying, In what is Christ a better teacher than Sankya Muni or any other moral Reformer? This is the state of the case in our day, and calls for a courageous admission that the fault lies in ourselves, and in the dogmatic unethical presentation of the old truth. The average preacher of some dry dogmatic theology seldom pauses to ask, Is this the doctrine which is according to godliness? It never occurs to him whether these theological formulas, *crambè repetita,* ever commend themselves to the conscience of those that hear him. His theological teachers have early warned him not to attend to such texts at all. What is conscience in the natural man? Are we to be told of a verifying faculty in every man; and is a tribunal to be set up in the pews by which to pronounce on the dogmas of the pulpit? It is in this sheep-like frame of mind that our popular shepherds expect us to take their utterances as the last word of the lively oracles. There are some men who will not take truth at all on these terms of authority, as if we are to take or leave it, but may not discuss it. These accordingly are "Church-outed," as Milton described himself; while not a few educated men go to church and regard religion "regulatively" as the best safeguard for popular morals. There must be a religion for the people, but it will be a sad day for truth in England when Christ's religion is treated thus, and betrayed as the Son of man was with a kiss.

If we only have the courage to say this out, it is not yet too late to reseat faith again on its old foundations of personal conviction. Instead of setting out with terrorising men to flee from the wrath to come, as Jonathan Edwards did, let us take the more excellent way of Christ and His apostles. Let us persuade men by commending our gospel to the conscience. Some consciences, it is true, will not respond; the lock will not always fly open when the key is applied. Are we, then, to conclude that the key does not fit every conscience, or should we not rather infer that the lock may be rusted? The key is true to the wards, but neglect of use has brought the lock into such a rusty state that Christ will have to stand at the door and knock, and sometimes knock long and loud in Providence, so as to alarm the sleeper within, before the door is opened.

But when it is opened we see the correspondence of Christ and the conscience, and how well the key fits the lock. As soon as this is perceived, then we understand why we can dispense with dogma, and are content to sit at His feet as the alone true teacher. The dogmatic method of authority falls back, and Christ stands out, seen in His own light and in the self-evidencing power of truth. Then ethics and theology, instead of distinct truths, are seen to be only different aspects of the same truth. The restoration of belief and the reformation of theology thus go on side by side. It is the old paths which we have to get back to, when every single dogma of theology was tested by its ethical truth and *in foro conscientiæ.* Were it found to be a dogma only, outside the needs of daily life, then it has to be rejected, or at least revised. In most cases, it will be found that the restatement of the dogma in its primitive doctrinal aspect will save it from this indignity of rejection as a corruption or error. Take the term "grace," which has been hammered on the anvil of later Augustinianism out of all shape, with its original aspect. There is grace of congruity and grace of condignity, prevenient grace, and, in its final form, an efficacious or saving grace. Are these all different names for the same thing, the favour of God to sinners in different stages of their approach to Him? Or does grace mean the phases of faith as it passes from unbelief to filial trust and confidence? The Realists of dogmatic theology have discoursed on grace till, as Joubert remarked, they have almost made of it a "fourth Person of the Trinity." But a return to doctrinal simplicity disposes of all these afterthoughts of later Augustinianism. Grace is seen to be only the good old Hebrew phrase, favour, and which reappears in Jochanan (our John) as the favour of Jehovah. That favour deepens, of course, the nearer we approach Jehovah, as the triune blessing suggests the true meaning. "The Lord bless thee and keep thee," God's general favour to all as the Father of all. "The Lord make His face to shine on thee," His favour as He draws nearer to us in the Son of His love. "The Lord lift up the light of His countenance on thee, and give thee peace," when we are brought so near to God that we see Him face to face in the One who is the express image of His person, and of whom we can say, "He that hath seen me hath seen the Father also."

The remedy, then, for dogmatism, let us add in conclusion, is to bring dogma back to its primitive sense of *δόξα*, or private opinion. Why and how the doxa of one age became the dogma of another we have already seen. The Church only followed the schools of philosophy in this transition from the aorist to the preterperfect sense of the term *δοκεῖν*. The intensive form of the verb *δογματίζω* marks the third and last stage of the development, on which we need not to enlarge, since there is scarcely a divine who will not admit that to dogmatise is a degenerate type of thought. It is, in a word, co-ordinate in time and place with that stage of the Church which we describe as Byzantinism. It was against this contentious polemical temper that Gregory of Nazianzen uttered his memorable protest: "Wouldest thou become a theologian? Keep the commandments. Conduct is the key to contemplation—*πρᾶξις ἐπίβασις θεωρίας*." One of the causes, perhaps the principal cause, of the decline of Christianity in the East was the running to seed of gospel truth in dogmatism. It wasted itself in dialectical subtleties. Not content with affirming the human and Divine in Christ, and that in Him dwelt all the fulness of the Godhead bodily, it went on to ask in what sense was this *σωματικῶς*.[1] How could the human will coexist with the Divine? And when it reached the definition that there were two natures in the one Person, "without mixture, without change, without division, without separation," a sentence which excluded alike Nestorianism and Eutychianism, it was easy to see that this all-round negation, instead of healing the breach, would only widen it. The Nestorians broke away in one direction and the Eutychians in another. The Monophysite Christians of the far East and the Jacobite Church among the Copts alike point to the futility of such nice distinctions. Dogmatism had dug its own grave. The Eastern Church, which is nothing if not orthodox,[2] seems to have shrunk

[1] Greg. Naz. xx. 12.

[2] *αὐτοσχέδιοι δογματίσται*, off-hand dogmatisers, such is the description which Gregory of Nyssa gave of Constantinople during the Council of Nice: "If a trader was asked the cost of such an article, he answered by philosophising on generated and ungenerated being. If a stranger inquired the price of bread, he was told the Son is subordinate to the Father. If a traveller asked if his bath was ready, he was told the Son arose out of

into the shell in which it had encased itself, like the hermit crab; and there it is found to this day, orthodox and little else, with a name to live and it is dead.

Singularly enough, the West, rejecting the term orthodox, takes up the designation Catholic as its equivalent. The genius of old Rome, with its boast, *Imperium sine fine dedi,* repeats itself in the Church, which claims to be both Catholic, Roman, and Apostolic. The *semper ubique* and *ab omnibus* are supposed to form its triple crown of orthodoxy. All roads lead to Rome; and all empire flows out of it, as the river runs into the ocean and thus waters the whole earth.

Thus far we have traced the development of dogma as an afterthought of theology. It was the first stage of the descent from the primitive standard of doctrinal teaching. It is an unpardonable liberty with language for those who mean only doctrine to describe it by that other phrase dogma. The one begins and ends with apostolic teaching, the other goes on to Conciliar authority. This dogmatic teaching may be true or erroneous, but we should not confound it with that which is doctrinal only. The late Edward Garbett, in his Bampton Lectures for 1867, made this mischievous confusion by defining his thesis as "the dogmatic faith, or an inquiry into the relation subsisting between revelation and dogma." What the preacher really meant was not so much the dogmatic as the definite faith. His position was the sober stand taken by the Reformed Church of England as soon as she built up her basis of belief on the one foundation of the sufficiency of Holy Writ. Mr. Garbett is emphatic on this one criterion, that it is the faith once for all delivered

nothing." Can we wonder that the lively Greek intellect, wearing itself out over subtleties of this kind, should sink into a shell of orthodoxy out of which it has never since emerged?

to the saints, and winnowed and kept pure from later traditions and errors introduced under the specious guise of developments. It is unfortunate, then, that meaning one thing, he should define it by another, and lend his respectable name to shield the position of those who are dogmatists pure and simple. Such confusion of thought brings with it its own swift retribution; and if Mr. Garbett and writers of his school, in their zeal against that nebulous thing known as "modern thought," find themselves hunting it down in company with reactionary Church authority teachers, they have no one to blame but themselves. They have gone a mile, and they will soon he compelled to go twain. Beginning with the position that the Church is the keeper of "Holy Writ," they are soon forced on unwillingly to admit that she is the witness, so that questions of the canon and so forth are uncritically to be decided off-hand; and that from antiquity, authority, and tradition, when so united, there is no appeal.

Against all these insincerities there is only one remedy, which is to bring theology back behind its afterthoughts into the first thoughts. Neander in his *History of Dogma* quotes a remarkable admission of Marcellus of Ancyra which decides the meaning of the phrase dogma. The term dogma, Marcellus observes, "has in it something of human purpose and opinion." To mix, then, dogma and doctrine, is to mix clay with iron; and we know that the image whose supports are thus mixed, not as metals in the ore, soon falls to pieces. Well would it have been for the Church if she had never developed out from the doctrinal into the dogmatic stage. The last of great doctors, in the strict sense of the term, were the two great heads of the catechetical school of Alexandria, Clement and Origen. With them ended the doctrinal, and soon after began the dogmatic stage, which is slowly dying out in our day after an unbroken reign of sixteen out of the eighteen Christian centuries. Our hope is that the "new theology" will hark back to that type which is the oldest of all; and should this hope be realised, we may again realise that ideal of Christian perfection, when the scribe who has been made a disciple in the kingdom of heaven, and has moved on from the Old Testament to the standpoint of the new, is as a householder bringing out of his treasure things new and old.

CHAPTER X.

AFTERTHOUGHTS ON INSPIRATION.

WE have laid such stress on "Augustinian afterthoughts," that some would suppose our complaint against afterthoughts in general began and ended with that famous Carthaginian Father. But this is not so. The same temper was at work in the Church ever since. It leavened the Schoolmen; it leavened the Reformation; and it has come down almost unchanged to our own day. One hypothesis has been set up to explain another till we can understand the saying of Newton, *Hypotheses non fingo.* It was a protest wrung from him as he glanced right and left, as well at the theology as science of the Cambridge of his day. Of the two the condition of theology was much more deplorable, for what was an idle guess in science became a dogma in theology, which, to dissent from, entailed penalties temporal and eternal too terrible to be named. We pass lightly over all this in our day as if it meant nothing at all in that day; but it was no light matter to think our own thoughts in an age when those who broke away from the bondage of an infallible Church only did so to set up the second bondage to an infallible Book, taken literally to teach all that men need to know of their origin in the past and of their destiny in the future.

The second class of afterthoughts, then, which we have now to deal with grew out of popular Protestantism. It is not merely in its Augustinian or doctrinal aspects, already discussed, but on its formal side as a book religion. To Augustine, the Church, as the keeper and witness of Holy Writ, was the final authority; but the Reformers, in breaking with the Church, and so far parting company with the one Church Father whom they cared even to quote, had to set up some ultimate authority. This to them was the Bible, "the Bible the religion of Protestants," though not quite in the Chillingworth sense, for Chillingworth was one of the small sect of latitude men who anticipated the Cambridge Platonists in thinking their own thoughts. But even here we must be just to the true Reformers. It was not so much the first as the second generation of the Reformers who set up a theory of inspiration as a new court of final appeal with which to combat Church authority. To the men of the first age, from 1520 to 1580, the Reformation was still fluid, and spiritual faith in a living God and His eternal decrees was the one formative principle. This was the heroic age of the reform, when men died, or were put to death, as Calvin did Servetus, all for the glory of God. It was an age of martyrs and massacres, and it is not for us to say what was persecution when all alike were ready to call down fire from heaven. But in the second generation, when the new faith had settled down and crystallised into rigid forms of its own, men began to ask what was the ultimate principle of Protestantism; and, afraid to own to such a purely spiritual principle as the inner light of conscience (which was the discovery of a later age), they fell back on the letter of the record, and had to set up a theory of book inspiration, which it has tasked modern criticism either to explain or explain away.

It is not our intention to discuss inspiration theories as such in detail, but simply to assign it its place among those afterthoughts or hypotheses which have kept up the credit of dogmatic theology till the age of true criticism has come to sweep it all away. By criticism, let us add, is meant—not that word-criticism which limits itself to discussing documents, their age, authority, and so forth. This is mere palæography—an important aid to discovery; but it is only the apparatus of the true critic, rather than the higher judgment which intuitively sifts out truth from its accretions of fable. The "higher criticism" only deserves the name when it goes to the heart of the question, and, after disposing of inspiration as the last word of Protestantism, goes on to show what it can set in its place as the verifying faculty of the enlightened conscience, the lamp of God in the heart of man. We have then to show that, besides Augustinianism proper, there is the popular Protestantism of a book religion which calls for careful restatement.

The afterthoughts of theology are nowhere more seen than in the changed bearings of the age to what is known as book religion. Almost every age has its own mode of settling the relations which must exist between the letter and spirit, between the document and its teachings, the scribe deposit and its authority as a rule of faith. To discuss inspiration, much more to enter on the canon and its details, would be beside our subject—specialists have taken this in hand; and since the able epitome of the last results of modern criticism by Canon Driver on the subject of the Old Testament canon, it is impossible to sit down any longer at the old dogmatic standpoint. We no longer dare to assume that the canon has been settled over our heads long ago. The Jews, it was assumed, were the official custodians of the Old

Testament Scriptures, as the Christian Church was of the New Testament. To these authorities we must submit, and abide by their decision. The Hebrews may reject the New Testament, and the Christian Church may depart from the Hebrew standard of the Old Testament, by admitting the Apocrypha to a co-ordinate position with the canonical book; but in both cases we are told that they are exceeding their authority. We may accordingly disregard as much the errors of Christians with regard to the Old Testament canon as of the Jews with regard to the New Testament. All we have to consider is that, on their own ground, the testimony of each is final. This was the old line of apologists, but all is changed now. Criticism has stepped in and challenged the trustworthiness of Hebrew traditions with regard to the canon of the Old Testament, as much as of Church traditions with regard to the New Testament canon. In the latter case we have accepted the challenge, and passed one by one every book of the New Testament through the fire of criticism. The negative school have done their worst, but the New Testament has stood the ordeal, and with, perhaps, the exception of the Johannine authorship of the fourth Gospel, the fires of this controversy have begun to smoulder down. It is now the turn of the Old Testament to pass through the same testing furnace. The authorship of the books themselves, their threefold division into Law, Prophets, and Psalms, the date of the books, and the eponymic names to which they have been traditionally assigned, all this has come up in our day for a fresh decision, and we may assume, from the changed tone of the public mind towards Professor Driver's courageously outspoken and free criticism on the subject, that a certain latitude of opinion is to be allowed in future, which would have been impossible to ask for a generation ago.

For much of this increased liberty we have cause to be thankful. Truth has nothing to fear from free inquiry. The frank admission that the date and authorship of most of the early books of the Old Testament canon are all open to question—that the unity of Isaiah, of Zechariah, and of Daniel are alike matters of dispute, on which even the most orthodox may keep an open mind —this is no small gain. It is an advantage that should be used with moderatiou, and not pushed too far, as it seems to us it has been in the case of the far too peremptory decision to post-date the authorship of the Psalter by Professor Cheyne. Where we are to draw the line between too great stiffness in refusing to yield, and too great laxity in rejecting traditional views,—it is not easy to say off-hand. But it is fair to take our stand at this point, that the onus of proof in every case lies with the negative school. A tradition so venerable as that of the canon of the Hebrew Scriptures is not to be lightly set aside, unless on very good grounds. The latest attempt at reconstruction, the Graf-Wellhausen theory, may have much in its favour; but it is too arbitrary and subjective for the more cautious conservative instincts of the average Englishman. We do not wish to prejudge the matter either way; but we venture to think that we can offer a suggestion or two on the side of intuitive spiritual theology which may go far to allay the fears of the old orthodox party, as well as to moderate the too defiant tone of the new negative school.

In the first place, we set out with the statement, not that the Bible *is*, but that it *contains* the word of God. This amounts to saying that the letter in every case in part reveals, but also in part conceals, the living spirit which lies underneath. Revelation, in a word, is a curtain or veil, and through this curtain we may pass into the inner sanctuary of the spiritual sense of the whole. Of making theories of inspiration there has been no end. Partial and plenary-verbal dictation,—and the mere elevation of the spiritual consciousness, differing only in degree from the inspiration of Dante or Shakespeare,—theories of this kind have covered the entire ground from the highest mechanical down to the lowest dynamical explanation of the equivocal term inspiration. After sifting all these out, there remains this unique fact, that the Bible, which in one aspect is like any other book, is also in another aspect wholly unlike, and with a character quite its own.

"Thou seemest human and Divine," is the conclusion we must come to of the Bible, and of the Christ who is its glorious end and aim. The testimony of Jesus is the spirit of prophecy. *Ob sie Christum treiben,* do we come upon Christ? is the book Messianic from cover to cover? —this was Luther's test of inspiration, and it ought to suffice us. The last struggle of the Church on the person of Christ, turned on the dispute with the Monophysites. It long seemed an unthinkable mystery how human and Divine could combine the union of two natures in one person; and so it was from the mere Deist point of view. The Divine must absorb the human, as the greater contains the less; or the human must so dim down the Divine that Deity sinks away, swallowed up beneath its veil of flesh. The *communicatio idiomatum,* or, as the Greek phrase went, the περιχωρησις, seemed only an expression of a dogmatic decision to hold on to two opposing truths, and to clasp contradictories together, and at the same time to deny that the admission of the one implied the exclusion of the other.

In the same way, the Church with a true instinct has upheld that the human and the Divine elements coexist and cohere in the Bible in the same way as they do in the person of Christ; but we are unable to produce any adequate explanation of the union in either case. It has held fast to its dogma of *communicatio idiomatum* in both cases, but is unable to offer any adequate explanation. But it occurs to us that the *Kenosis* doctrine, which relieves much of the mystery on the subject of the human and Divine in Christ, may also throw light on the subject of inspiration. The orthodox Church has been practically Eutychian on the subject of Christ's person,—not formally so, we admit, but in the recoil from the Nestorian extreme it has inclined much more to Eutychianism. This arose not so much from any wilful exclusion of the human element, but from sheer inability of thought to call up any intelligent conception of "two natures in one person." The ground of this inability lay in the equivocal term "nature." It was assumed (as all Deists must do) that the nature of the Infinite must be incommunicable to the finite. Between Creator and creature there is much more than disparity, there is a gulf fixed which no theory can bridge over. The Incarnation, in a word, from the Deistic point of view, becomes an unthinkable mystery—it goes farther back still, since, in fact, creation itself must be unthinkable; for how can the Creator, if Infinite, pass out of Himself into the finite and conditioned? Hence we have to fall back on such senseless phrases as that He made the worlds out of nothing, and creation at last becomes a bald affirmation of a fact for which reason by itself can offer no explanation which is not merely verbal. The early Gnostics felt this difficulty, and so they set to work to invent a Demiurge, a Bathos, a Pleroma, and other hypotheses which as hypotheses have gone the way of all brain cobwebs. The orthodox East clung, however, to the conception of the Logos either as ἐνδιάθετος, as before creation, or προφορικός, as going forth in creation. It was this Logos doctrine which carried the East safely through all the labyrinths of thought, as well on the subject of creation as of redemption. Thanks to the preface to St. John's Gospel, that most precious jewel of God's word, the arcanum of arcana, all was explicated, and the bald dualism of God and matter bridged over, or rather absorbed in that higher Monism in which the Eternal is ever proceeding forth through the Logos and entering into time relations, and so delighting in the habitable parts of the earth.

The *Kenosis*, then, which is the key to the Incarnation, is also the key to our conception of God in creation. The Eternal Father is ever communicating, in condescending love through the Son, some of His perfections to those lower orders of being whom we call His creatures. It is His nature and property so to create in condescension or self-emptying, much in the same way as it is the nature and property of the sun to shed his effulgent beams out into space. *Kenosis*, then, as much in creation as in redemption, at once suggests the key to what we go on to describe as the self-effacement of the Divine in a human consciousness. God spoke by the prophets—so the Creed affirms; but we are nowhere asked to define the mystery, or to go into psychological puzzles as to the meeting point of human and God consciousness; nor does the Divine imply a temporary suspension of ordinary self-consciousness. We find in Christ the human was so absorbed by the Divine, that on one occasion when the disciples said, "Master, eat," His reply, was "My meat is to do my Father's will, and to finish His work." In His case we must assume perfect simplicity and entire transparency of character. Hence, that He should forget hunger and thirst in the absorbing spirit of His work, is what much lower minds than the Christ attain to every day. But the *Kenosis* goes farther than this; it implies that He emptied Himself of His glory, and took a servant form. If this had been only in His Incarnation, and for three short years, then it would seem a unique, perhaps incredible mystery. But the Logos has been ever so emptying Himself. It is self-abasement, exinanition of the full glory of Godhead, when He paints the lily, and fits an insect's eye to the tiny operations of the insect world. Hence it is that, to mere Deism with its design and argument, it seems perplexing to find perfection from the least to the greatest of God's works. The notion of condescension in the Most High, that He "humbleth Himself to behold the things which are done in heaven and earth," seems strange to Deism, to whom humility seems only the shadow of the cross; and that is "foolishness," as we know, to the mere natural man. On these grounds we see that unless we set out with this key-word *Kenosis*, we shall never unravel the mysteries either of creation, redemption, or of that mode of communicating the mind of God to men which we define as inspiration. But this one master-key opens all these three locks. It is the same Logos who is the link in creation between the finite and Infinite, whose goings forth in redemption are that He has become one flesh with us that we may become one spirit with Him, and who is also the source of the old prophetic fire, the one fountain of light and love in inspiration.

The mistake in theology has been the same as in science, by isolating a single truth, and then to try and wrestle with it as with Proteus, and to wring its meaning out in single-handed fight. The sciences will not thus be won by direct assault. Their flank must be turned.

In laying a subject aside and in thinking of some other thing, a side light will sometimes enter the mind, and one theory thus open the door to another. So Newton found it, as he passed from one theory of physics, where his calculations had failed him, to another theory of optics; and, after exploring the one domain, he was able to re-enter the other as conqueror, and to hold his ground there. It is the same in theology. Inspiration and the Incarnation throw light on each other; and now that we have got hold of the Incarnation by the right aspect, in the phrase of the *Kenosis*, it will be strange if we cannot use the same conception to lead us on to the right meaning of inspiration. In the *Kenosis* of Christ's person we hold that the wisdom and goodness of God dwelt in Him bodily. In no mere Apollinarian sense (though Apollinarianism is not such a heresy as it seems) the wisdom and goodness of the Logos dwelt in the man Christ Jesus, and were to Him His Pneuma. When we speak of a *human* pneuma we are using words with no meaning; we are like the disciples on the Mount, not knowing what we say. The Pneuma itself is the Divine inherent in the human; it is itself a prophecy of the Incarnation—the ground and sufficient cause of the Incarnation becoming credible and intelligible, and not a mere mystery jarring to all our sense of truth. In our Lord Jesus the Christ, a Messianic element was the plenary indwelling of the Holy Ghost, not given to Him by measure as to other sons of men. But this does not imply either omniscience or omnipotence. These are attributes of pure Deity, which must be, and were, laid aside when He emptied Himself of His glory; and if equal to the Father as touching His Godhead, He became inferior to the Father as touching His manhood. Under false reverence to shrink from this frank confession of the *Kenosis*, is to fail to grasp the true meaning of the Incarnation. This is why, as observed already, the popular orthodox view is still Eutychian, and explains the outcry of some hyper-orthodox champions of the old school at the measured and well-weighed words of Mr. Gore in the *Lux Mundi* on the subject. That they were an offence at all, is an index of the depth of popular ignorance of the true Catholic doctrine of the Incarnation. Till the *Kenosis* is understood, the Incarnation must remain an unassimilated dogma.

It is the same with inspiration. It also stands apart among unassimilated faith formulas until we see that the Divine can only enter the human by some act of condescension. Accommodation is the old phrase. Men say that God accommodates His teaching to the imperfect faculties and immature judgments of men. At a low stage of culture He meets them with animal sacrifices and rites and ceremonies which to us seem burdensome. As the ages advance, He lightens the burden of ritual-teaching, becomes more oral and less ocular, and at last the prophet and scribe supersede the priest altogether. Even Judaism had reached the Rabbinic stage before Christ's coming. And how strange a decline it was when Christ's religion sank back again into the beggarly elements, and the commemoration of His death in the Eucharist feast was lowered again into a repetition of the type after the antitype, and described as the sacrifice of the Mass! We must go on to see in inspiration these advancing stages through accommodation, or else we shall never understand the Bible as a book human and Divine. To throw all the books into pie, so to speak, and read them in a lump, finding the Trinity in Gen. xix. and the doctrine of the Mass in Malachi, this is that kind of uncritical use of the Bible which we need not waste time in exposing. It is too out of date to find excuse for it in the uncritical use of the Old Testament by the Fathers of the early Church. Inspiration, in a word, is the unfolding purpose of God for the education of the race through a chosen people, that people themselves only learning the mind of God through an elect race of prophets and teachers. Thus, within the election there is an election, and the prophets themselves had to search what and what manner of time the Spirit of God which was in them did signify. They had to grope, in a word, after the meaning of their own sayings. They uttered dark sayings of old, because God-consciousness always enters in at first to dim self-consciousness, and a man inspired must be for that very reason in a sense beside himself, though always "sober for your sake." Inspiration was always much more than mere mantic phrenzy, we admit, though it often seemed to approach the dangerous limits between sanity and insanity.

High views of inspiration are generally assumed by devout people to indicate high views of God and His glory. In reverence for His word written our views cannot be too high, just as our reverence for the person of the Lord Jesus. Only in both cases we are to avoid the Eutychian extreme, much more common among the orthodox than the Nestorian. Two natures exist in one person; but the natures are, since the Incarnation, so fused and intermingled that He is no longer twain but one Christ; this is orthodox theology with regard to our Lord Jesus, who objects to the expression the indwelling of the Eternal Word in the man Christ. For the same reason we should be content to speak of the book as "containing" the word of God. By that expression we mean that in that library which we call the canon, every book has its place and purpose: each is part of a whole;

and if, to us, some part seems insignificant, it is because we fail to see organic unity. It is as with our body, in which some members seem more honourable than others, but all are tempered together and bear reference to the whole. Such is inspiration. As to the *literature* of the canon, there are certain rights of criticism which have their place, but they are quite subordinate to and apart from the spiritual use of the Bible as a book of devotion. On that point Canon Driver has taken his stand on strong ground. He is within his rights as a Canon of Christ Church and Hebrew Professor to discuss and to deal with the Palestinian as much as with the Alexandrian Jew's revision of the canon. He may show grounds, if there are any, why the most negative German critic may be in truer touch with the spirit of the old book than the Massoretic or any other Hebrew school of the older criticism. But he must not forget, as the negative school too often do, that the *onus* of proof lies with those who advance novelties. Presumption is always in favour of the occupying holder, since possession is nine points of the law. Some of our younger critics, in the first flush of excitement, forget that it is easier to assert than to prove. Negation becomes thus quite as dogmatic and far more offensive than the old traditionalism, which maintains that a position must be true because it is long established. There is, we admit, an immense presumption in its favour, since the general shut up in a garrison with ten thousand men may expect to hold his ground till another with twenty thousand men comes against him.

But, like Canon Driver, we draw our line at the *literature* of the Bible. *Libros Canonicos ad leones* is a modern version of the *Christianos ad leones.* Let the young lions of criticism work their will on the letter of the record, and we fearlessly say that what remains after negation has done its worst is that "word of the Lord which liveth and abideth for ever." To us, for instance, this new phrase, the Hexateuch, is as unimportant as the old phrase Pentateuch: it seems like pulling down one house of cards to set up another. If the orthodox had not been so ill-advised as to fall into Bibliolatry, this kind of attack would have never been made. It was the same when the old orthodox school were Creationists, and evolution seemed to set aside the hand of God and the necessity for a first cause. But as soon as the defence ceased the attack died down; and so it will be with much of this itching ear for the last novelty of negative criticism. As soon as it ceases to alarm by our taking higher ground of inspiration than the old school did, so soon will it sink into the contempt it deserves. The archives of Israel are historical documents, and therefore must go to the school of history there to be tested in the usual way. To fear the result is to show very little faith. If the New Testament canon has come out of the fires of criticism, what have we to fear for the Old? We shall no doubt have to give up something, especially the uncritical order and ground on which Jerome arranged the Vulgate, borrowing partly from the Hebrew and partly from the Greek arrangement of the books, putting them out of their true order, which was mainly chronological, and so giving fictitious importance to some semi-canonical books, such as Daniel and Koheleth, which were probably of later date than their eponymic authors, and among the Antilegomena.

All this will soon be over, and then inspiration will be seen to be a growing truth; and that as Jesus increased in body, soul, and spirit, so there is harmonious orderly growth of the letter and spirit of the Bible. In all the books there is a theopneustic element, the test of which is that it is profitable for doctrine, for reproof, for correction, for instruction in righteousness. The *Didaché*, in a word, is elenchus, or evidence internal of its truth; this leads on to *Paideia*, or education, and that established state which he fitly describes as ἐπανόρθωσις, or maturity in the faith.

CHAPTER XI.

REMEDY.

We must come back to Kant—We must come back to Christ. Strange as it may sound, these two cries of morality in stress for a true basis, and of religion for a living centre of authority, alike spring from the same source. They both express the same need, the one for an immutable morality, the other for an intuitional theology. We shall have no difficulty in pointing out how they correspond each to the other, how they express the same need for foundation which cannot be shaken in the two departments of duty and God, where alone the conscience has a right to a final decision.

In the first place, let us glance at the meaning of this last word of sound moralists, "We must get back to Kant," and see how it expresses this need. Ethics had been shaken to its basis by two tendencies in the opposite direction. There were some who had pushed the Egoity of the Ego to its breaking point. Starting from Fichte, they have passed through Hegel up to that dreary extreme in which self is its own God. We not only think our own thoughts, but thought itself becomes its own object, the thing in itself, the *ding an sich*. As for "duty," it has been sublimated into a law of mere self-consistency. The "right" is that which is right in our own eyes. The ancient Stoic touched the point of apathy, but the new Stoic of subjective morality is not merely superior to pleasure and pain, he is a proud, passionless thing; he is more than this, he is an "intellectual all in all." God and the world are not merely outside him, as the old Stoic taught—he is his own God, his own universe, and quite in a new sense as he thinks in his heart so is he.

But this extreme subjectivity has brought with it its own corrective—it has called out a reaction in the opposite extreme. This is that "Monism" in which both Schopenhauer and Hartmann have drowned us in the depths of pessimistic despair. A new God has been invented whose name is "Will;" but it is "Will" divorced from all moral conceptions, or even from self-consciousness. It is Buddhism over again, as Fichte and Hegel's ethics were Stoicism under a new name of Egoism. This new Buddhism is quite as atheistic as the old. The world is *Wille* and *Vorstellung*—the world rising up out of unconsciousness and only groping after consciousness in man. This is his misery, that he attains self-consciousness, and, like a guilty creature surprised, tries to hide himself from self, to escape from his own shadow, as in Chamisso's weird tale of the man without a shadow. No wonder that the last word of this desolate theory is pessimism. It is like Buddhism, weary of selfhood, and longing to get off the wheel of life and to dream itself back into nothingness. The modern Nirvana is annihiliation, and the goal we get on to is to fly off like spray from the fountain, and so not to fall back into the basin to be thrown up again in the eternal round of sinking and rising. Negations like these bring their own remedy. The cry of outraged human nature is to get back to a basis of some theory which is not false to the facts of life, and in which love, conscience, and duty are more than mere *ægri somnia.* That basis of immutable morality is found in the Kantian axiom of the categorical imperative. There is a voice within (we may as well at once name it by its right name, conscience) that calls out that right is right and wrong wrong by an eternal sanction. "For ever, O Lord, Thy word is settled in heaven." As in Wordsworth's grand Ode to Duty, which has the true Kantian ring—

> "Thou dost preserve the stars from wrong,
> And the most ancient Heavens through Thee are fresh and strong."

No other basis of morality can be set up than this. If its precepts are not inviolate and binding under every condition, we are ploughing the sand and sowing the salt sea. Casuistry, especially confessional casuistry, began to sap the foundations of ethics, right became right because it was commanded; and the same power which bound could, of course, also loose. Ethics have thus been absorbed in dogmatic theology; and the same divines who set up the commands of an absolute Jahveh as justifying the slaying of the Canaanites, consistently enough taught that to the chair of Peter such a dispensing power belonged. As the Vicar of Christ, he might within limits lay down what was right and what was wrong. This, of course, was limited at first to indulgences from certain ceremonial duties; dispensations from fasting and other external obligations were bought and sold. But it soon went on to touch the foundations of morality itself. Under Jesuit teaching the Pope became absolute master of the ethical as well as the ceremonial code of duty. When pardoners had gone round Europe daring to sell pardons for sins past and prospective, it was time that Luther came and knocked a hole in Tetzel's drum. It was a case like that of Israel in Egypt when Pharaoh doubled the burdens of the taskmasters, then Moses came; so, when theology dared to tamper with the foundations of morality, and treat the immutable and eternal law of right as something mutable or mere *mos pro lege,* then the Reformation arose, and the rights of the common conscience of mankind were vindicated among the German and Gothic races at least, if not among Latins and Sclavs.

Immutable morality has thus, at least since the Reformation, become the heritage of all who are on the side of the Reformation; and when Hobbes in this country, from his cynical, sceptical point of view, began to tamper with these foundations of all truth, Cudworth was stirred up to write that *Treatise on Eternal and Immutable Morality*[1] which is probably the only work of Cudworth which has a right to live. Of Cudworth's learning in the *True Intellectual System of the Universe,* it seems, to borrow the phrase of a recent competent editor, "to resemble the knight clad in complete mail, the armour was admirable as a defence against the enemy, but often smothered the wearer. His other works contain merely an expanded and very diffuse application of principles already proved in the *Treatise concerning Eternal and Immutable Morality.*" "Further," as Mr. Scott goes on to observe, "this latter work has an especial claim upon a British public, for it has not yet had a fair field. The first edition was published long after the death of the author, when his memory and a vague respect were all that was left of him; while the last edition formed a mere appendix to the *True Intellectual System of the Universe,* and was thus put out of the beaten track of the philosophical student.

[1] See an *Introduction to Cudworth's Treatise concerning Eternal and Immutable Morality,* by R. W. Scott of Trinity College, Dublin. London: Longmans. 1891.

With regard, then, to the ethical foundations of theology, we regret that we cannot say, "We must get back to Cudworth," and have to repeat the expression, "We must get back to Kant." It was the fault of all the Cambridge Platonists, that they made too much smoke of the fire which they kindled — they were smothered by scholarship. The Puritan divines were one and all intolerably tedious. It has been said of Orton, one of them, that while Orton was striking a match a Bunyan would set the world on fire. The same *tedium theologicum*, transferred to Platonist philosophy, lay heavy, like a Dutch mist, on Cudworth and his school. He has not left his mark, as he deserved to do, as the first and best opponent of that debased gospel of expediency and opportunism of which Hobbes was the proto-evangelist, and Locke and Paley only later imitators. To do the mystics and inner-light men of the seventeenth century, and above all the Cambridge Platonists, justice, they saw and seized on this defect of popular Protestantism, and raised a standard against it. More especially we find in Whichcote the sentiment that there is a "seed of a deiform nature" in every man, the Divine image or root of goodness, and on which our union with God and conformity to His nature must depend. Culverwell, Worthington, Rust, Patrick, Glanvell, Norris, all followed on the same lines, and laid stress on the same class of truth. The late Principal Tulloch, who was the first to call up these noble names out of the obscurity into which they had undeservedly fallen, describes them as a "narrow stream running between high banks of authoritative dogmatism." Whichcote's aim was to point out the correspondence of reason and religion; in a word, to make faith reasonable, and to fuse morality and religion in one. J. Smith, the golden-tongued, as he was named in his day, attempted a revival of Christian Platonism, with, it must be admitted, not a few neo-Platonic elements, which in that uncritical age were mixed up together, the early Plato and his Alexandrian imitators being often confounded. Cudworth, again, dealt far too ponderously with that forgotten theory which he calls Hylo-zoism, and which, under a changed name, is reappearing among us as Monism. In More the Cambridge Platonists declined into something like theosophy and pure mysticism, and this is probably the true reason of their falling into contempt during the whole of the eighteenth century, which prided itself, more than anything else, on its "common sense" and its contempt for enthusiasm in any form. Coleridge truly observes of this Cambridge school, that "they were more Plotinists than Platonists. The theosophic reveries of the Alexandrian school fitted more aptly their own supersensual imaginations, and so they passed from the original to a later type of Platonist writings with the most indiscriminating indifference. They missed the light Greek airy tone of the original Plato, and took up instead that style of profound but sombre and unwieldy thoughtfulness which shows that no one can wholly escape from their surroundings." As the modern Yankee has been described as a cross between a Puritan and a pedlar, so we find the same cross in these Immanuel-men (for with one exception, that of More, they all came from the same Puritan foundation) of the Puritan and the Platonist. They tried, in a word, to recast the popular Augustinian theology of the seventeenth century by introducing the missing element of a pneuma or verifying faculty in man, the voice of God in every man naturally born in the world.

The attempt failed, as perhaps it was bound to do. It was born out of due time; but no such movement perishes because it does not carry on a corporate life of its own with a visible succession. Spiritual movements pass on into other forms, and the mystics of the Church in all ages have been a fertilising element even in cases where they seem to have died out, leaving no successors. If in our day a spiritual philosophy is possible, and an ultimate concordat between reason and faith, it is because other men laboured, and we have entered into their labour. Spiritual philosophy, we are thankful to say, never was left without a witness, even in the thick night of the *seculum Deisticum.* The lamp of intuitional truth passed on from Shaftesbury to Hutcheson and Butler, and so through a thin thread of witnesses, chiefly the Scotch psychologists, till in Kant we meet with the true protagenist of ethics. He was awaked from his dogmatic slumbers by the scepticism of Hume, probably in the same way as Hobbes aroused Cudworth; and his assertion of the "Categorical Imperative" was the same high-water mark from the end of the eighteenth century that Cudworth's assertion of eternal and immutable morality became for the age of Charles II. In any case, whether Cudworth or Kant are to divide the honours, as Leverrier and Adams have done in astronomy, as pathfinders of the lost planet, we must so describe eternal immutable morality as the missing link, wanting which all theology labours under the one fatal defect of dogmatism. It wants verification, and we know the position which verification holds in the so-called positive sciences. It is the one brand, wanting which no science can be even hall-marked as positive. Earnest men are lamenting, in notes loud or dulcet, that theology is a poor captive Hecuba, and no longer Queen of the sciences. But whose fault is it but their own? No one would dream of setting up a new set of notions about God, dogmatically constructed out of crude Bible interpretations, reinforced by traditional theology, into a Queen of sciences. To state such a claim is to dismiss it as absurd. But let us reach a theology based on our spiritual intuitions, and these resting on the rock of a morality eternal as God Himself, and immutable as His "yea and amen;" we are not sure that the age would not alter its note, and treat such a theology with something more than the languid interest with which it listens to the attempts of modern Churchmen to galvanise old-world conceptions of a magical view of the priesthood, and those politic Privy Council decisions how to keep divines, Anglican and Evangelical, tethered to the same rack, and eating out of the same manger.

We have seen that immutable morality is the first support of a theology of the future. Expediency, eudæmonism, and the prudential ethics of self-interest here and hereafter, must all go, like the rotten pillars of a house built on the sand, before we even begin to build. The next pillar to set up is intuitional theology. On these two supports of immutable morality and the theology of intuition of our spiritual concepts as self-evidencing, we may begin to build. Wanting these two, we had better remain where we are, and believe in the Bible as "inspired" because it says it is so, and in the Church as a true teacher because a corporation of clergy under that name offer to be our guides. This provisional way of looking at things must go on unless we put a little more courage into our convictions, and say, like the slave at the whetstone, in the Roman story, *Seca.* The indolent acquiescence of educated men in dogmatisms on which they stake no real belief, lies at the root of the sceptical temper of the age. Young men "play at priests," and old men on the bench bear rule by their means, and my people love to have it so. We ask with the prophet of Chebar, who saw wheels within wheels of the mystery of God's enfoldings and unfoldings, "What shall be the end thereof?" Would that we could go on to say, We must get back to Christ, as we must get back to Kant. We have pointed out a definite meaning to the one phrase; let us see if we can fix as distinct a meaning to the other. To get back to Christ can only mean—if we take the true Christ meaning of the term—that we get back to the point in which we see in Jesus of Nazareth the Anointed of God. Messiah in the Old Testament has a very definite sense, and we must not slip away from it in the New Testament. St. John, who was much more Hebraistic, even in his Epistles, than many suppose, lays stress on the "anointing which we have received of Him which abideth in you, and ye need not that any man teach you." Can we forget that this anointing is the same Christus, the *salbung*, the consecration chrism which made the Christ what He was. Mystical as that sounds to many, the only question should be, Is it true? Is there any meaning in His prayer for His people, "I in them, and they in me"? Dogmatic theology has forgotten all these conceptions; especially since Cyril's day she has sunk into a Eutychian sleep, miscalled orthodoxy. She has so forgotten true Athanasianism, which is the union of God and man in one person, without confusion of nature, that her explanation of that mystery ever since Cyril (the Augustine of the East as Augustine is the Cyril of the West) summoned the Council of Robbers at Ephesus. Theology has gone astray. It has not lapsed into heresy, God be thanked; but it has become practically Eutychian. We do not know where to look outside the mystics for a single theology East or West which is not tainted with Cyrillism, as we prefer to call it. By this we mean that hyper-orthodox temper which is so set on extolling the glory of Christ as God that it forgets the meaning of its own term, Christ as the "anointed" of God. All that Augustine did to debase theology in the West, and even more, Cyril has done in the East. He was the same maker of heresies that Augustine was, and succeeded to perfection, by his polemic temper, as his Carthaginian contemporary, in patching up one hole by making another. Eutychian-Nestorian were a sad battlefield in the East as Augustine and Pelagius in the West. We should be unfair to Augustine's memory to leave him to bear the whole load of our theology of afterthoughts. The Patriarch of Alexandria, whose *parabolani* were the religious wonder of their day, and whose murder of Hypatia has never been cleared up, stands branded in the page of secular history; and till Churchmen write history as God's book describes the sins of holy men, we shall have two versions of the same event,—the solemn sneer of a Gibbon, and the still more saddening attempt of a Canon Bright or a Canon Robertson to whitewash characters that never can be white as long as History is true to her office.

But enough of this censure of afterthoughts. In getting back to Christ we must get back behind Cyril's orthodoxy as much as Augustine's. We must lay hold of the person of the Anointed One, who is to anoint us, as He has been anointed of His Father. This can only mean that we have a witness within; that we know Him that is true, and we are in Him that is true. All these phrases are lightly passed over as part of some mystical inner-light religion which has very little to say to faith and practice, as to what an orthodox Churchman has to believe, and what he has to do. Alas! that faith and practice have got so far asunder, that, as in death, "we cannot hear each other speak." The creed of the average Christian is a list of long and abstruse theological propositions, of which there is no apter summary than the *Quicunque vult*, now sung in churches, where it is much better not read. As for his practice, it is only the common morality of everyday life salted with a few phrases about grace, but out of which the taking up the cross daily and of imitating Christ is quietly dropped. It is not workable outside convent walls, even if it is within. But theology will never be Queen of the sciences unless Christ is King again in our lives, and the lord of every motion there. Formal theology is no more capable of this than man is able with one dead lift to raise himself up aloft and walk on air. To get back to Christ is what the saint, at the end of a lifelong struggle against the flesh, sees; it is like land ahead to the sailor who has crossed a stormy ocean. We have not yet attained, and none is as yet perfect, and those who are nearest perfection are those Paul-like spirits, who groan within themselves, waiting for the adoption, to wit the redemption of the body. To "get back to Christ" means so much that it is the end, not the beginning, of a long journey. But a step may be taken which at once enfranchises us, and sets us on the right track. We have to break with all afterthoughts on theology. Luther, Calvin, Cranmer, doctors of all types, have made the simple crabbed, and the sublime scholastic. A narrow scholastic intellect belittles all it touches. First the poetry, then the philosophy, at last even the common sense of religion dissolves away in the mud-pool of technical divinity. Until a healthy scepticism of traditional methods begin, we can promise no true therapeutic in theology. "Wash and be clean" must be the beginning of the new gospel, as it is of the new therapeutics. All our best hymns brim over with this sentiment, "Thou, O Christ, art all I want." What a pity that as soon as the hymn is ended a sermon begins, which sets up a scholastic plan of salvation, often so technical, that were it not for some fire of love and personal appeal, which the preacher, if a born orator, infuses into it, it might be a sermon on stones to stones. All this must be laid aside; and when, having ourselves found Christ, we go on to preach Him to others, let us not go to bodies of divinity or models of master-preachers, but let us try our appeal on the touchstone of the human heart. Does it lift men to a self-renouncing life, a level altogether above the old dead level of turnpike road morality, then it is a power of God unto salvation. If not, it will only be like that preaching of morality which Selden laughed at in his day, in which the mastiff of unregenerate human nature is meek as long as we stroke it, but flies at our throat the instant that we threaten or offend it.

Immutable morality and intuitional theology, in a word, must thus work together. If combined, the play of two such forces would be simply irresistible. But, as the world is constituted at present, we see little or no hope of their being given free play. Religion is not yet out of that "regulative" stage in which men of the world wish to keep it. It has been debased into a subtle form of utilitarianism, a "scheme of salvation." It is not an end in itself, but only a means to an end, a mode of securing felicity and escaping suffering here and hereafter. As long as the gospel is so debased, instead of being abreast of the higher morality, it actually falls short of it. As long as it is a kind of disguised eudæmonism, is it possible that it can attach to itself any nobler ethical system than that of the greatest happiness of the greatest number? It comes, then, to this, that a pure ethical theory, such as that of Cudworth and Kant, must lead up to a disinterested religion of love. The editor of *Lux Mundi* well points out the three evils of dogmatic deductive theology under these heads—(1) Christianity is no longer devotion to a living persón, but acceptance on authority of a system of theological propositions and ecclesiastical duties. When Churchmanship, as the writer well observes, assumes this degenerate form, Christianity is not destroyed, but we fall short of the true spirit and temper of sonship. (2) In the next, the adoring contemplation of our one Lord and Master is interrupted by undue exaltation of saintly intercessors. As an illustration of this last, he adduces Alphonso de Liguoris' Glories of Mary, in which the Madonna, as a kind of second Saviour, almost eclipses her Son. When she conceived the Son of God in her womb, and afterwards gave Him birth, she obtained half the kingdom of God, so that she should be Queen of Mercy and He King of Justice. That this hyperdulia of Mary should lead direct to something like the blasphemous assertion that justice and mercy have parted company, or at least are divided between mother and Son, is only what we shall expect. (3) The third illustration of degenerate religion, when it is pushed in an unduly subjective direction, is true; but we have remarked on it already, and need not pursue the subject further.

This testimony of Mr. Gore is all the more striking, since the tendency of his teaching is unquestionably in the direction of external authoritative Church teaching. It is all the more satisfactory, as a proof of the candour of a writer who is too true a follower of Christ to allow any lesser guide to usurp His place as the one Sun of the soul. The only theology, in a word, which will stand the test of time is that which has been from the beginning. To purge away afterthoughts, we must work down into the stratum of first thought. We must know God as He is, and as revealed by the Son through the Spirit; and in this sense, and in this only, will an intuitional theology and an immutable morality be found to harmonise. We shall "get back to Kant" and get back to Christ at one and the same time. The time has come to replace this "regulative" theology of plans of salvation, all derived from "three Carthaginians," with something simpler and deeper, at once more human and Divine: the Christ of history, who is also the Eternal Logos, is the light of all men. The time for timid compromises and half-truths has gone by. A theology for the age must be a theology of conscience, with a God revealed in His Son by His Spirit, and with none of those "trailing clouds" of Manichean pessimism still clinging about Him, with which Augustine entered the Church.

Why is it, we sometimes ask, that poets, and not theologians, are so often the best interpreters of the theology of any age? Dante in his day, Milton in a later day, and now Tennyson and Browning, seem to have that same intuition, the vision and faculty Divine, which made the Hebrew prophets what they were, not only God's messengers to men, but also the interpreters of the age to itself. It seems the same in our day, in which the prophets of the theology of the future are those poets who would ring out the darkness of the land, ring in the Christ that is to be, or, to borrow from another of these modern oracles—

> "I go to prove my soul;
> I see my way as birds their trackless way.
> I shall arrive—what time, what circuit first,
> I ask not; for unless God send His hail
> Or blinding fireballs, sleet, or stifling snow,—
> In some time, His good time, I shall arrive:
> He guides me as the bird in His good time."

There is a note in these lines to which men like Gordon, the soldier-mystic, find a mellow music, beside which our old orthodoxies seem out of tune and harsh. The reason is, because from Augustine's day downward the Church has ceased to be a witness of the Logos or Christ within. We may add that, all but a few mystics and Christian Platonists, such as that small Cambridge sect who were forgotten almost in their own day, the whole world went after the dogmatists. Predestinarianism and sacerdotalism were the toys of children. "Opinions," as Glanvill, one of this small sect of Platonists, observes, are "the rattles of immature intellects." But the world has outgrown these scholastic rattles, and sullenly stands aloof from theology, because it has nothing better to give than these toys of childhood.

The remedy, then, as we have seen, is simple, if we have only courage to say it out. It is contained in the old Cato phrase, *Delenda est Carthago.* If we could only agree to take three Church teachers off their stools of authority, Tertullian, Cyprian, and Augustine, the Church of the future will have little trouble in making an accommodation with all the rest of the Fathers. The remedy for afterthoughts, then, let us repeat it, is to get back to first thoughts; but it is not so easy as we suppose to think ourselves up into the first thoughts of a theology which has come down the stream of time, gathering accretions with every age which it passed through. This is not easy, but it ought not to be impossible; nor is it, if we are on our guard against the oldest of all fallacies, the mistaking the connotations of terms for their denotation or definition. The fallacy of the dictionary, as the late Bishop Fitzgerald once termed it, lies as heavy as ever on the popular mind to this day. The English reader of the New Testament meets with such terms as "faith," "grace," "election," "salvation," "the Church," and so forth; and, scarcely suspecting that it is so, he reads into these terms a Lutheran, Calvinist, Anglican, or medieval meaning, perhaps as foreign to the mind of the inspired writer as our age and its ideas are foreign to the first age of the Church. To borrow Dr. Johnson's sturdy phrase, we must clear our mind of cant of this kind. It is more difficult to do so than we at first suppose, and yet the only remedy for these afterthoughts of theology lies in getting back to the first draft of truth, so as to see things with purged eyes and unprejudiced minds. This is not easy, but it is also not quite impossible. Every day we hear of converts to the faith in the mission field, who get a grasp of Christ and His gospel first hand; and what a grasp it is! how firm their faith, how simple and childlike their conceptions of the love of the Father, the grace of the Son, and the fellowship of the Holy Ghost! Sad to say, in their case, as in ours, Church tradition and a theology of afterthought soon enters in. The traditional eschatology, which has scarcely been challenged since Augustine's day, the sacramental system, with its sacerdotal efficacy, salvation itself, as a far-off result of the day of judgment, conditional on a certain discipline of faith and works—all this enters in in the second, if not in the first generation of missionary effort, and so the Christianity of the far East pales into a weak reproduction of the Christianity of the far West. We are back again in the school of traditionalism, that type of old diluted Judaism from which Christ has in vain set us free.

It is sad to think that it is so; but we shall gain nothing by pretending that it is otherwise. Men can only give what they have got. The missionary, trained in a theological hotbed at home, can only plant out the same seed which he has received. The Divine archetype and its dogmatic transcript are to his mind inseparable. He would suspect the more highly trained teacher who even hints that afterthoughts are not quite the same as first thoughts. But the cause of truth calls on us to deal plainly with uncritical minds of this type. In their consciences they desire to be Bible Christians, and certainly believe that they are. They may not have passed through the same storm and stress as Chillingworth, and so reached Chillingworth's position, that the Bible is the one authority, and so that the religion of Protestants is a safe way to salvation; but they certainly can subscribe to Chillingworth's noble declaration, that this presumptuous imposing of the senses "of men upon the words of God, the special senses of men upon the general words of God, and laying them upon men's consciences together, under the equal penalty of death and damnation; this vain conceit, that we can speak of the things of God better than in the words of God; this deifying our own interpretations, and tyrannous enforcing of them upon others; this restraining of the word of God from that latitude and generality, and the understandings of men from that liberty wherein Christ and His apostles left them,—is, and hath been, the only fountain of all the schisms of the Church, and that which makes them immortal, the common incendiary of Christendom, and that which tears in pieces, not the coat, but the bowels and members of Christ. 'Take away these walls of separation,' and all will quickly be one. Take away the burning, persecuting, cursing, damning of men for not subscribing the words of men as the words of God; require of Christians only to believe Christ, and to call no man master but Him only; let those leave claiming infallibility that have no title to it; and let them that in their words disclaim it, disclaim it also in their actions. In a word, take away tyranny, which is the devil's instrument to support errors and superstitions and impieties in the several parts of the world, which could not otherwise long withstand the power of truth. I say, take away tyranny, and restore Christians to their just and full liberty of captivating their understanding to Scripture only, and as rivers, when they have a free passage, run all to the ocean, so it may well be hoped, by God's blessing, that universal liberty thus moderated may quickly reduce Christendom to truth and unity."[1]

It may be that we are nearer this reunion of Christendom, on the basis of an open book consulted by all, with an open unbiassed mind, than was possible in the days when Chillingworth wrote. A few Latitude men, two or three at most at Oxford, four or five perhaps at Cambridge, of the same school of forethinkers in an age of afterthinkers, caught a glimpse of this Sangreal of Reunion, on terms of comprehension which would make short work of dogmatic theology. But the age was not ripe for this happy result. The Bible itself had to be passed through the fires of criticism, and the canon itself broken up and recast in a furnace heated seven times, before we could say what we are dealing with, in asking Christians to set up the Bible as their one standard. Chillingworth's position has to be restated before we can give it unqualified acceptance. At last, however, in our day, the whole of the New Testament has passed through the fire, and Christians at least may know what are the books they may depend on, and that they are genuine transcripts of the original authors. As for the Old Testament, they can afford to wait till results of recent criticism have reached the same stage of settlement. Alarmists of the uncritical school have raised the cry that their faith is in danger, because the Old Testament is undergoing

[1] Chillingworth, chap. iv. § 17.

the same sifting process as the New Testament. But this treating the Bible as a whole one and indivisible, this committing of Christians to a blind uncritical acceptance of the Jewish canon, is unfair on the face of it. The common conscience of Gentile Christendom revolts at this going behind Christ and His apostles. We are Gentiles, not Jews. The lively oracles of the second covenant look back on and reflect the same teaching as the oracles of the first covenant. But farther than this we need not go. To do so is to "build the bridge much broader than the flood;" it is to stake the truth of Christ's mission on one of the minor issues as "to whose are the fathers." Traditional theology has hampered itself with too much baggage of this kind, and its line of march has constantly been exposed to forays of the negative school, against which its only defence has been to halt in some entrenched camp of dogmatic authority. The Church vouches for the canon, and to oppose the canon is to deny the witness work of the Church, and so the controversy ends in a lame conclusion of this kind.

But at last we seem to be emerging from this blind alley of opposing dogmatism and doubt. Christians are coming to see that these theological afterthoughts, whether about the Church or the Bible, are not what they were baptized into; and they are beginning to ask whether their baptismal belief is not enough. Is it not as safe a way of salvation, to use Chillingworth's phrase, as any Roman, Anglican, or Genevan after-copy of it can be? Happy decision, blessed interim standpoint, certain concordat of a settlement of all controversies in the future! In the name of the Father, Son, and Holy Ghost, I, the follower of Jesus Christ, renounce the world, the flesh, and the devil. A threefold confession, and a threefold renunciation, such is the first word of the early Church, and to this the last and best thoughts of this nineteenth century can say Amen. Religion within the bounds of morality, this was Kant's demand in his day, only refused, as we hold, because Kant had narrowed the sense, both of religion and morality. By religion he understood the dry and dessicated *caput morbum* of Deism, even then going off before the attacks of the young intuitional school of Jacobi and others. But worse still, his idea of morality was limited by the narrow circle of duties between man and man which just escape enforcement by statute law, and which the old school of ethics therefore described as of imperfect obligation. If we take religion to be Deism, and morality to mean a duty to our neighbour with a policeman in the background, we can see that such a settlement of the claims of both never could be listened to. It excuses the fear of dogmatists when philosophy offers reconciliation on these terms. But Kant's accommodation is now forgotten; and, readjusting the meaning of the two terms, morality and religion, by the light of intuitional morality and spiritual philosophy, we see no reason why we may not bring the two together again. If the keynote of religion be God's general fatherhood, and the keynote of morality be man's general brotherhood, why may not an accommodation be made on these terms, and an accommodation which will prove the basis for the ultimate reunion of Christendom, on the simple basis of love and loyalty to one Master?

Let us see how such a revised theology would work; how much of the old it would cut out, and how much retain. The Trinity, for instance, understood as triunity and purged of all its later scholasticisms, which bring it perilously near Tritheism, would, of course, stand. To what were we baptized to, unless into the name of One who is to us tripersonal as Father, Son, and Spirit?

Let us forget Sabellian and anti-Sabellian disputes, and limit ourselves to the one phrase in which Augustine spoke more as a Platonist and less as a dogmatist than usual—*Homo imago Trinitatis*, and we shall see in the triunity of man, body, soul, and spirit, the psychological adumbration of the great theological verity which so many stumble at because misrepresented. So far for one half of the baptismal formula, the confession of the name we adore. Next for the other half, our triple renunciation corresponding to our triune confession. Religion here passes into morality, as morality becomes animated with an enthusiasm other than its own. So true is it—

> "Unless above himself he can
> Exalt himself, how mean a thing is man!"

This fusing of morality and religion into one, is indeed that return to primitive New Testament Christianity which the age asks for, but does not see its way to. As a matter of fact, simple lay Christians, men and women, have solved the problem, as they do the simple problems of geometry, without knowing there is any problem at all. They walk through them as Pascal and Newton did through the first books of Euclid, solving by intuition what to commoner minds seem to ask for laborious proof. So it is that those who find joy and peace in believing, learn by intuition that they have a great need, that Christ as Saviour can supply all their need, whether they call it pardon, purity, or peace. In idea they sometimes speak of these stages at which all the afterthoughts of theology enter in. There is a pardon stage, at which they ought to stand like penitents at the brazen altar at the porch, and learn of Christ's imputed work. Next, there is a purity stage, at which the merits of Christ once accepted at the golden altar within the veil, return to them in a steam of acceptance, and they are filled with the fragrance of the sacrifice. Lastly, there is a peace stage, in which holiness, first imputed, then inherent, leads on to union with God, or fellowship with the Father through the Son by the Holy Spirit.

Now, all this, which is spread out by our theologies into systems, each marking successive stages of Christian experience, is seen at a flash as one intuition of the spiritual mind. The devout scarcely suspect that they leaped to this conclusion just as Pascal and Newton passed at a bound through all the laboured demonstrations of the early books of Euclid. To an intuition, whether from the spiritual or intellectual side of our nature, the conclusion is contained in the premises; to state the problem is to demonstrate it. Now, the return to primitive Christianity implies the abandonment of all afterthinking theology, but not the abandonment (as simple souls in their fears suppose) of the best truths which this theology in all its leading types, Roman, Anglican, and Genevan, are agreed in. All that we insist on is, that in any statement in which one of the three theologies differs from the other two, we should call a halt, and insist on some special proof. This is what Chillingworth demands of the Church of Rome. Does that Church propose dogmas which are at least far-fetched, not easily derived from the sacred page, and which, even if true, do not touch the needs of daily life or concern the conduct of the man of mankind—these we may relegate to the theological lumber-room. They are among those vanities which Milton said—

> "Fly o'er the backside of the world, far off
> Into a Limbo large and broad, since called
> The Paradise of Fools; to few unknown
> Long after new, unpeopled and untrod."

We may take Chillingworth's test, and apply it to the divergencies of Churches from each other and from the truth. In the few points on which they are agreed we may see the note of Catholic consent; where they begin to differ, there we may at once ask ourselves, Are not all these afterthoughts? As Churches diverge, so they grow dogmatic, and the measure of their dogmatism is also the measure of their departure from primitive truth. It is too late now to regret that the Reformers vied with each other in setting up creeds and confessions. Every Church was a Church State with a confession of its own. Helvetic, Belgic, and even separate cities or cantons, such as Basle or Zurich, laid claim each to its own *formula consensus.* A better mind now and then dawned on them with the suspicion that division was a sign of weakness. In the year 1552, when the Council of Trent was framing its decrees against the doctrines of the Reformation, Archbishop Cranmer invited Melancthon, Bullinger, Bucer, and Calvin to a conference in London for the purpose of forming an Evangelical Union Creed. To this Calvin replied, that for such an object he would willingly cross ten seas, and that no labour and pain should be spared to remove, by a scriptural consensus, the distractions among Christians, which he deplored as one of the greatest evils.[1] But the danger past, and Trent having uttered its seven thunders in vain, these, in petty national Churches, fell asunder as before, and so far from syncretism gaining any ground, the dissidence of dissent, and a Protestantism which divides the West, because, like the queen in Hamlet, it "protests too much," became the order of the day down to the end of the *seculum Dogmaticum.* Then, in sheer weariness,

[1] Quoted from a paper by Dr. Schaff on the consensus of the Reformed Confessions, *Christ and Christianity,* by P. Schaff, p. 153.

men and theologians even fell back into the *seculum Deisticum*, the end of which only came when Deism itself paled away as a poor ghost of the past before the rise of Kant's *Kritik*. Ours may be described as the critical age of the Church, when all is passing through the fire, dogmas and documents alike. What survives that testing and stands the fire, may be described as Catholic doctrine, and the deposit of faith which may be handed on to the future as its theology.

How much will live, and what will pass away as dross, it is too soon to say; but it is reassuring to know that if much will go off as afterthinking theology, much will remain. The simple test of that which endures is this, that it centres around the person of Christ, and our love and loyalty to that Supreme Centre of all heart homage. To the earliest type of Christians, such as are glanced at in the Epistle to Diognetus, that gem of the sub-apostolic Church theology, all lay wrapped up, like in the form of that Babe of Bethlehem to which wise men came from the East to lay their gifts at His feet. We often say, Would that the Church could return to this theology of one creed, and that the shortest, the least explicit. But to utter the wish is not to go on, as too many do, to admit that it is a barren wish. So it is, and must be, as long as we go on tagging anthropology on to theology, as the whole West has done ever since Augustine led the way. "Grace" is a charming sound, harmonious to the ear; but we wish to hear of grace more in a theological, less in a metaphysical sense,—*Charis*, that is, as it flows from God's free goodwill to men, His kindness and philanthropy—and less of grace as an abstraction, the logical antinomy to freewill in man. As for those long discussions, in which Pelagius and Augustine left an evil legacy to the Church, they are of the schools scholastic, and remind us of Sir

W. Hamilton's key to such discussions, that no controversy of this kind has ever emerged in theology which has not previously emerged in philosophy. What Sir W. Hamilton was thinking of, was that thorny quickset hedge of afterthinking theology which Augustine had planted, and Calvin tended down to our day. As for theology, in the strict sense of the term, that theology which goes out as the subject of pure Deity, of His personality and perfections,—His loving care over all His works, and His relationship with man, since He breathed mysteriously into man's nostrils the breath of two lives, a sentient and a spiritual,—on this subject, so far from having too much, we have had too little theology. In the early Alexandrian school this makes up nearly the whole of their teaching. Theirs is theology, as the teaching of the West turned chiefly on anthropology, and it remains to be seen which is most in harmony with the best thoughts of our day.

What the age requires in religion more than in anything else is simplicity. A creed should be short, and not concatenated, article upon article, inference upon inference, until belief breaks down beneath its top-load of dogma. Such a creed is that earliest symbol which passes by the name of the Apostles' Creed. Its articles are few, and the teaching is simple; it is like those circular stone temples, open to the sky, of the age of the Druids, in which each stone is a monolith, and on which the ring of the hammer or mallet of controversy has never been heard. It has no chisel marks; and we are left to conjecture how it came there, and who drew the sacred circle, into which we can easily pass in through open gates, as if into a temple not made with hands. Simplicity, then, is the first note of a true theology, which is at once old and new. The next and most important note is that all turns on the Person of Christ. A theology which is largely notional is, as a rule, little emotional, and so we are working with the wrong instruments, and seeking to enter the citadel of the soul by open assault, not by sap and mine—*non in dialectica complacuit.*

This golden saying of an Ambrose is even truer to-day than when first uttered; for what has the march of mind for centuries taught us but this, that the wider the circle of knowledge, the vaster the horizon of our ignorance opens on us. The dream of reaching the earth's circumference is a dream of childhood; we have, or ought to have, long since outgrown it. Vast, too, as has been the expansion of our intellectual sphere, it is as nothing to the discoveries which we have made as to our mental limitations. The new criticism has set up walls which we never can climb, and between which we only can pass. Antinomies of reason and paralogisms of thought are set up by Kant, new like the *flammantia mœnia mundi,* which we can never pass. Nor are these terms the mere jargon of modern metaphysics. According to Kant, an antinomy means that natural contradiction which results from the law of reason when we seek to know the absolute, passing the limits of experience. Pure reason, again, has its antinomies, which are like the *sic et non* of Abelard, the thesis and antithesis are each logically sustainable. It is the same with the practical reason. The antinomy of the practical reason is that virtue ought to be happy, but cannot be so here. This is answered by the doctrine of the future state, which is a postulate of the practical reason. We only glance at these Kantian distinctions here, to enforce the lesson that reason never can be, and never was meant to be, the organ of the religious faculty. It is instead to close the eye in the act of adoration; not merely to shut out the lower world sense perception, but also to hush to rest that inquisitive dialectical faculty which we sometimes call reason and sometimes understanding; but whether in its lower or even in its higher function of pure reason, we never can find out the Almighty to perfection, and which, if allowed free range, only lands us in logical contradictions out of which there is no escape. It is only the spirit by which we know or are known of God. This is an intuition above reason which searches (*ἐραυνα*) the deep things of God. This spiritual faculty, which is love in its purest, most sublimated form, knows God only so far as it loves Him. This is the best side of Augustine's teaching, in which, with happy inconsistency, he forgets his dialectical disputation tendency and temper, and falls. "Caritas inchoata inchoata justitia est, caritas provecta provecta justitia est, caritas magna justitia est, caritas perfecta perfecta justitia est,"[1] is a golden saying, which may be set off against tomes of his polemical treatises. Indeed, it may be said of Augustine as of Toplady, one of his most logical disciples, if he had written more hymns and less polemics, he would have left a richer legacy to the Church. But let that pass; the lesson which the age asks is that of those Greeks who said, "Sir, we would see Jesus;" and when it has been led on to know the Risen Saviour by the Holy Spirit, then its craving is still the same—"Show us the Father, and it sufficeth us." A religion must centre around a person to find acceptance in an age suspicious of logic and wearied with word strife. As long as religion presents itself as a school of metaphysics—Scotch or German—to the schools, it must go and share the fate of these little systems which have their day and cease to be. The wider, and therefore more modest, mind of our day knows its limits too well to put

[1] Aug., *de Natura et Gratia*, chap. lxx.

up any longer with these dialectics which passed for theology, and which the Highland woman, who called on Norman Macleod to go over her fundamentals, will soon be the last surviving relic. Let not sincere souls fear that faith will sink when a theology of fundamentals is found out to have overlooked the one fundamental point of all, that God is love, and not mere sovereignty. It is probable that theology, rid of this incubus of a Determinism, which is neither scientific nor spiritual, but an unnatural amalgam of both, will then rise as if with wings into its true sphere, the awakened conscience, using intuitions of its own which are purity of heart, faith working by love, and prayer which clasps God, so to speak, by the feet. To the pure and praying spirit heaven is opened; it is such who see God, and who know Him, because they love Him and trust Him, because truth needs trust, and they have tasted His truth by living experience. This is religion in the exact sense of the term, the tie which binds us back to God. Theology suggests a chain of many links, and man-made religions all make the scheme of salvation long and painful; it is intellectually difficult to grasp, ethically and experimentally it is still more difficult to lay hold of in the right way. The line of the saintly Cowper here comes in, and no one suffered greater tortures than he from leaders of this type—

> "Oh, how unlike the complex works of man
> Heaven's easy, artless, unencumbered plan;
> Luminous alone by the light they give,
> Stand the soul-quickening words, Believe and live!"

Simplicity on the intellectual side, and living trust on the ethical side, are the marks of the faith once delivered to the saints. The purity of a theology may be almost tested in this way. It is seen in a descending scale of second, third, and fourth century theology. After that the darkness of dogmatism becomes so great, that we may almost gauge the ignorance of monkish commentators by the violence of their vituperation against any who went before and who happened to bear the brand of heresy. It is said Celsus' treatise against Christianity is forgotten but for Origen's reply. In the same way Origen himself has, to a great extent, perished on account of the ignorant copyists treating his commentaries as unworthy of notice. "Throughout the 'Middle Ages,'" as Mr. Bigg remarks (*vid.* Bampton Lecture, *The Christian Platonists of Alexandria*, p. 277), "the name of Origen was a by-word in the East, and the margins of his MSS. are found scrawled over with fierce execrations of his heresies and his blasphemies."

May we not measure by this single remark the contrast between primitive and debased theology,—those conceptions of God which may be classed with apostolic times, and those latter-day conceptions of an age of afterthought, when dogmatism had dimmed and asceticism soured those God-implanted instincts in us by which the soul turns to God as a flower to the sun? We are not concerned in a defence of Origen, much less of Origenism. The Bampton Lectures of 1886 have at last done tardy justice. We can see the true Origen through some clearer medium than the uncritical abuse heaped on him ever since the age of Justinian and the so-called Fifth General Council. It is only as lending point to our comparison between early and after ages of Church history that we single out Origen, the most misunderstood of early Fathers, because least in harmony with the reigning ideas of later ages, which were all cast in an entirely different mould. But the question remains, Which of the two theologies, that of the early Alexandrians or the later, is most in harmony with modern thought? If we ever ask ourselves, as only a few do, what shape the Church of the future will take, will it be dogmatic and traditional, or spiritual and intuitional? the answer is obvious. It will certainly not reflect that type of monastic Byzantinism under which the Church became enslaved to one form of bondage and the State to another, until, between these corruptions, society perished, and the sweep of the Saracen's scimitar laid both low together. The Church of the future will look out on a new world, with conceptions so enlarged, purified, and, at the same time, simplified, that it will smile at those complex theories in science, politics, and religion which once weighed down the human mind and held it in such bondage to a dull and spiritless tradition. The so-called sciences are found all to interlap: forces are so correlated, that while the details for specialists become more minute every day, the great unifying principles grow more simple. It is the same in law and politics: rights and duties are seen to be correlative, and a new jurisprudence is growing up on this basis. Lastly, theology itself will have to take a hue from the age it enters on. It will be more humanitarian; but will it, therefore, as the timid suspect, lose the sense of God's nearness as the all-Father, and of our relationship to Him, indissoluble as the parental tie itself? It is a tie which, so far from being broken by death, will then only attain its full fruition and meaning.

With regard to the Church of the future and the theology of the future, there are two superlatives, optimism and pessimism, which hitherto have held the field between them, but are alike unmeaning as expressions of God's dealings with the race. Into the history of these phrases we need not enter. The use, or rather abuse, of the one provoked the other, and the true solution lies in the middle term meliorism, on which we feel disposed to take our stand. The reigning Augustinianism has ever struck a pessimist note with regard to the mass of mankind. The sentiment of the apocryphal writer Esdras has passed current for orthodoxy, at least in the West: "I will tell thee a similitude, Esdras: As when thou askest the earth, it shall say unto thee, that it giveth much mould whereof earthen vessels are made, but little dust that gold cometh of: even so is the course of this present world. There be many created, but few shall be saved." [1] Nor is it strange that a pessimism of this kind, with regard to the mass of mankind who are non-elect, and for whom it is better they had not been born, should lead straight to the other extreme of an almost immoral optimism. The age which has rejected the theology of pessimism has lapsed in an unthinking, unserious way into a kind of bland optimism. We are not universalists *ex professo,* and those whose thinking all leads straight in that direction are loud in disclaiming a phrase which sprang up in America, and has too much the ring even there of a reaction against the Determinism of the school of Jonathan Edwards. All things are of God; He is the one Will of the universe. This modern phrase of what is called the Monothelite heresy reigned in the West without a rival. But since Determinism of this kind seemed to make God the author of evil, and carried with it certain reflections on His perfections which no mere appeal to God's sovereignty can get over, men began to twist the argument right round. Since it is unworthy of the one Will of the universe that only some should be saved, let us conclude as consistent Monothelites that it is His sovereign will that all should be saved. In this way the age consciously or unconsciously has

[1] 2 Esdras viii. 2, 3.

dropped out of pessimism into optimism. It is a sweeter note, we admit, and one more in harmony with all we are taught of the Headship of Christ, and that He must reign till He hath put all enemies under His feet. But all the same we are forced to say that this optimism is only Augustinianism turned inside out. The American universalist is only a revolted Calvinist; and we are confirmed in this conclusion by remarking that it is the most Calvinistic Churches which lean most in the new direction. In the East, which was even more Pelagian than Augustinian, it has always been so. Evil is a quality of the freewill of man; it is an awful endowment of his nature that it can so determine in time its destiny for eternity. In this the so-called Arminians of the West are in harmony with Alexandrian theology as contrasted with the Determinism to which Augustine set the type in the West. Now, it is instructive that the three types of theology which are non-Calvinistic, as we may say the Lutheran, Anglican, and Wesleyan Churches are, do not lean towards universalism, which, as we have seen, is the inevitable reaction from Calvinism.

There must be a cause for this concomitance, and it is easily seen what it is. The Determinism of the Augustinian theology throws on the one Will of the universe all the issues of life and death, temporal and eternal. In the most logical type of it which Hopkins, who went as far beyond Edwards as Edwards surpassed Calvin, and Calvin Augustine, it has come to this, that even right and wrong are sublimated into varieties of the one same thing, which is the will of God. To the followers of Hopkins, heaven and hell were alike for the glory of God; and the occupants of the dungeons below as of the palace chambers above of the Great King would alike sing the same Song of the Three Children, Benedicite.

To argue with one-sided men of this type would be a waste of reasoning. It only confirms what sober thinkers ever have held, that to run a single thought out to certain logical conclusions, is to forget that we can only reason at all within and between certain antinomies of thought. It is no sign of sanity, but the reverse, thus to be ignorant of our own ignorance; and the disease of theology has been this, that some of its brightest lights have forgotten that if any man "thinketh he knoweth anything, he knoweth nothing as he ought to know." Our guesses in the dark may or may not be approximations to the truth, but the instant that we dogmatise and denounce others, as Augustine did Pelagius, we are certainly in error ourselves, and, like the blind, only lead the blind until both fall into the ditch.

Nothing strikes us so much as this contrast between the theology of the New Testament and that of later times. The note it strikes is neither that of the optimist nor the pessimist. Meliorism, or an increasing purpose in the ages to come, the education of the human race by slow successive stages of advance, corresponding to the six days of creation, this is the true note of the New Testament, not the mere "now or never" note of the theology of later ages. The soul-saving theology, with belief and baptism standing between us and the awful gulf of eternal death—this was the afterthought of a later age. As is always the case, men read out of the Book what they had themselves first read into it; and the result was an amalgam of Biblo-scholasticism, which has passed current until a more critical age has passed the whole through the furnace to test what is primitive and how much yet are the additaments of later thinkers. The result is instructive. The residuum is so small that it is all contained in one short creed, and the clauses of that creed so enigmatic that they seem to cover almost any kind of interpretation. Jesus and the resurrection, this is the sum of the apostles' teaching; but what vistas these two words open up! The person of Jesus, human and Divine, covers the whole ground of theology proper, and the Anastasis throws light on all that we mean by man and his destiny. He is at present "in the flesh," but there are unfoldings and capacities as yet latent, all of which the term Anastasis covers and throws light on when Anastasis is understood in its widest sense.

Thus it is that the eschatology of the New Testament does not so much differ from the popular eschatology in detail, as in its general drift and direction. It has been the endeavour of trained theologians from the first to attempt to bring the two into textual harmony; and it would be strange if they had not succeeded in this, especially as dogmatic theology only professes to draw its teachings direct from the well-head of the Holy Book. But there may be a certain surface of agreement when there is no inner harmony. The finer ear of one musician will detect any discord which passes for harmony to another. Much of music is mere noise, for this reason, to the trained and too sensitive ears of a few. So it is that the eschatology of old and new theology strikes quite a different note to those who only judge of man's hereafter from the few pregnant hints of the New Testament. Not to go into detail, the contrast is all summed up in this, that in the New Testament all centres in the person of Christ. He is the Anastasis and the Life, whether here or hereafter. Later theology sets out with assuming, as Martha did, the Pharisaic dogma—which is Platonism run into a Hebrew mould—of an Anastasis at some last day or judgment, as if in some valley of Jehoshaphat. Our Lord neither contradicts nor corrects Martha. He simply takes the phrase out of her mouth and lifts it into a higher plane of thought. "I am the Anastasis;" the difference in terms is slight, but the point of view is wholly changed. We seem to see the same truth, but with changed eyes. It is like a man returning to the scenes of his youth—

> "Dost thou look back on what has been?
> As some divinely-gifted man
> Whose life in lowly scenes began,
> And on a simple village green."

The eschatology, then, of the New Testament brings us out of all theories of the immortality of the soul, the resurrection of the body, the duration of rewards and punishments, and all those battlefields strewed with the castaway weapons of old combatants. When we get into the mind of Christ and draw near the heart of God, we begin to wonder how such small dogmatisms could have filled our mind at all. Take the term rewards and punishments, how miserably inadequate such a phrase sounds to express the relation of spirits with the Father of spirits! It is excusable as a phrase of the old schoolmaster and magistrate stage of our training. The law was such a schoolmaster, and it passed us on to the governmental view of God, who will no doubt reward every man according to his works. He is the righteous Judge, who will certainly recompense men as they have deserved —indignation and wrath, tribulation and anguish upon every soul that doeth evil; while to them who by patient continuance in welldoing seek for glory and honour and immortality—eternal life. Rewards and punishments, as the best thinkers have long seen, thus grow out of the nature of the case. In Butler's phrase, they are natural, *i.e.* not arbitrary. Moral laws, like material, execute themselves. To call in the aid of some public judge and executioner, is to reduce God to the level of a magnified man. Anthropomorphism must stop short then—we speak of the eye, the heart, the finger, and hand of God; but to make Him a mere magistrate to enforce His own sentences, would be to fail to see the meaning of that law which cannot be broken, but in violating which we are only ground to powder.

The eschatology, again, of the New Testament lifts us at once above the old disputes of Sadducee and Pharisee as to the immortality of the thinking principle on the one hand, and of the necessity of a material framework on the other hand, with which to carry on identity and personal consciousness. Plato, as it has been often remarked, reasoned well as to the immortality of the soul; only too well, since he overproved his point, and left us with a sense of existence *a parte ante* as well as *a parte post.* But he failed, as Aristotle pointed out, to give us that sense of personal identity, wanting which our desires for immortality are mere visions through the ivory gate. Aristotle came after Plato and pierced his air-bladder of immortality with the needle point of criticism. He showed that the rational soul of man is immortal but impersonal, while the sensitive soul is conversely personal but not immortal; and so the deepest thinkers stood beside the grave, and had to say with the women, "Who will roll us away the stone?" for it was very great.

Here the eschatology of the New Testament enters in with the true explanation. Our Anastasis after death is an entire Anastasis of both rational and sensitive soul, and our personality which inheres in the latter will thus be complete. This Bishop Butler, in his essay on the subject prefaced to the *Analogy,* has entirely missed, and so has failed to see the true reconciling point between Plato and Aristotle's theory of the soul and its immortality. Nor is Bishop Butler alone in this capital error. Theology in its afterthinking way has too often mistaken, as Martha did, the true kernel and centre of the whole subject, that our Anastasis is bound up with the Anastasis of Christ; so much so, that if the one fails the other also fails, as the apostle argues, *ex abundanti*, in those verses of the Corinthians where he shows, first, that our resurrection depends on that of Christ; and that, secondly, His resurrection would be unmeaning, nay impossible and false, unless the Anastasis of the whole human race had been designed as part of the eternal plan of which Christ's resurrection at Easter was strictly the first-fruits, followed by that of every man in his own order.

There have been many criticisms and exposures of the popular theology for which we cannot be too thankful. Archdeacon Farrar, the late Dean Plumptre, Canon Row, and others too numerous to mention, have cut away the chief excrescences of error which made the outlook into the hereafter too dismal to be taught, until a general scepticism on the whole subject had crept into and at last possessed the popular mind. But this scepticism unfortunately cast back a shadow on the New Testament, chiefly because writers were not careful to show that the inferences of theology were not taken direct from the fountainhead in the teaching of Christ and His apostles. Their silence as to restitution and recovery hereafter, was taken to mean that the state of man was eternally fixed at the moment of death. Hence the crude opinion that some last act, whether of sin or repentance, would fix, and fix for ever, the condition of a soul in eternity. The continuity of character was lost in a magical idea of sudden conversion in the act of dying. This took the place of every other. Our poets, who, if not our theologians, are at least the abstract and epitome of the age they live in, show us this. Hamlet's argument, that it would never do to slay his uncle in the act of praying—

> "Now might I do it, pat, now he is praying;
> And now I'll do't:—and so he goes to heaven;
> And so am I reveng'd:—that would be scann'd."

Such conceptions of heaven and hell, turning on the last act in life, are only seen in their crude literalness when bluntly put by a master poet holding the glass up to nature, and giving the very thoughts of his age in its own words. It is by the help of this thinking aloud that we understand what theology really teaches, and are able to point out where the confusion of thought begins. What the New Testament teaches is continuity of character. Such as we are as a whole in this life, such we pass into the life eternal. But it is rank superstition to suppose that a last decision will determine our state for eternity. It is this heaven or hell alternative in which the popular theology built up systems more or less misleading.

But enough of these errors of afterthought, which will all pass away as soon as the true exegesis of the New Testament is laid hold of, not by scholars only, but by the people at large, through more enlightened pulpit teaching. This must be a work of time; but we need not despair. Slowly a better, benigner conception of God and His dealings with all His children is filtering down into the public mind. It is not in a day that Rome is either built or overturned. It is not all at once that the misconceptions of ages pass away. As a matter of fact, they are never argued down; they go out of themselves like candles that burn out in their sockets. The well-meant attempts of reformers to write down the "popular theology" are to a great extent "love's labour lost."

But the fact remains that the heretics of yesterday become the orthodox of to-day, and perhaps the masters of sentences of an age yet coming: so true is it that Wisdom is justified of all her children; their ashes, flung out, are gathered in "history's golden urn"—

> "And spite of praise,
> As one who feels th' immeasurable world
> Attain the wise indifference of the wise."

CHAPTER XII.

THREE TESTS OF AFTERTHOUGHTS—1. UNPRIMITIVE; 2. IRRECONCILABLE WITH HIGHER LIGHT TO BREAK FROM GOD'S WORD; 3. METAPHYSICAL STAGE OF THOUGHT.

In the first place, these afterthoughts are unprimitive, if not uncatholic. The first test of afterthoughts lies in this. What the creeds contain may be said to be *de fide;* what the creeds omit or pass by may be treated as afterthoughts. The two most widely known are that of Chalcedon, commonly called the Nicene Creed, and that of the Roman Church, commonly called the Apostles'. The first is that which was drawn up at Nice on the basis of the Creed of Cæsarea by Eusebius. Large additions were made to it at Nice to define the full Deity of the Son, and it concluded with anathemas on all who pronounced the Son to be of a different hypostasis from the Father. Another creed much resembling this, but with extensive additions at the close, and with the omission of the anathemas, was said to be drawn up at Constantinople, but was first proclaimed at the Council of Chalcedon. The only addition to this made by the West was the addition of the *Filioque* clause, emphasising the double procession of the Holy Ghost. The shorter creed of the Roman Church came to be called the Apostles' Creed from its originally consisting of twelve clauses, to which each of the apostles threw in one, hence it was a *συμβολή* for *σύμβολον.* It was successively enlarged. First was added the "remission of sins," next a "life eternal;" then came the "resurrection of the flesh," which we have rightly softened down to "of the body;" and lastly, the "descent into hell" and the "communion of saints." This, then, is the Catholic faith. All beyond deserves the name of afterthought. Now, it is observable that this creed, whether in its Eastern or Western form, leaves out of view altogether such questions as the necessity of episcopal succession, of the origin and use of sacraments, the honour due to the Virgin Mary, inspiration, predestination, and other articles which bulk large in the later Confessions of the Reformed Churches.

How are we to account for this? Either we must close the door, and so shut out both the errors of later times with the defences and replies to these errors, or we must open the door, and so admit that the draft of the faith by Catholic antiquity was incomplete. A door, as the French say, must be open or closed. It will never do to admit some and reject others. The Roman Church consistently admits development. The Immaculate Conception and Papal Infallibility were pious opinions as late as a quarter of a century ago. Now they are dogmas which we dare not question if we are to accept the Roman obedience. On the other hand, if we close the door and take our stand on the one Catholic draft of doctrine as contained in the two historical creeds, of which the *Quicunque vult* is confessedly only an expansion, we have to shut out as mere afterthoughts the whole of sacramental theology on the one hand, as we do the distinctive teachings of later ages, as the atonement, its extent and application, and also of the Bible and its authority.

It is clear, then, there is a wide room for this question of afterthoughts. We are forced to ask ourselves, Was the first draft of the faith, as summarised in the two creeds of the East and West, sufficient and precise, or did it slur over intentionally those questions which strike us in this day as all-important, both as to the means of grace and whether certain sacramental channels are essential? Or, on the other hand, were these creeds mere provisional summaries—a compendium of theology good enough for these days, but requiring to be largely supplemented by the maturer thought of later ages? To this test of afterthoughts we now turn.

It certainly seems as if East and West, Greek and Latin theology, had diverged from early times. It is an old remark that the Roman took a practical view of life, the Greek the speculative; the one, therefore, developed anthropology, the other kept to theology proper. This is so true that we have nothing to add to it. But if so, how is it that the creeds of the East and West (for we assume the Epistles is the Latin draft of the creed) are both alike objective and historical, and pass on one side all that we now regard as the "way of salvation" theology? The very term "grace" is not so much as named in any of the creeds. It certainly seems that we are here on the track of these "afterthoughts." To a simple faith, sin and the Saviour are not two experiences, but one. Salvation and the felt need of it grew up in one identical act. It is a flower with two stalks, and we cannot grow the one out of any other root than the other. But it may happen, as in Augustine's remarkable exceptional experience, that sin and striving with sin may go on for a long time without any felt need of a Saviour, any perception of a remedy outside our own will to repent. The result is that Augustine's experience became a kind of bed of Procrustes on which theology was laid. Sin was set forth as a single truth breaking up into original and actual sin, with all their endless ramifications, by-ends of controversy, and disputed issues, so that men in discussing sin lost hold of salvation, and had to pick it up afterwards almost as a distinct subject. This lingering long in the forecourts of sin was not only experimentally hurtful to Augustine afterwards, for repented sin leaves something more than an outward scar, it "petrifies the feeling," as Burns calls it; but the mischief lay deeper for the Church at large. It led to the development of an elaborate hamartiology and soteriology, which, so far from fitting in together and being coextensive, were set each under separate headships of a first and second Adam. What misery this has wrought, what heart-searching as to the coextensiveness or not of sin and salvation, none can say till the last day. The *durus pater infantum* had doomed all to perdition alike; as an Amalek of old, the doom fell on old and young, infant and suckling. This was chapter one; then came chapter two, when out of the doomed race an elect remnant was spared, though whether by electing grace or the action of our will, or both combined, this was left open, on which theology might wander in endless mazes lost. These are the afterthoughts, as we have already seen and stated. They all date from Augustine, and stand and fall with his teaching. But they are uncatholic, or at least post-catholic, as not contained, explicitly at least, in any of the creeds; and for this reason, when we appeal to antiquity, we are on safe ground in saying this old theology of Augustine is not old enough for us, who do not desire to go behind or beyond the teaching of the great creeds of the teneted East and West.

Another simple test of the truth or error of afterthoughts in theology is this—How would it fare with them, had God, as we may trust is the case, more light to break out of His word, the hidden gospel, for instance, of the larger hope? Tested in this way, we see at once what are and what are not afterthoughts. Let us glance at the outlines of the popular creed, and see what would stand this test and what would go off in a mist of words like the baseless fabric of a vision. Seen in the light of the larger hope, or of æons of education beyond, such a doctrine as that of the Trinity remains unaffected. Athanasianism would stand when the overhanging edifice of Augustinianism is shaken to its foundations. The dogmatic afterthoughts of the East, such as wander away into Eutychian and Nestorian errors right hand and left, which neutralise each other, they are left far behind. Dearly has the East paid the penalty for afterthoughts of this kind, which brought in the flood of Mohammedanism and swept them all away. Deism avenged itself for these misreadings of the mystery of the Incarnation, by having none of them, and shutting the whole East up for centuries into little Monophysite or Nestorian sects too insignificant for the general historian even to record their existence. To the ecclesiastical antiquarian they are interesting, as all relics of the past are and must be. But to the progressive mind, which asks what the Christianity of the future will be when the Euphrates is dried up and the Moslem heresy, based on bare Deism, has lost its power, the problem is quite obscure. But in any case, as we have said, the East will have less to cast off than the West when she shakes herself from her sleep of centuries, awakes like the seven sleepers of Antioch in the legend, and descends from her cave of dry, out-of-date dogmatism, to be greeted again with the word, "We are all Christians here."

But in the West it will be otherwise, where Augustinianism in one form or other covers the whole ground of orthodoxy. Sad to say it, but much which now passes for sound Catholic doctrine will then be found strangely uncatholic and sectarian. Much, on the other hand, which passes in the cant of the day as "painfully humanitarian," will be found to be as theological as it is humane—

> "Thou seemest human and Divine,
> The highest, holiest manhood thou."

Tested in this way, we have to ask which of our current theologies will stand and which will pass away. It was one of Burke's wisest sayings, that to find out what the young men are thinking of,—the young men who will make public opinion a decade or two hence,—this is the secret of political prophecy. We know what young Oxford was thinking of in the forties, and so in the seventies and eighties we had it full blown in Anglicanism, based, it is true, on unquestioned acceptance of Augustinianism and its conclusions. But the young Oxford of our day is again dreaming dreams and seeing visions; but they are very unlike those out of which the Tract party sprang up, under leaders so venerated that the name of one is given to a large and flourishing young college, and the name of another to a theological house or hostelry, which has shown hospitality sometimes to tendencies not quite in harmony with those of its patron saint. Stern and unbending orthodoxy is sometimes like stern and unbending Toryism, subject to strange reactions. Enough of this—the theology of the future, liberating itself on the side of eschatology from the cramping creeds of the past, will emerge as the mountaineer, who gets above crag and forest into an upper air where the survey will be as wide as surprising. He will still see, but far below his feet, the village which he left, with its tinkling chapel bell; and the only thunder which he will hear will be the voice of God in the awful avalanche. But what of that? for beyond him is Italy. He is passing out of one zone into another; soon will he change his climate and breathe larger, freer air. Such is the contrast between old and new in theology which we are entering on in our day, and the question for the educated man to ask and answer is, What baggage of the past is he to carry with him? Is he to descend into Italy, so to speak, a simple crag-climber, with axe and knapsack only; or is he to pass like a Hannibal or a Napoleon, carrying an army with him, and prepared to roll into one again the whole of Gaul, trans-Alpine and cis-Alpine? This, to put it shortly, is what the theology of the near future has to settle with itself; and it has shuffled off coming to a decision far too long. The Protestant sects, it is true, who make short work with the past, and laugh at the law of continuity, have settled it in their own rough-and-ready fashion. What is East or West, Athanasius or Augustine, to them? If these worthies of the past agree with them in their version of the Bible, so much the better for these worthies. For this reason, Calvin, finding Calvinism in Augustine, as Luther found Lutheranism, agreed to extol Augustine, and set him on a plane apart from all other patristic authorities; and this not because they wanted help from the Fathers, as a Jewell or a Hooker might have done, but because they were pleased to find one at least of the Fathers who had not gone down into the general apostasy. This, it is needless to add, is the tone of popular Protestantism to this day. It wants no side light from antiquity, it makes no account of this principle of continuity. But we of the English Church, who pride ourselves that we are neither

Philistines nor Pharisees, like the mere sects, have to ask what baggage of the past we shall take with us into the theology of the future. We have already pointed out what that is. We must go to the East rather than the West for the pattern of a theology in harmony with the *Zeitgeist* of the future. Even in the East we must stop short with Athanasius, last of the Fathers. He had not sunk into a stupid contempt for philosophy. It was the true pædagogy of the Greeks, as Moses was of the covenant people. The law of continuity compels us to make a breach somewhere, and to decide what to take over and what not. Even the judicious Hooker (or judicial rather, if we were to assign him his true epithet) hints, as much as he dared do in his day of dominant Calvinism, that the yoke of Augustine was too heavy for some to bear. "The heresy of freewill," he observes in his sermon on Justification, "was a millstone about the Pelagian's neck; shall we give, therefore, sentence of death inevitable against all those Fathers in the Greek Church which, being mis-persuaded, died in the error of freewill?" To the same effect is the oft-quoted saying of Jeremy Taylor: "Original sin, as it is at this day commonly explicated, was not the doctrine of the primitive Church; but when Pelagius had puddled the stream, St. Austin was so angry that he stamped and disturbed it more. And truly I do think that the gentlemen that urged against me St. Austin's opinion, do not well consider that I profess myself to follow those Fathers who were before him, and whom I forsake, as I do him, in the question."[1]

The testimony of these two eminent men, which we could easily enlarge if we cared for catenary authority, points to the real root of bitterness in the old orthodoxy, its strange theory of birth sin, its distortion of the

[1] Jeremy Taylor's Works, vol. ix. p. 396.

doctrine of heredity by inclusion of an innocent posterity in certain consequences which the conscience refuses to see are moral, and which, therefore, stamp the whole Augustinian system as non-moral. Forensic and federal, they are mere phrases, the flags under which Luther and Calvin led their followers; but the intelligent thought of Germany has rejected the one as Switzerland has the other. And so the age as a whole is non-theological; not because indifferent to these subjects, as is commonly said, but because theologians have not carried out the sifting process carefully enough, and thoroughly gone through doctrine by doctrine, as the tribe of Judah was taken man by man until the son of Zerah was taken, and with him was found the strange garment on the floor of his tent. Then it will be seen that a doctrine which lands us in inconsistencies such as these, that we are free and not free, responsible for our sin yet not responsible, free to do evil but not free to do good, with an inability, as some call it, which we can deepen down till it becomes a disability,—such contrarieties as these carry their own sentence. They are darkening counsel without knowledge.

The third test of these afterthoughts of theology is that they betray their origin. They spring up in the metaphysical stage of thought, when the mind mistakes its notions of things for the things themselves. Intruding into things not seen, assertions and explanations of matters which lie behind the veil and beyond the record, queries about quiddities only existing in the scholastic brain, and a general curiosity, half-feminine like that of Queen Caroline, to know the why of the why,—this is the true note of the afterthinker in theology. The problem of evil, its origin and ultimate destiny, is just such a subject as suggests itself to this half-trained thinker, impatient of the limitations of mind and the conditions of thought itself. The curse of theology has been, that it has too often turned adjectives into nouns, and made the names or qualities of things identical with the things themselves. To some extent this delusion, this fetishism of mind, has been dispelled by science; it lingers on in theology only. Who now speaks any longer of colour as an entity? The rose is red and the violet blue by some entity of redness and blueness when science was in the metaphysical stage. We now know, so far from a quality inherent in matter, colour is only the result of the action of light on certain bodies, whereby (and here lies the mystery) they absorb some and reject others of the rays of the spectrum. It was not till long after the decomposition of light by Newton that this simple account of it dawned on the scientific mind. That colour is the rejected and residual matter of sunbeams, not some inherent property of matter, clears off at once a whole class of entities which lay like rubbish in the path of science.

May it not be so in theology? It has not purged itself of so much metaphysics, which make up three-fourths of its afterthoughts. Evil is the same unsolved problem to the theologian which colour was to the physicist till the early years of this century. We set out with assuming the existence of evil as an entity, or at least a quiddity, a quality inherent, that is, in certain moral agents. Then we go on to ask its origin, and never leave off till we have settled to our own satisfaction some theory of its final absorption or extinction. The fine lines of Milton well indicate this personification of evil—

> "But evil on itself shall back recoil,
> And mix no more with goodness, when at last,
> Gathered like scum and settled to itself,
> It shall be in eternal restless change
> Self-fed and self-consumed."

We at once cut our way out of this forest, pathless as that in which the lady of Comus was lost, when we refuse to speak of evil at all as an entity, and go on personifying abstractions, as Milton does sin and death. Sin is, like death, a mere condition or relation of a moral agent to himself and others. Just as colour is only a modification of light, the rejected rays of certain absorbent but non-luminous bodies, so evil is the result of the action or rather repulsion of God's light on certain of His moral agents. Sin, the apostle is careful to explain, can only exist where law enters; where there is no law there is no sin. Sin, in a word, is the result of law, which is like light meeting that which is repulsive to it in our lower animal desires, and so are formed what we call the colours of good and evil. All the shades and hues in the world of right and wrong, the myriad twisted beams of conduct up and down the moral scale, from the savage to the saint, are only the action and reaction of law and desire, flesh and spirit, on each other. Evil would cease and disappear if either of the two conditions which keep man midway between an angel and an animal were to cease. He would subside into the brute, and so sink below moral evil, if the law ceased to be the ox-goad of conscience, and he found it hard to kick against the pricks. He would rise above moral evil if there were no flesh, and so no evil desires betraying him into secret rebellion against good.

Such, then, is man, a pendulum between two opposite tendencies; and the good that he allows, and the evil which he allows not, but yields to, are only like colours, not light itself so much as light resisted and rejected. Character, we admit, is thus made; and the possibility of the formation of character, and so of its perpetuity in some fixed type of good and evil, as long as the mind endures, so stamped with a character or quality of its own, this is as far as we can go and need go. But theology, in its afterthoughts, has gone much farther. It has dealt with character as with colour, as a quality inherent, *per se*, in moral agents, and thus has been led to draw out the horizon with the eternity, or at least the possible eternity, of evil much farther than the safe warrant of Scripture allows. This it does, on the assumption of the indelibility of the hues of moral good and evil—an assumption which, as we have seen in the case of colour, is pre-scientific, and of the metaphysical age of thought. Any gardener will show us how we may turn and twist the hues of plants, and so condition the colour receptivity of flowers that they may absorb rays they once rejected, and reject others which they once absorbed. Are we to say less of human nature under a heavenly gardener? Unless we fall back on the sullen theory of reprobation, and forget that it is not the will of our heavenly Father that one of these little ones should perish, we fail to see the meaning of these gloomy hues in which the old school in their helplessness paint the perpetuity of evil. It is pitiable to hear that he that is filthy must be filthy still, and so forth; because, forsooth, as we know is the case, there is no self-remedial power in human nature. It may be ever so true that the Ethiopian cannot change his skin, or the leopard his spots; but who ever said that it was so, or that the remedy lay in ourselves? There is no self-adjustment in the plant to change its environment, and so make white roses blush into red. But red roses are as much the skill of the gardener as white; and the whole question of man's hereafter really turns at this point, where theology shows its little faith in the fatherly character of God and His educational purposes with regard to the race as a whole. It is the question, Is God the heavenly husbandman or not? does He purge all His plants that they may bring forth more fruit? and, lastly,—a truth by no means to be blinked,—does He turn the vine stocks which bear no fruit into fuel, and burn them up with an everlasting burning?

These are issues which dogmatic particularism as much as dogmatic universalism has never looked square in the face. Butler's gloomy ratiocinations, that possibly evil may be as much the eternal order of things, hereafter, as it is at present, rests on a basis of mere naturalism, the legitimate outcome of which is atheistic pessimism of the Schopenhauer type. In Butler, it certainly seems as if there was a defective sense of the all-goodness of God, an unevangelical taint from the age of Deism, which he so recoiled against, but yielded to, partly from constitutional melancholy, to which he was the same victim as Gray and Cowper, but principally from his lack of spiritual sunshine. Had he basked more in the beams of Christ's victory over death and sin; had he seen the headship of Christ over humanity, and His purpose of gathering all in Christ,—he could never have looked on the problem of good and evil in the pessimist light which he has done. Turning his eyes on the gloom of abounding wickedness, and seeing no remedy in or around, here or hereafter, he breaks out into almost despairing language (*Analogy*, Pt. II. chap. v.) on the inability of sin to bring forth aught but retribution, which, as he wisely cautions us, is not so much arbitrary on God's part as inherent in the nature of evil itself. This is very true; but it is only one side of the truth, the unevangelical side of the problem. Were there no Father to send the Son to seek and to save that which is lost "till He find it," we should echo this *de profundis* of the melancholy Butler as to evil abounding.

But to a Paul, who sees that sin abounds only that grace may much more abound, the universe presents a wholly different aspect. Butler is the November, in a word, of an age dying under Deism. Wesley is that world just awakening out of its January sleep; and we, in our day, with the gospel of a larger hope in our hands, may lift up our eyes and see that summer is nigh.

Let us then get beyond these afterthoughts of theology as to the personality of evil, or, which is the same thing, its inherence in fallen beings as a quality inherent and inseparable from them as such. Augustinianism, with its Manichean conceptions of matter and its inherent evil, laid the train which afterthinkers down to our day have fired. Evil may be, probably is, only good in the making, the potter's vessel marred on the wheel; the true moral from Jeremiah's much misunderstood metaphor is not that the potter preserves these marred specimens as tokens of his failure, proofs that he is but a "'prentice han'." To argue so of the All-wise, All-good, sounds like flat blasphemy, though men do not mean it so, merely because they repeat phrases the meaning of which they have not rung out. What the potter does, is to render back the unbaked clay, when marred on the wheel, into the lump again, then to turn it a second, perhaps a third time on the wheel; and then only, when at last it is a vessel unto honour, and worthy of the potter's skill, is it put into the fire and baked for final use. The inference from that sadly misunderstood phrase in the Romans, so far from leading up to Augustinian particularism, opens the door the other way. To understand it, we must go on to the 11th chapter, where Israel's blindness is seen to be blindness in part, and not judicial or final; so that when this partial blindness is taken away, Israel shall be restored, the fulness of the Gentiles brought in; and the apostle concludes with the adoring exclamation, very unlike the gospel of particularism, "Oh the depth of the goodness and riches of God!"

The late Dr. Hatch, whose early loss Oxford still regrets, remarks on this subject in the Hibbert Lectures of 1888, that "the afterthoughts of theology may all be traced up to these two sources. First, the tendency of the Greek mind to transform belief, or the simple trust in God, into an intellectual conception. It is requisite that a man should define his beliefs; that it is as necessary that a man should be able to say, with as minute exactness, what he means by God, as that he should say, 'I believe in God.' It is purely philosophical. A philosopher cannot be satisfied with analysed ideas."

"The second conception comes rather from politics than from philosophy. It is the belief in a majority of a meeting. It is the conception that the definitions and interpretations of primary beliefs, which are made by the majority of Church officers assembled under certain conditions, are in all cases and so certainly true, that the duty of the individual is not to endeavour, by whatever light of nature or whatever illumination of the Holy Spirit may be given him, to understand them, but to acquiesce in the verdict of the majority. The theory assumes that God never speaks to men except through the voice of the majority. It is a large assumption. It is a transference to the transcendental sphere, in which the highest conceptions of the Divine nature move, of what is a convenient practical rule for conducting the business of human society. Let the majority decide. I do not say that it is untrue, or that it has not some arguments in its favour; but I do venture to point out that the fact of its being an assumption, must at least be recognised."

These two misconceptions of the essence of religion, the one removing it from the region of the affections to that of the intellect, the other from the private conscience to the public decision of the Church in council sitting, go far to explain all that we mean by afterthoughts in theology. Dr. Hatch has here, correctly enough, diagnosed one of the errors of later theology as arising out of the super-subtle love of the Greek intellect for definitions to put in the place of faith in a living God. But he has failed, as we think, in tracing all the evils of dogmatic theology to Greek character. The second defect of dogmatism, by the right of the majority to rule and bear down the dictates of private conscience, is much more Roman than Greek. Greece fell to pieces much more through anarchy than over-centralisation; and the earliest Churches, because Greek, were, like the Corinthian, much more in danger of that extreme than the other. It was Rome, on the other hand, which took up the regulative magisterial view of religion, and *Roma locuta est* was soon—much sooner the note in the West than it ever was in the East. Greek theology, it is true, fell under the oppressive yoke of Byzantinism; but this was because old Rome had migrated to Byzantium, and carried with her her methods "in Church and State." With this important qualification, there is much in Dr. Hatch's theory which we can accept and agree with.

As an illustration of the "all or nothing" style of reasoning in which the dogmatic deductive school of divines argue, the following extract from one of the ablest preachers of that type will suffice. The late Dr. Liddon, in a sermon on "the Justification of Wisdom," observes truly enough, that when men now-a-days reject Christianity, they reject it, as a rule, bit by bit. "A single truth, say the grace of baptism, or the atoning value of our Lord's death, or the transmission of original sin, or the union of our Lord's two natures in one Person, or the eternal punishment of the lost, is supposed to present insurmountable difficulties. What always or almost always happens is, that the truth is detached from the general body of Christian doctrine; it is treated as a thing complete in itself, having no necessary relations with other truths; it is taken to pieces; it is then, from whatever reason, pronounced incredible. And what wonder? It is subjected to a strain which it was never meant to bear; it is placed under conditions which, except in the mind of its critic and rejecter, do not anywhere belong to it. Most assuredly the truths of the Christian creed are not, and may not be treated as these detached isolated atoms. They are parts of a great whole. They shade off one into another by almost imperceptible gradations. They are linked one to another by common underlying principles, by love of contrast or love of correspondence; they are just as much a whole as is the world of physical nature, only, of course, an infinitely grander and more overwhelming whole; and the Eternal Wisdom, whose mind they are and on whom they harmonise, reaches across them from end to end, mightily and smoothly and sweetly ordereth all things." Much of this we can heartily go with, and honestly admire in its fervour of undimmed faith in the gospel as a whole; but this analogy from physical science as a whole and the gospel scheme as a whole, is only true in so far as we say of both, as Butler does, that the scheme of nature is imperfectly understood as that of revelation. To turn round on all doubters, as Dr. Liddon does, and to charge them with bit by bit rejection of revelation, because Church dogmas, either as to infant baptism or eternal punishment, fail to convince,—this is that perilous type of dogmatism which only genders the very unbelief it declaims against. "Unfaith in aught is unfaith in all," is a line often quoted in this connection, but unfairly so. There is unfaith in moral character which is the root of jealousy, and works like madness in the brain; and we may harbour the same unfaith in God's perfect goodness, which makes us cry out, Shall not the judge of all the earth do right? For unfaith of that kind, the remedy lies, not in mere dogma, such as Dr. Liddon enumerates, but that display of the Divine goodness when, in the phrase of the old Book, God made all His goodness to pass before Moses.

By a singular coincidence, the Hulsean and Bampton lecturers for 1885–86 took up the subject of Augustinian and Alexandrian theology respectively. Their treatment of these two widely constrasted schools of thought was fair and impartial, and nothing was left unsaid on either side to set forth the distinctive merits and defects of the great Father of the West by the Hulsean lecturer, and of the two great heads of the catechetical school of Alexandria by the Bampton lecturer. What we were disappointed with in not meeting in both cases, was a discussion of the causes which led to the almost entire effacement of the Alexandrian type of theology even in its native home, the East, while the Augustinian reigned without a rival through the entire West almost down to our own day. To understand the cause of this eclipse of Clement and Origen, and this one-sided Augustinianism of the West, we must bear in mind that to the practical Roman intellect, to the still ruder intelligence of the barbarians who succeeded, the Greek type of thought was as strange as its tongue. The Latins neither knew that nearly perfect vehicle of expression, the Greek tongue, nor the thoughts which eirculated by means of it. They had a profound distrust of philosophy, especially of Platonism, and never forgot that the so-called orthodoxy of Clement and Origen was only Gnosticism thinly disguised. Clement professed to teach what the true Gnostic was in contrast with the pretended. This alone was enough to excite suspicion, which Origen's conjectures on the stars and their inhabitants certainly did nothing to allay.

What is desired, then, is a thorough-going criticism of the contrasts between Greek and Latin theology as a whole. As monographs on the subject of Clement and Origen on the one hand, and of Augustine on the other, these volumes are full of instruction; but we want more than a monograph, we desire to see East and West set side by side, and the merits of each fairly and fully set forth. A thorough-going criticism of that kind is still a want of the day.

The usual defences of Augustine move on the same lines as those which make out in the same way that Luther was no Lutheran, Calvin no Calvinist, and which only amount to Wilkes' impudent saying, "Your Majesty, I am no Wilkite." *Un sot trouve toujours un plus sot qui l'admire,* is as true of wisdom as of folly, of saints as of sages. Imitation, which is the sincerest form of flattery, never stops till it lands the followers of some great man in an absurdity which he would have been the first to expose. But it still remains the case, error has its germinant force as well as truth; nay, if *humanum est errare* have any meaning, truth genders error much more readily than error ever winds back up to truth. For this reason, too, Augustinianism prevailed in spite of its forbidding aspect to the outside mass of men, that it fell in with the prevailing terrorism of the times when Rome was rocking to ruins, and men crowded into the Church to escape the fate of a perishing age and generation. A century before, a nobler, more disinterested view of the Church prevailed. It was then regarded as the *cœtus fidelium,* but there, as Bigg remarks—

"Probably Luther, whose passionate phrase, *Origenem jam dudum diris devovi,* is one of many which lie heavy on the great Reformer's fame, is the only man of eminence that ever spoke of Origen in language like this; though the Augustinian divines of the sixteenth and seventeenth century were scarcely more just to the great Alexandrine than were the *Græculi* of the Lower Empire. Even Methodius, even Theophilus, were diligent students of his books. Augustine, Bede, Bernard, respect the memory of one with whom they had little in common but learning and greatness of soul. Origen's name has been a kind of tombstone. There has been no truly great man in the Church who did not love him a little. Let us add to this Erasmus' testimony: 'Plus me docet Christianæ philosophiæ unica Origenis pagina quam decem Augustini.'"[1]

[1] Bigg, p. 279.

EPILOGUE.

Two theories, that of evolution and that of the education of the human race, are so entirely master of the field, that to attempt to disturb them by calling in a third and rival theory would seem presumptuous. The two amount to much the same thing. Lessing's education theory is the older of the two: it is historical, and has even a certain Biblical ring about it; at least it falls in with the Pauline conception of the long minority of the race under the law, when we were under tutors and governors. But the evolution theory of Darwin has at last thrown Lessing's conception of education into the shade. In a sense we may say we are all evolutionists now. If there are any who cling to the old-world conception of special creation, and of that as spread out over six successive stages or days, they so modify their mode of stating it that it shall not conflict, in name at least, with the new notion of the advance of lower forms into higher by some internal force which we may describe as evolution. Between day and day, or stage and stage, there is no longer supposed to be a gap of time. The old Hebrew metaphor, "and it was evening and it was morning," as if God had left off at night time, and the work stood still till next morning, when a fresh creative start began, this is now regarded as too anthropomorphic. Creation is admitted to be continuous. There are no pauses—no gaps to fill up; and though Darwin and his school admit that they have not in every case found the missing link, they have no doubt that it has existed, and the theory stands unshaken although complete verification in all its details is at present not forthcoming.

But the evolutionists overlook the fact that Nature has other aspects besides that of orderly growth upward. She has a record of degeneracy—of type fixed only to relapse back to some more primitive type—of differentiation done and then undone, as if the standard were too high, too artificial, to endure under the strain and stress of actual life.

If this is so of pigeon-breeding, need we wonder that it is so in a still more marked degree of human nature. Once or twice in history has a small community like Athens, Rome, Carthage, and one or two centres of culture, reached a pitch of refinement at which it was unable long to maintain itself. The standard was too high, the ideal too noble for human nature's daily food, and so it sank back exhausted after its first effort. Hybridity is the fate which overtakes any variety of plant or animal too highly trained. It comes up, and is cut down like a flower, and never continueth in one stay. Evolution, then, without degeneracy is only a half truth; and his followers, more Darwinian than Darwin, who harp on the one note of perpetual progress, find themselves confronted with awkward facts which they can neither explain nor explain away.

But to those who have no special theory to sustain, this degeneracy of higher types into lower is only what we might expect. The better sinks back into the worse much sooner than the worse rises up into the better; *humanum est errare.* Not truth, but guesses at truth, error and imperfect conjecture, and fiction or false theory, that mixture of a lie which ever delights mankind,—this is the sad heritage of us cave-dwellers, who, as in Plato's grand myth, catch only the distorted images of things on our prison walls, and mistake these idols for the realities beyond. This being so, what can we expect but that men's afterthoughts soon take the place of the first thoughts of God in the case especially of such a sublime revelation as that of Jesus Christ. It could, at best, come to us under the guise of symbols and parables, for we are but broken lights, and our little systems have their day, and cease to be. As long as we recognise this, and in all humility admit that it is so, no harm can come from our little systems. If "little," they are no more heady than a little learning is, as long as we do not fall into the conceit that it is anything more than a shallow draft, and that drinking deeper will sober us again.

This is the true lesson of Church history. It seems destined to pass through these three stages, two of which are over, and the third and last we are only entering on since the law of the limitation of our faculties has been better understood. The hint on this subject which Locke threw out, which Kant afterwards formulated, and Sir W. Hamilton finally began to build up, a new philosophy based on the law of relativity,—this is now accepted everywhere. We have only to name this law of the limitation of our faculties, and the whole of Augustinianism is seen to be a sand-heap thrown up by children playing on the shore, while beyond are the mighty waters rolling evermore. To demolish these dogmas of predestination with limited salvation of the elect alone, is to take them for what they are not. They may be left to time, and the next tide, which is already fast rising, will sweep away this scholastic theology.

We are entering, as we have seen, on the third and

last age of Church history. The primitive age of *Didaché* held its ground till the Alexandrian school of catechists had to yield before the deepening need for an organised Church under a hierarchy, and falling back on general councils as a high court of appeal. This was the œcumenical or Catholic consent stage of Church history, which under serious limitations, arising from the revolt of Protestantism, has come down almost to our day. But modern thought since Descartes' day has made a breach in this Church continuity theory. Men were called on for the first time by this father of modern thought to cease dogmatising, and to pause and answer one question, What is the Ego? The Cartesian answer, that the Ego lay in self-consciousness, did not quite go to the root of the difficulty; and down to Hegel's day, and since, the sphinx is ever at us repeating the same question, to which all the schools and sects of philosophy send back each its own reply. At last, however, Scotland and Germany is to select two names—only Kant and Hamilton have helped us to an answer which seems to spell finality to this tormenting sphinx question. It lies in the relativity of knowledge. All science is regarded only as so much reclaimed land, with the moorland of nescience lying beyond. We know in part, and the instant that we forget this and begin to dogmatise, the curtain drops, and we are again plunged in darkness. This is so in all departments of knowledge. In the sciences properly so called, details so crowd in on us that we cannot see the wood for the trees. We are oppressed by "specialism," and no museum will contain the multitude of "sub-orders" and varieties which advance on us like a plague of locusts,—none breaking their ranks,—so that even to catalogue them is more than science can attempt.

But it is when we turn to the science of sciences, the knowledge of God and of our eternal state, that the mind sinks under the sense of its own limitations. Here our faculty of "comprehension" soon finds itself comprehended, and we have to reverse the usual order of mathesis, a science which is itself to know, and then to know that we know. In Divine things we can only apprehend that of which we are apprehended. Here the Gnostic and the Agnostic stand face to face; and the one apparently has as good right as the other in this sacred precinct, where both seem intruders. At every turn our knowledge of Divine things is met by mystery. The veil of Isis is on theology, and the Agnostic scornfully asks, Do we intend to tear off the veil, and to forecast from the life here what the life beyond the veil can be? For these reasons the old worn-out dogmatism of the Church's childhood is so out of date that it is a pity to disturb it. To write out a set of anti-Augustinism teachings, would imply that we feared that the African doctor was more than half right. The day has gone by for replies of that kind. Are we, then, to leave the ancient traditionalism of Catholic consent undisturbed, as the old orthodox ask us to do, and pass it off on the age as a good and safe "regulative theology"? We might do so but for the growing demand for some readjustment of the old claims of reason and faith. If "faith" would only confine itself to what is purely spiritual and subjective, on the lines of immutable morality and intuitional theology, we should have an easy task to reconcile the two. The conflict of ages would come to an end, and the age of apologetics pass away with the need for defences of a truth seen and felt to be true by its own inherent self-evidence.

But we are far from that consummation at present, and have still to ask, What can be the end of these afterthoughts? What is to replace them when they are seen to be out of date, when we are on the look-out for something to set up in their stead? Here the old French saying, that first and third thoughts are of God, but second thoughts of the devil, may throw some light on what we are seeking after. It may be that our third thoughts, the after of afterthoughts, may bring us back to first thoughts, and to that primitive type of *Didaché* which was before dogma, as it is bound to live after the second dogmatic stage of Church history is past. Too long have utilitarian ethics and prudential soul-saving theology lived on together, and lent each other a helping hand. The builders of afterthoughts of this kind reared a theological Babel, earliest type of confusion, where they took bricks for stone and slime for mortar. What utilitarianism produced in the hands of a cunning workman like Paley, this university knows only too well. Theology of that type, backed up by a system of rewards and punishments, made it worth the while of the self-regarding eudæmonist to serve God, who would send him to hell if he did not, and who kept in store the glories of heaven with which to reward His followers. Had this account of the gospel scheme come from some scoffing Celsus or Lucian, desirous to hold it up to ridicule, we should have refused to reply to it. But that this came in perfect good faith from the clearest and most candid of thinkers, the ornament in his day of this university, enables us to measure the depths to which unspiritual orthodoxy had descended in the days of our grandfathers. Happily this reward and punishment theology has passed away with that hangman's code, the vindictive jurisprudence of the past, of which, perhaps, it was the consistent outcome. The hanging code and the theology of terrorism, which failed even to terrify, much less to deter, have both had their day. As Sir H. Maine remarks, we have outgrown the state of society which regarded terror as its one instrument for the repression of crime. Consistently enough, terrorism here and hereafter lived and died together. They were born of the same brood of hard evil thoughts concerning the All-good, and, like other unconscious blasphemies of men against the Son of man, they are now forgiven for the Son of man's sake. They were at least not sins against the Holy Ghost, since many of these worthies in law and theology seem not so much as to have heard whether there was any Holy Ghost. What a spiritual religion becomes when it passes into unspiritual hands, and living doctrine is fossilised into dry dogma, we have only to turn to Church history to see by many and repeated examples.

Let us hope, then, that the last or third thoughts of theology will suggest some corrective to the worst effects of those afterthoughts or second thoughts, which are in most cases not best, but worst. On this subject a remark of the venerated Charles Simeon deserves notice. It raises him in our esteem, and it shows how far removed he was from that narrow standpoint of the merely orthodox divine, that *ne quid nimis* temper of dull moderatism, which, professing to strike the golden mean, ends in touching only that of a leaden mediocrity. Simeon held on other points besides the Calvinist and Arminian controversy, which was alive in his day as it is now long since dead, that the right way of dealing with certain questions was not on a *sic aut non*, but on a *sic et non*. He was disposed to say "Yes" and "No." So far from shrinking from extremes, he insisted on pushing every principle to its extreme conclusion, provided only he was at liberty to take up some opposite principle, and also drive it home in the same way. He held that the only reconciling point for truth was by letting warring shades of opinion say their last word, and when all were honestly taken up and laid down, we should arrive at last at a sound body of working sentiments. The errors, in a word, of some men are more helpful to us than the platitudes of those who venture little because they believe and love little. The fine song of Montrose—

> "He either fears his fate too much,
> Or his deserts are small,
> Who dares not put it to the touch,
> To gain or lose it all,"

is more than a mere cavalier's sentiment. There is in it this dashing cavalry charge way of thinking the root of something not far off from the mind of Christ. We have to cast ourselves into the waters, as Peter the disciple did more than once, if we would come to Christ; and if, beginning to sink, we raise the cry of little faith, "Lord, save me, I perish," the Master will be at our side, and His word will be, "It is I, be not afraid."

The afterthoughts of theology, then, are not to be corrected by simply recalling them, but by going on to discover the compensating truth of which they are at best but the first draft, rudely drawn and distorted by our fears. There is this to reassure us when our heart condemns us, that God is greater than our hearts, and knoweth all things. The Church has been narrow, distrustful of her Lord, and too ready to teach for doctrines the traditions of men. But what of that? We all know and deplore it, but we are coming to see that it could not be otherwise. The Church stepped into the derelict seat of the Empire, and took on her all the imperial airs of the old Roman world. She affected the *urbis et orbis* note of stand and deliver; and when this over-centralisation failed of its effect, she broke up, in the opposite extreme, into sectarianism and separateness, in which the old dogmatism repeated itself under conditions which made Geneva a kind of "little sister," or bad imitation of Rome, that Tityreus in the Eclogue describes his native Mantua—

> "Urbem quam dicunt Roman Melibœe putavi
> Stultus ego huic nostræ similem."

We have not yet lived down all this reaction, but we are coming on to a time when an accommodation will be possible. The two reactions—the first against Rome, and the second reaction of our day back into her arms as the one visible centre of unity—have both by this time nearly exhausted their strength. There are new forces in our day entering the field which promise to put a new complexion on old controversies, now nearly worn out. The science of comparative religion has sprung up in the wake of comparative philology; it may be said, indeed, to be its direct product. Both teach the same truth, and point to the same conclusion in a future not very far off. They point to a common spring out of which humanity arose in the past, and a common destiny to which it is tending in the future.

Comparative theology teaches much the same lesson as comparative philology. It points to a threefold stage of advance in our conception of God, corresponding to a threefold division of tongues—the Turanian, Semitic, and Aryan. The lowest types of ethnic religions, generally speaking, fall under the first category; they are gross, sensual, fetish forms of worship, and the only steps to their altar up to God are the generative symbols of the visible world. It is at this low stage of calf-worship that idolatry most signally fails as symbolism; it loses the spiritual in the sensual, and thus ends without bringing the worshipper into the presence-chamber of the Unseen and Eternal. The second stage upward is that attained by the Semitic races, to whom the vision was vouchsafed of a one absolute and supreme Ruler of the universe. This, the monotheistic stage of religion, roughly speaking, has adapted itself to that family of languages known as Semitic for reasons which it is not easy to explain. The necessary connection between Monotheism and the Semitic type of tongues is not as obvious as the partisans of the parallelism between theology and philology would have us suppose it is. Still less can we go with those who see in Christianity, as the reconciling point of nature-worship and Monotheism, the product of that higher type of culture which the Aryan races have advanced to in their spread over the world from East to West. Such generalisations as these, which make the growth of the religious sentiment co-ordinate with the development of language, from the mere agglutinative and monosyllabic stage of the Kalmuc on to the inflected and syntactical type of the educated European, are at least premature. But it is enough to say that there are three leading types of religious sentiment, more or less harmonising with the three great linguistic families of men. It is a dead lift out of Polytheism into Monotheism, as great as the passage from a Turanian to a Semitic type of speech. It is no less a dead lift for a stern Monotheist, who worships a transcendent Deity such as the El of the Hebrew, the Allah of the Moslem, to get on to that secret of the Incarnation of Deity who is immanent in the spirits of men, and who has shone out in all His glory in the one Son of man who was also Son of God.

If these three stages of comparative theology, corresponding to three stages of comparative philology, are ascertained to be correct, the inference is obvious, if we may assume progress under continuity to be the law of the evolution of man and the education of the race. We may expect Turanian types of thought to merge into Semitic, which again, in their turn, are to give way to that last generalisation of thought when the Author of nature is no longer adored as a transcendent Deity, but when the tabernacle of God is to be with men, and He is to dwell in them and they in Him. Not as yet has even Christendom, with the exception of a few saintly and mystical spirits, realised the deep meaning of its own dogma of the Incarnation. It is still regarded from outside: we see the hard shell of dogma which encloses it; not a few reject the shell because unaware of the precious kernel of universal truth which it contains. To say that a deistical age like last century should have lapsed into Unitarianism in all but a hollow lip profession, is to say only what we suppose must be the case. Supernaturalists accepted this and all other dogmas of their creed, but they never attempted to assimilate them. To the question, *Cur Deus homo?* they gave the Anselm answer, which only goes half-way, and breaks off exactly at the point where a real solution is craved for. If God became man merely for a purpose, *i.e.* to give worth to a sacrificial death, otherwise of insufficient value, to atone for all the sins of all men, we can well dismiss such a doctrine of the Incarnation as one of many possible plans of salvation. It may be true, but it certainly cannot be the whole truth. On the contrary, it is such a teaching as opens a door for explaining away, first the Atonement, then the Incarnation itself.

Dogmatic theology, as we have seen, failed to recognise that in Christianity there was something more than an advance on a monotheistic religion. Lessing's *Nathan the Wise,* with its story of three rings, all facsimile, Hebrew, Moslem, and Christian, being simply different versions of the same truth, was legitimate enough from the deistical standpoint at which Lessing stood in common with his age. But this age of Deism is over, and the Christ of history is seen to be the Pleroma, the fulness of Him who filleth all in all. There is not a single glimmer of truth, not a stray spark of God-given light, in any the oldest of the old ethnic faiths, which does not find its fulness in Christ. This is not mere eclecticism, which is a poor, shrivelled conception of the true glory of Christ, of Him who never breaks the bruised reed nor quenches the smoking flax. All voices, however, without meaning to us, are crying in the wilderness, "Prepare ye the way of the Lord." All sounds are preludes of a great concert, when the trees of the wood are to break forth into singing. What is more instructive still—monotheistic creeds never can understand polytheistic. They cannot assimilate them; their last word to them is negation, an abhorrence of idolatry. But spiritual Christianity has a wide sympathy for all. It is the true reconciling point, not only of these monotheistic faiths, in face of which God and nature stand apart in hopeless dualism. It also opens its wide heart of sympathy for the childish faiths of our forefathers who worshipped stocks and stones. "Whom ye ignorantly worship, Him declare I unto you." It lightly passes by their image-worship; it has no harsh word of iconoclasm to say against it, but fastens on the one symbol, the altar of earth with the inscription, "To some unknown Deity," and makes this the point of departure for the one new and true, because universal, religion.

The ultimate universalism of Christianity has, of course, been held from the beginning, but held in a sense in which it is very little in advance of Hebraism. To the true Jah every knee should bow, every tongue should swear. This somewhat narrow draft has been the hope of the Christian Church. Gentiles are to come, but only as proselytes, and through the gate of baptism, and so to enter the Church of the living God. So far the vision of God on these latter times has not been given horizons much wider than those of Isaiah and Ezekiel. But the seer of Patmos also, when rightly understood, has a vision of a city lying four square, and on each side three gates. Twelve gates thus lie open day and night, *i.e.* to the enlightened and to the ignorant, and open at all the points of the compass. There are north and east proselytes, and also those from the south and west. Every breeze that blows wafts some to these happy shores, where is the gathering of the nations, and where our contentions cease.

There is, then, a new theology to be born, which shall unify and absorb into itself all the contradictions of the old. The river of God has been parted into four heads, as it flows out of its early Eden, and they will never meet again till they meet in the all-embracing ocean. But we already discern where the meeting-point is to be. Hitherto missions have been conducted on mere proselytising and soul-saving lines. To gather heathen into the Church and to save their souls from hell, it is on these lines, and these alone, that missionaries, Roman and Protestant alike, have gone out up to the present. It is feared that any society which appealed on any other ground would receive small support from the home oracles of the religious world. But the ablest missionaries who are in the field see farther than their zealous but narrow supporters at home. They see that God fulfils Himself in many ways, and that the stages of genuine conversion are so many, that they spread over many generations. The education of the human race is the last thing in the world which can be hurried. If nature does nothing *per saltum*, how are we to expect the kingdom of heaven to grow in any other way than first the blade, then the ear, then the full corn in the ear? Thus a universal religion is slowly preparing, and of which we can barely trace the outline at present. For this reason, that some of the building is well above ground, while large parts of the temple of the living God in China and India is at present only to be seen by tracing its foundations. But as soon as India and the East has brought its treasure and riches into the New Jerusalem —as soon as a new Christendom has sprung up coextensive with the bounds of the now known and habitable earth—is it supposable that the old theology of that Augustinian Christendom, coextensive with the Roman Empire and reared out of the ruins of Rome, can be so enlarged and become so elastic as to contain the East and its faith philosophies? To name such a supposition is to answer it. "The bed is shorter than that a man can stretch himself on it, and the covering narrower than that he can wrap himself in it" (Isa. xxviii. 20).

What, then, follows but this, to which all our remarks lead up to—the theology of the future will be some grand amplification of the old theology, some fresh relaying its foundation verities, some embracing its scholastic and mediæval afterthoughts in a wider synthesis, out of which nothing essential is left out, but which contains a humanitarianism to which Augustinian theology in all its shapes is strangely unreceptive and unsympathetic to.

"Largior hic compos æther, et lumine æstit purpureo."

We shall breathe freely in those days under the sense of

recovery of two primitive verities, which the Church of Christ early lost hold of in her Atalanta race after the golden apple of greatness. We shall receive the sense of God's Fatherhood and of man's brotherhood. At present, not only do these two truths stand apart, but those who hold the one slight or disregard those who hold the other. The brotherhood of man has been till the other day a kind of dream on the part of the Rousseaus, Mazzinis, and others who, as humanitarians, stand far aloof from any conception of God corresponding to that of the God and Father of our Lord Jesus Christ. Yet, rightly regarded, the two are correlative, and consequent the one on the other. God is the Father of the human family only in so far as they stand in a new and filial relation to Him through the sacrifice of Christ. On the other hand, Jesus is the elder brother by whom we, the younger and outcast children, are brought back into the family of God. We need not here discuss that distinction, on which Scotch theology has laid so much stress of late, whether God is the Father of all men simply because all men are made in the image of God, or the Father of men because they have been brought into a new covenant relationship with Him, of which sonship is the test, by the redemption of His death. Virtually the two come to mean the same thing, since we are only redeemed because we are made in the image of God. The original sonship in creation and the adopted sonship of redemption both alike assume that there is a spiritual element in man which entitles us to say—"For we are also His offspring."

Theology, then, as soon as it begins to revolve on these two polar points, the Fatherhood of God and the brotherhood of men, will present itself in a new light to inquiring and candid minds that now stand outside the Church and aloof from religion. Socialism, as it is called, has generally shown itself extremely averse to positive religion in any of its dogmatic types. In vain the Churches try to woo and win the Socialists, and charm away their distrust of definite religion. Latterly, all the Churches without exception have strained their exclusiveness almost to breaking-point, in the hope that they might win those who hold the brotherhood of men into coupling this with the thought of the Fatherhood of God. This was the aim of the so-called Christian Socialists, who, in Germany at least, did not escape the charge of a certain sickly sentimentality. It was said that, disguise it as they might, they were after all suspected to be agents of the police, and employed to break up certain anarchic forms of combination by holding out counter attractions of a higher brotherhood and of a new Socialism. To put Christ at the head of the movement seemed to the artisan to be the same artifice as that of Richard II. offering to be their leader when the king of the mob, Jack Cade, had been felled to the ground by the mace of Lord Mayor Fitzwalter, turned into a battle-axe. But a better spirit is rapidly coming over both sides of the subject of this attitude of the Church to Socialism. No one is thought the worse of as a Christian for claiming to be a Socialist. On the other hand, the Socialist lecturer does not feel bound to rail at religion as the log across the stream of progress, damning the current, and compelling it to overflow its banks. This change for the better on both sides is a sign that the new theology is beginning to take the place of the old. We are on the eve of such a mighty change that we can only speak of it as the "regeneration" and the preparation for the second coming of the Son of man. Humanitarianism, in a sense undreamed of before, has entered in and is permeating our theology.

This was regarded at first as the entrance of an enemy. The Church having forgotten our Lord's humanity, and lapsed unconsciously, of course, into what was practical Patripassianism, the excluded truth entered in as a heresy at first, and only recovered its footing when the Church saw that it had forgotten one of the clauses of its own creed. The result of this awaking to a fresh study of Christ on the human side is seen not only in the success of such a book as *Ecce Homo*, with many inferior imitations, which follow it as the jackal the lion; it is seen in a desire to face fairly the difficulties of working men, not only as to the Bible, but also as to those class distinctions which have passed from the world into the Church, and so have lowered its ideal of our oneness in Christ.

As soon, then, as the standing quarrel between the Church and Socialism has been adjusted, as it seems likely to be in our day, we may be prepared for a new attitude of the masses towards Christianity, the effects of which no one can forecast, much less assign limits to. But it is no exaggeration to say that it will be as life from the dead to our sleeping Churches. It will lift us at once into a larger and purer air, where we shall rise above old outworn magisterial conceptions of God and separatist views of our fellow-man. It will be seen in the light of humanitarianism, that the old probation theory of man's destiny breaks down, and that the only key to the Divine dealings with man must be some education theory. Education, with eternity to work in, at once alters our whole standpoint; one after the other the old safeguards which the old theology brought in will be seen to be no safeguards at all. Their effect has been the exact opposite. Instead of keeping the sheep in the fold, it has tempted many to stray off to strange pastures, and hindered others from coming in who might have stood had they heard no other voice than that of the "Good Shepherd."

Hard theology, as it is known in New England, led, of course, in the reaction straight away to what, in their phrase, is called soft-shell theology. Let us hope that in this country, at least, where the door has never been closed to the hope of God's general Fatherhood by the remorseless logic of a theology improperly so called, we shall adopt without strife the theology of the future. Any theology deserving the name of a doctrine of God must exhibit a whole God in an entire Christ. There must be no passing, as if through a prism, of the white light of God's sevenfold perfection with some of the rays seen more refracted than others. This pencil of refracted rays, such as comes from writers on the attributes of the old school, like Charnock and others, must be produced no more. Unless in every case, and to all alike, God is represented as holy and just and good, we shall begin to doubt whether this is the light of God as it streams from heaven. Because the old school drew sharp lines of distinction between God in Christ and God out of Christ, casting the red wrath rays at one end of the spectrum on the non-elect, and the violet rays of colourless compassion on the predestinated, a reaction set in towards Universalism, which has been nearly as paralysing to sound scriptural faith as the original error from which it was a reaction. We must live all this down as we are doing. The second thoughts of theology, ending in themselves in blind negations such as we have glanced at, must be succeeded by those third thoughts which, as being lasting and final, can be said to be of God, as only first and third thoughts are.

This is the consummation we must lead up to; but the theology of the future sets us asking about the Church of the future. It seems to us a question whether the men of this age, with a few bright exceptions, are prepared to welcome either such a new Church and theology, at least, not in England. In Germany, where men of the type of Richard Rothe—to name only one—abound, and where the calm culture of the university type of man is the rule and not the exception, such an attitude of waiting for the kingdom of God is not uncommon. But Englishmen, who have the faults of their qualities, are prosaic in the same sense as the old Roman world was. They hold the captive East in fee, and excusably enough think that the political masters of India must give and not borrow from the East. We evangelise there and we educate, but schoolmaster and missionary, secular and spiritual alike, go out with a quiet sense of our own vast superiority, and with almost a spirit of condescension. We never suspect that the faith and philosophy of the West has something to learn from the East. It is a sense of the *Deus immanens* which will profoundly modify the *Deus transcendens* class of conceptions which have dominated the whole West: when this comes it will set the doctrine of the Incarnation in a new light. The conversion of the Jew is to be, in the language of the apostle, as life from the dead. But what is the stumbling-block to the Jew, as well as to the Moslem, but that hard, unbending type of Monotheism which, out of a sublime truth, has evolved a sterile negation which ends in itself? The gathering of the nations and the fulness of the Gentiles all point to the same result, when East and West shall flow together, and Jew and Gentile meet and mingle like rivers long parted. This is the consummation of all things; and when this blessed day of gladness and reunion of Christendom in one wide embrace and kiss of charity shall arrive, then, in the language of prophecy, there shall be new heavens and a new earth, or, to drop metaphor, a new Church to contain a new theology. It was mere self-will, unsupported by a general consensus of the best thoughts of the best minds, when Swedenborg in 1757 proclaimed that the new Church had descended like the Bride of the Apocalypse out of heaven adorned for her Bridegroom. But extravagant as the claim was, and unsupported by later evidence, this much must be said for it, that a new theology seems to call for a new Church as its witness and keeper. To Swedenborg, perhaps to others a century ago, the festering bodies of the Reformed and the Roman communion seemed, like the bodies of these two witnesses, to have lain in the streets of the great city, which spiritually is called Sodom and Egypt, where our Lord was crucified. It seemed to him the resurrection of these two witnesses could only mean the new theology which a new Church was raised up to proclaim. To a new doctrine there was to be attached a new discipline, and those who admit the one claim will not raise much difficulty as to the other.

Ægri somnia is all we can say of these dreams of Swedenborg. But the day is coming for the new theology and the new Church, but traced on wider, more world-embracing lines than the ingenious Swede, who himself was before his time, ever dreamed of. Men are wearying in all directions of those provincialisms which shut men up in political units called the State, and of those theological departments called the Church, with their several concordats or alliances, offensive and defensive. The Ultramontane ideal of a Church supreme, with the civil power as its deputy, has had its day and ceased to be. It can never return. The new ideal which Rothe ended his days in groping after, was some perfectionised civil polity into which the Church should merge. It was the old

Ultramontane turned inside out, a type of Erastianism *in excelsis.* We only glance at it here to indicate the tendencies of modern thought. They are all towards some new generalisation which shall assimilate all that is good in the old, leaving only the dross behind. In science we are wearying of specialisms. Too much detail is turning men from studies in which a library cannot contain all that is written on one small subsection of entomology. It is disheartening to know that no book on physiology ten years old has any other place than the lumber-room. Unless re-edited or re-written, its place is in the cellars and no longer on the shelves. This is the pace which kills a science. In mental philosophy there are still, it is true, a few classics left; and men who can edit a dialogue of Plato with notes may still set up some modest claim to be students in psychology. But all this points to only one conclusion, that we must, in very weariness of the iteration of the old, under assumed airs of novelty, get on to some grand new generalisation which shall be at once, in the best sense of the term, both new and old—

> "One God, one law, one element,
> And one far-off Divine event
> To which the whole creation moves."

Is it too extravagant to pitch our expectations high on the dawn of the twentieth century. There is an increasing purpose as the centuries go by. Any gain is real gain, and the relapses are few. Science has firmer hold and has truer methods than when Bacon began to point the way without so much as suspecting the true path of discovery by imaginative insight, not by perpetual plodding over "experiments solitary." It is the same in politics and social science. The old political economy of industrialism, the true wealth of nations advanced by self-help alone, is now seen to be a half truth. The complementary half of State help or co-operative industrialism is now recognised, and so a full-orbed ideal is at last attainable.

Are we to be told, then, that the comparative method, which has raised anatomy and philology into exact sciences on lines which Bacon never suspected, and which has made advances in social science beyond the reach of Adam Smith and Ricardo, whose method was deductive only on a scanty basis of induction, that nothing remains for sacred science so soon as she shall take up the same instrument of a higher research? Comparative religion, based on anthropology and comparative philology, has only crossed the threshold of preliminary and tentative guesses, and has scarcely yet made her voice heard in university pulpits. But the day is not far distant when the comparison of Christ and other masters will be pushed to lengths which such genial teachers as the late Archdeacon Hardwicke would have smiled approval on could he have lived to see that day, before whose very dawn he died. We shall see Japanese scholars trying to find the key to our occidentalisms in the same stumbling fashion as we guess at the inner philosophy of the East. These guesses at truth will be found in the first attempt to strike wide of the mark. But, like all approximations, they will mark ground gained, and which we shall never have again to give up. Not one of our political ameliorations but has its reflex action on theology. To name only one already glanced at. The reformatory theory of pnnishment has replaced the vindictive, marking, as Sir H. Maine has pointed out, the third and last stage of jurisprudence, when man becomes again in a better sense his brother's keeper. We should be as stupid as the Bourbons, and remember nothing and forget nothing, if we could delude ourselves to suppose that a theology which lags behind jurisprudence could escape early extinction. In an age when such phrases as the "new chemistry," the new jurisprudence, or the new political economy, are on every one's lips, what can be the use of shutting ourselves up in old scholasticism, miscalled theology? Let our note rather be to set our faces forward towards the coming day—

> "They are tired of what is old,
> I will give it voices new;
> For the half has not been told
> Of the beautiful and true."

In this way only can we deal with the afterthoughts of theology, not by sweeping them away, but by coupling on more last words. Such is our Epilogue; Prometheus, not Epimetheus, must be the keynote for the Church and theology of the future. It is summed up in a phrase of Teucer's address to his comrades in exile in the well-known ode—

> "Nil desperandum Teucro duce et auspice Teucro."

Nil desperandum should be our note in navigating unknown seas, and in seeking a second Salamis, a fresh island home. Our countrymen launch out over the seas at the rate of a thousand a day to found new Englands at the Antipodes, and under new constellations and seasons reversed, summer when we have winter, winter when it is our summer. There they find that all that is worth retaining in Church and State at home will bear repeating in colonial life. The lesson is not to be lost on us. Our motto should be "Forward," and on our flag the heroic phrase, *Nil desperandum*—

> "Cras ingens iterabimus sequor."

In a few years at farthest we shall each one by one join the long procession to the grave. We shall ourselves pass within the veil, and there learn the deep meaning of things that have been. There we shall for the first time fully put away childish things, and know even as we are known. There we shall smile at our crude attempts by conserving old out-worn dogmatisms, and so keep up the divisions of Christendom. Soon, very soon (permit me as one of the elders to say so), we shall see with Baxter, who mellowed as he aged, that the controversies of early and middle age are in most cases mere logomachies, and that our battles of the nineteenth century are only too like those ghosts in the clouds seen for nine days after the battle of Chalons, the afterglow of the strife of Hun and Frank already over. We shall wonder at the long-suffering of our Father, so gently leading us up out of our modernisms, which were only mediævalisms under another name—the ghosts of slain enemies contending together in the air. All this may seem cynical; and so it would be, if, when that which is in part is done away, we had not that which is perfect to put in its place. Perfection may not be the note in politics or religion, as finality is certainly not the note in science. But meliorism is a safe note to strike in both. In politics a new jurisprudence has made short work of vindictive punishments. Theology will soon adopt the same methods, and at once there will pass away a whole code of terrorism, such as has dimmed with tears the eyes of the best of men. A Dean, too much respected to be named here, once said to the preacher, that unless he held the natural immortality of the soul and the eternity of future punishment, he could see no sufficient reason for the coming of the Eternal Son in the likeness of sinful flesh. This is that type of religious rationalism which insists on a sufficient reason for everything, and which lies at the root of all our plans of salvation from Anselm's day to our own. It is these afterthoughts which, as soon as seen to be afterthoughts, will go off of themselves. Then we shall see the central truth that God is love, and see it stand out in its own light. Then the line of the mystic poet Gellert will be understood—

> "I sometimes think the man
> Who could surround the sum of things, and spy
> The heart of God and secrets of His empire,
> Would speak but love:—to Him the vast expanse
> Of intermediate things could melt in one,
> And make one thing of all theology."

This was a favourite line of the saintly Thomas Erskine, at whose feet I have sat for a lifetime, and whose theology is to my thinking the one type which has any future. To his revered memory I inscribe these thoughts. I can only trust, that as the education of man in place of his probation was the keynote to that theology of the Cambridge Platonists, so in this famous school of learning, where all arts are liberal and the blight of dogmatism has withered theology less than elsewhere, this attempt to declare that one is our Father, and all ye are brethren, will be accepted as the one education theory which we are prepared to hail as the theology of the future.

Mr. Cunningham in his Hulsean Lectures of 1885 tries to point out that Augustine's doctrine of Predestination was little more than an assertion of Divine foreknowledge, which at once reduces it to a meaningless truism which it is not worth while either to affirm or deny. "God, who foresees all things, sees also that there are some who never receive the message of grace, and some to whom it is brought. He has provided the means of salvation; He foresees how far these shall be rendered accessible to any generation, how far each man shall avail himself of them, and thus there are some who are predestined to salvation, since God knows from the first that they will work out their own salvation with fear and trembling. It is because God foresees what man will do that He predestines; and thus it is by the use of the means of grace that human beings accomplish the destiny which He has foreseen. The doctrine of Calvin, however, by ignoring the distinction between foreknowledge and predetermining, seems to take all reality out of the ordinances of Christian life. Why should I listen to preaching if I am predestined to damnation? Why should I seek to discipline my body or to seek God in prayer, if I am predestined to salvation? It is thus that the doctrines of Predestination may give an excuse for Antinomianism, if it be regarded as an arbitrary decree, not a foreknowledge which has its grounds in the Divine prevision of the actual occurrences in time. It is because St. Austin holds so firmly to the real efficacy of the sacraments as means of accomplishing God's purpose of love towards the world, that he does not regard Predestination as a mere arbitrary decree, but as prescience of the actual course of the ministration of Divine grace through a defective human agency."[1]

This attempt to exculpate Augustine's Predestinarianism by explaining it away as mere foreknowledge, is not the line of defence which any genuine Augustinian would accept. Dr. Mozley distinctly accepts Augustinianism on both sides, and sees a reconciliation between its bare Predestinarianism and also its sacramentalism, which to modern minds seem wholly divergent types of thought. But there was no such contradiction between the law in Augustine's mind. The late Dean Milman throws a flying bridge over between the two which is as satisfactory as any other.

"Latin Christianity in its strong sacerdotal system, in its rigid and exclusive theory of the Church, at once admitted and mitigated the more repulsive parts of the

[1] Cunningham, *St. Austin*, p. 126.

Augustinian theology. Predestinarianism itself, at least to those within the pale, lost much of its awful terrors. The Church was the predestined assemblage of those to whom, and to whom alone, salvation was possible. The Church scrupled not to surrender the rest of mankind to that inexorable damnation entailed upon the human race by the sin of their parents. This is the key to the real reconciliation. Augustine was not as illogical as he seems to us, who see old theologies in the light of later afterthoughts. In Augustine's day there had not been time for the distinction to develop between the Church, or the little company of the saved, and the mass of nominal and baptized but unregenerate professors. Hence it was no such inconsistency to hold that all who were so baptized, were also among the little company of the elect and the predestined. How difficult it is, when we have to deal with afterthoughts upon afterthoughts, such as modern Calvinism or old Augustinianism, to thread our way through the labyrinth!"[1]

With regard to St. Augustine not being an Augustinian, which is Mr. Cunningham's contention, some remarks of the *Church Times* (July 29, 1887) are very much to the point. "This thesis is urged with persistent ingenuity, and in a very plausible fashion, all the more plausible from the entire conviction of the writer; but, nevertheless, it must be qualified as only an exceptionally brilliant piece of special pleading. Nevertheless, we are convinced that he has not been unfairly charged with the responsibility of generating the system which ordinarily goes by his name. He is the legitimate father of Calvinism, Baianism, Jansenism; he is as truly the parent, though not so legitimately, of the Lutheran doctrine of justification. It is his bastard child, as Calvinism is his lawful offspring." The writer goes on to show that Prosper of Aquitaine, who pushed Augustinianism to its extreme consequences, was never rebuked for his heresy as the East would have regarded it; on the contrary, when he brought out of St.

[1] Milman, *Latin Christianity*, i. p. 146.

Augustine's writings a high-flying supralapsarianism, which Toplady might have called his own, we have proof of St. Prosper's status, that he was chosen at Rome, whither he had betaken himself to hunt down Pelagianism there, where it had taken a strong position, to be secretary to the Pope,—by that Pope himself the most illustrious theologian then living, being no other than Leo the Great.

With regard, too, to Luther and Calvin finding their theology almost full blown in the writings of Augustine, the writer remarks: "When either Luther or Calvin quoted Augustine on his side, he is not seeking a certificate for himself, but benevolently throwing the shield of his patronage over the elder writer, and graciously excluding him from the number of those who were so unhappy as not to set forth Reformed doctrines in their writings. They literally did not care twopence for any one's opinion but their own; and the presumption, therefore, is altogether that when they do quote any writer outside the Bible as making for them, they have a strong case in favour of their view of his opinions."

The conclusion which a reviewer in the *Church Times* comes to is naturally this, that there are two St. Augustines, or two distinct bodies of divinity infused by the same spirit, but which it is impossible to homologate and fuse into one. The sacramental teaching of Augustine, that is Catholic and primitive; but the predestinarian was his private heresy. During the scholastic period of the Church the two struggled on together; but at the Reformation they were rent asunder, and each branch of the Church claimed to be the possessor of this St. Martin's cloak. This we consider to be a fair account of the whole matter. In any case we agree with the reviewer, that all Mr. Cunningham can make out for his patron saint, St. Austin, is a verdict of not proven; and if a verdict of guilty must be brought in, that a strong recommendation to mercy be added to it.

The strong anti-Augustinian because anti-Calvinist bias of this reviewer is seen from the following: "In fact, Western Christianity will never be what it should be till frank abandonment of St. Augustine's specific theology, as complete as, for instance, the abandonment of St. Anselm's theory of the Incarnation, has been, involving no censure on him for propounding it, taken up as a final position. To call St. Augustine the "doctor of grace," to recommend the *Summa* of St. Thomas, wherein Augustinianism is dominant, and then to anathematise Le Bay and Jansen simply for restating it less aggressively than St. Prosper did, is neither honest nor logical. But Mr. Cunningham has made as good a fight as the case permitted. In this we heartily agree; but it is not the first time that it has been St. Augustine's fate to be not only misunderstood himself, but the source of misunderstanding in others. The propositions which Jansen drew up as an epitome of Augustine's teaching, were declared by the Jansenists not to be Jansen's at all, but a Jesuit perversion, till at last, like the cuttle-fish, we are lost as to fact itself in this ink of controversy.

www.ingramcontent.com/pod-product-compliance
Lightning Source LLC
LaVergne TN
LVHW020526100826
845148LV00010B/1354

* 9 7 8 1 5 9 7 5 2 1 1 6 1 *